Improving Measurement of Productivity in Higher Education

D1246408

Panel on Measuring Higher Education Productivity:
Conceptual Framework and Data Needs

Teresa A. Sullivan, Christopher Mackie, William F. Massy, and
Esha Sinha, *Editors*

Committee on National Statistics

Board on Testing and Assessment

Division of Behavioral and Social Sciences and Education

NATIONAL RESEARCH COUNCIL
OF THE NATIONAL ACADEMIES

THE NATIONAL ACADEMIES PRESS
Washington, D.C.
www.nap.edu

THE NATIONAL ACADEMIES PRESS • 500 Fifth Street, NW • Washington, DC 20001

NOTICE: The project that is the subject of this report was approved by the Governing Board of the National Research Council, whose members are drawn from the councils of the National Academy of Sciences, the National Academy of Engineering, and the Institute of Medicine. The members of the committee responsible for the report were chosen for their special competences and with regard for appropriate balance.

This study was supported by grant number 5793 between the National Academy of Sciences and Lumina Foundation. Support for the work of the Committee on National Statistics is provided by a consortium of federal agencies through a grant from the National Science Foundation (award number SES-1024012). Any opinions, findings, conclusions, or recommendations expressed in this publication are those of the author(s) and do not necessarily reflect the view of the organizations or agencies that provided support for this project.

International Standard Book Number-13: 978-0-309-25774-9
International Standard Book Number-10: 0-309-25774-3

Library of Congress Cataloging-in-Publication data are available from the Library of Congress

Additional copies of this report are available from the National Academies Press, 500 Fifth Street, NW, Keck 360, Washington, DC 20001; (800) 624-6242 or (202) 334-3313, http://www.nap.edu.

Printed in the United States of America

Suggested citation: National Research Council. (2012). *Improving Measurement of Productivity in Higher Education.* Panel on Measuring Higher Education Productivity: Conceptual Framework and Data Needs. Teresa A. Sullivan, Christopher Mackie, William F. Massy, and Esha Sinha, Editors. Committee on National Statistics and Board on Testing and Assessment, Division of Behavioral and Social Sciences and Education. Washington, DC: The National Academies Press.

THE NATIONAL ACADEMIES
Advisers to the Nation on Science, Engineering, and Medicine

The **National Academy of Sciences** is a private, nonprofit, self-perpetuating society of distinguished scholars engaged in scientific and engineering research, dedicated to the furtherance of science and technology and to their use for the general welfare. Upon the authority of the charter granted to it by the Congress in 1863, the Academy has a mandate that requires it to advise the federal government on scientific and technical matters. Dr. Ralph J. Cicerone is president of the National Academy of Sciences.

The **National Academy of Engineering** was established in 1964, under the charter of the National Academy of Sciences, as a parallel organization of outstanding engineers. It is autonomous in its administration and in the selection of its members, sharing with the National Academy of Sciences the responsibility for advising the federal government. The National Academy of Engineering also sponsors engineering programs aimed at meeting national needs, encourages education and research, and recognizes the superior achievements of engineers. Dr. Charles M. Vest is president of the National Academy of Engineering.

The **Institute of Medicine** was established in 1970 by the National Academy of Sciences to secure the services of eminent members of appropriate professions in the examination of policy matters pertaining to the health of the public. The Institute acts under the responsibility given to the National Academy of Sciences by its congressional charter to be an adviser to the federal government and, upon its own initiative, to identify issues of medical care, research, and education. Dr. Harvey V. Fineberg is president of the Institute of Medicine.

The **National Research Council** was organized by the National Academy of Sciences in 1916 to associate the broad community of science and technology with the Academy's purposes of furthering knowledge and advising the federal government. Functioning in accordance with general policies determined by the Academy, the Council has become the principal operating agency of both the National Academy of Sciences and the National Academy of Engineering in providing services to the government, the public, and the scientific and engineering communities. The Council is administered jointly by both Academies and the Institute of Medicine. Dr. Ralph J. Cicerone and Dr. Charles M. Vest are chair and vice chair, respectively, of the National Research Council.

www.national-academies.org

PANEL ON MEASURING HIGHER EDUCATION PRODUCTIVITY: CONCEPTUAL FRAMEWORK AND DATA NEEDS

TERESA A. SULLIVAN (*Chair*), Office of the President, University of Virginia

THOMAS R. BAILEY, Institute on Education and the Economy and Community College Research Center, Teachers College, Columbia University

BARRY P. BOSWORTH, Economic Studies Program, The Brookings Institution, Washington, DC

DAVID W. BRENEMAN, Curry School of Education, University of Virginia

RONALD G. EHRENBERG, Cornell Higher Education Research Institute, Cornell University

PETER T. EWELL, National Center for Higher Education Management Systems, Boulder, CO

IRWIN FELLER, Department of Economics (emeritus), Pennsylvania State University

BARBARA FRAUMENI, Muskie School of Public Service, University of Southern Maine

JULIET V. GARCIA, Office of the President, University of Texas at Brownsville and Texas Southmost College

MICHAEL HOUT, Department of Sociology, University of California, Berkeley

NATE JOHNSON, HCM Strategists, Washington, DC

GEORGE D. KUH, Center for Postsecondary Research (emeritus), Indiana University

WILLIAM F. MASSY, Independent Consultant, Florence, MA

CAROL A. TWIGG, National Center for Academic Transformation, Saratoga Springs, NY

DAVID J. ZIMMERMAN, Department of Economics, Williams College

CHRISTOPHER D. MACKIE, *Study Director*
STUART ELLIOTT, *Senior Program Officer*
ESHA SINHA, *Associate Program Officer*
MICHAEL SIRI, *Program Associate*

v

Acknowledgments

The work of this panel has been immeasurably assisted by the insight and counsel of numerous colleagues. In particular, we wish to acknowledge the reviewers. This report has been reviewed in draft form by individuals chosen for their diverse perspectives and technical expertise, in accordance with procedures approved by the Report Review Committee of the National Research Council (NRC). The purpose of this independent review is to provide candid and critical comments that will assist the institution in making its published report as sound as possible and to ensure that the report meets institutional standards for objectivity, evidence, and responsiveness to the study charge. The review comments and draft manuscript remain confidential to protect the integrity of the deliberative process. We wish to thank the following individuals for their review of this report: Julian Betts, Department of Economics, University of California, San Diego; William G. Bowen, President's Office, Andrew W. Mellon Foundation; Pat Callan, President's Office, Higher Education Policy Institute, San Jose, California; Charles T. Clotfelter, Center for the Study of Philanthropy and Voluntarism, Duke University; Don E. Detmer, University of Virginia School of Medicine; David N. Figlio, Institute for Policy Research, Northwestern University; Brent R. Hickman, Economics Department, University of Chicago; Michael McPherson, President's Office, The Spencer Foundation; B. Don Russell, Jr., Department of Electrical Engineering, Texas A&M University; and Burton A. Weisbrod, Institute for Policy Research, Northwestern University.

The review of this report was overseen by Greg Duncan, distinguished professor of education, University of California, Irvine, and Charles Manski, Board of Trustees professor in economics, Northwestern University. Appointed by the NRC's Report Review Committee, they were responsible for making certain that an independent examination of this report was carried out in accordance with institutional procedures and that all review comments were carefully considered.

Although the reviewers have provided many constructive comments, and improved the content of the report a great deal, they were not asked to endorse the conclusions or recommendations; nor did they see the final draft of the report prior to its release. Responsibility for the final content of this report rests entirely with the authoring panel and the institution.

Many others generously gave of their time in offering oral presentations at meetings and answering questions from panel members and staff, thereby helping us to develop a clearer understanding of key issues relevant to the measurement of higher education productivity and related issues. The panel thanks Lumina Foundation; they provided financial support for the project and, even more importantly, helped shape the scope of the study. From Lumina, Jamie Merisotis, Kevin Corcoran, Suzanne Walsh (now with the Bill & Melinda Gates Foundation), and Charles (Chip) Hatcher provided insights and guidance in their roles as initiators of the project. Kristin Conklin (HCM Strategists, LLC) kept the panel informed about Lumina grantees' programs to increase productivity and proposals for measuring the effectiveness of those efforts. The panel benefited from the open discussion of these initiatives.

During meetings and deliberations, the panel heard from a number of subject matter experts. Andrea Bonaccorsi, University of Pisa, Italy; Kevin Carey, New America Foundation; Hamish Coates, Australian Council for Education Research; Bo Hansson, OECD; Jorge Klor de Alva, University of Phoenix; and Donna Sundre, James Madison University informed the panel about efforts to measure higher education productivity, to design and implement accountability systems, and to improve input/output data at different levels of aggregation.

The panel could not have conducted its work without an excellent and well-managed staff. Connie Citro, director of the Committee on National Statistics, and Stuart Elliott, director of the Board on Testing and Assessment, provided expert guidance to the panel about the NRC study process. Program associate Michael Siri provided excellent administrative, editorial, and research support. Esha Sinha, program officer, provided valuable research and analytic assistance with her understanding of higher education data sources. Her knowledge proved especially helpful as we worked through some of the thornier measurement issues. The panel also benefited from the work of Kirsten Sampson-Snyder, Division of Behavioral and Social Sciences and Education, who was responsible for overseeing the review process. Amy Smith provided able editing of numerous drafts.

Christopher Mackie, the panel's study director, organized our meetings and facilitated communication among panel members, including a lengthy process of chapter revisions. His work required synthesizing and evaluating many disparate points of input, seeking what common ground could be found, and guiding the panel through careful discussion of the points of disagreement. He helped to develop the structure for the panel's final report, and he shepherded the report through the final review process.

Most importantly, the members of the panel deserve thanks for their patience, creativity, and hard work. There is a reason that higher education productivity is not currently reported in the national accounts. Reaching agreement on conceptual and measurement issues was difficult work. This report reflects the collective expertise and commitment of the individual members of the panel, each of whom brought a unique perspective based upon a scholarly discipline, research experience, and a lifetime of practice. Members were generous with their time and effort, and they struggled to understand and appropriately acknowledge the critical views of others. Our meetings provided many opportunities for panel members to learn from one another.

Teresa A. Sullivan, *Chair*
Panel on Measuring Higher Education Productivity:
Conceptual Framework and Data Needs

Contents

Summary

MOTIVATION AND PANEL CHARGE

Higher education is a linchpin of the American economy and society: Teaching and research at colleges and universities contribute significantly to the nation's economic activity, both directly and through their impact on future growth; federal and state governments support teaching and research with billions of taxpayers' dollars; and individuals, communities, and the nation gain from the learning and innovation that occur in higher education.

Effective use of resources is (and should be) a serious concern in the delivery of higher education, as it is for other sectors of the economy. In the current environment of increasing tuition and shrinking public funds, a sense of urgency has emerged to better track the performance of colleges and universities in the hope that their costs can be contained while not compromising quality or accessibility. Metrics ranging from graduation rates to costs per student have been developed to serve this purpose. However, the capacity to assess the performance of higher education institutions and systems remains incomplete, largely because the inputs and outputs in the production process are difficult to define and quantify. For higher education, productivity improvement—increasing the number of graduates, amount of learning, and innovation relative to the inputs used—is seen as the most promising strategy in the effort to keep a high-quality college education as affordable as possible.

It was within this context that this panel was charged to identify an analytically well-defined concept of productivity for higher education and to recommend practical guidelines for its measurement. The objective is to construct valid productivity measures to supplement the body of information used to (1) guide

1

resource allocation decisions at the system, state, and national levels and to assist policy makers who must assess investments in higher education against other compelling demands on scarce resources; (2) provide administrators with better tools for improving their institutions' performance; and (3) inform individual consumers and communities to whom colleges and universities are ultimately accountable for private and public investments in higher education. Though it should be noted that the experimental measure developed in this report does not directly advance all of these objectives—particularly that pertaining to measurement of individual institution perfomance—the overall report pushes the discussion forward and offers first steps.

While the panel is in no way attempting to design an accountability system, it is important to think about incentives that measures create. Since institutional behavior is dynamic and directly related to the incentives embedded within measurement systems, steps have to be taken to (1) ensure that the incentives in the measurement system genuinely support the behaviors that society wants from higher education institutions, and (2) maximize the likelihood that measured performance is the result of authentic success rather than manipulative behaviors. Clearly, a single high-stakes measure is a flawed approach in that it makes gaming the system simpler; a range of measures will almost always be preferable for weighing overall performance. While not diminishing the weight of these cautions, it should be noted that monitoring productivity trends would not be adding incentives to a world without them. Among the major incentives now in play are to enroll students, get research grants, improve in national rankings, raise money, and win athletic competitions. The panel believes that adding another incentive (and one more worthy than a number of these) will help round out the current set in a positive way.

THE PRODUCTIVITY MEASURE

Improving and implementing productivity metrics begins with recognition of their role in the broader performance assessment picture:

- Productivity should be a central part of the higher education conversation.
- Conversations about the sector's performance will lack coherence in the absence of a well-vetted and agreed-upon set of metrics, among which productivity is essential.
- Quality should always be a core part of productivity conversations, even when it cannot be fully captured by the metrics.
- The inevitable presence of difficult-to-quantify elements in a measure should not be used as an excuse to ignore those elements.

The first step is to define key terms by applying the standard economic concept of productivity to higher education. In the model developed in this report, the baseline productivity measure for the instructional component of higher education is estimated as the ratio of (a) changes in the quantity of output, expressed to capture both degrees (or other markers of successful completion) and passed credit hours to (b) changes in the quantity of inputs, expressed to capture both labor and nonlabor factors of production. The assumption embedded in the numerator, consistent with the economics literature on human capital (e.g., Bailey et al., 2004; Barro and Lee, 2010a), is that education adds to a student's knowledge and skill base, even if it does not result in a degree. Key to the denominator is the heterogeneity of labor and other inputs used in the production of education—and the need to account for it.

The proposed approach should be viewed as a starting point; additional research will be essential for addressing a number of thorny issues that impede full and accurate productivity measurement and, in turn, its value for guiding policy. However, it is not premature to introduce a statistical construct to serve as a foundation for work on the topic. Indeed, having such a construct will guide data collection and research upon which the measures must be based.

MEASUREMENT LIMITATIONS AND KEY AREAS FOR MODEL ENHANCEMENT

A number of complexities characterize higher education production processes. These reflect the presence of (1) joint production—colleges and universities generate a number of outputs (such as educated and credentialed citizens, research findings, athletic events, hospital services), and the labor and other inputs involved cannot always be neatly allocated to them; (2) high variability in the quality and characteristics of inputs, such as teachers and students, and outputs, such as degrees; and (3) outputs (and inputs) of the production process that are nonmarket in nature. As is the case with other sectors of the economy, particularly services, productivity measurement for higher education is very much a work in progress in terms of its capacity to handle these complexities. Because no single metric can incorporate everything that is important, decision makers must appeal to a range of statistics or indicators when assessing policy options—but surely a well-conceived productivity measure is one of these.

Joint Production

Reflecting policy information needs as well as feasibility-of-measurement constraints, this study focuses on the instructional mission. By not directly accounting for other contributions of higher education to society—perhaps most notably research—the baseline model developed in this report omits a central mission of a large subset of institutions. Commentators such as Jonathan Cole have argued that research capacity is the primary factor distinguishing U.S. universities from those in the rest of the world, and that the country's future depends strongly on the continued nurturing of its research-intensive universities (Cole, 2010). Indeed, this is why the federal government and state governments have invested and continue to invest billions of dollars in university-based research.

The decision to limit the report's focus to measurement of instructional productivity is not intended as a comment on the relative importance of teaching, research, and public service for institutions with multiple missions. However, the focus on instruction does come with the analytical consequence that the resulting productivity measure can provide only a partial assessment of the sector's aggregate contributions to national and regional objectives. For this reason, just as the performance and progress of the instructional capabilities of institutions must be monitored, measures should also be developed for assessing the value of the nation's investments in research. Even for a purely instruction-based measurement objective, an improved understanding of faculty resource allocation to research is essential because time use is not fully separable, and because research intensities may affect the quality of teaching.

Quality Variation and Change

Historically, institution or system performance has been assessed using unidimensional measures such as graduation rates, time to degree, and costs per credit. When attention is overwhelmingly focused on completions or costs, the risk is raised that stated goals will be pursued at the expense of quality. For this reason, input and output quantity measures should ideally be adjusted to reflect quality differences; that is, productivity should be defined as the ratio of quality-adjusted outputs to quality-adjusted inputs. However, such measurement is extremely difficult, which means that developing data and methods for doing so is a very long-term project. In the meantime, while accounting is incomplete, it is essential to monitor when apparent increases in measurable output arise as a result of quality reduction. For the foreseeable future, this will have to be done through parallel tracking of additional information generated independently by universities and third party quality assurance methods. And, until adjustments can be made to productivity metrics to account for quality differences, it will be inappropriate to rely exclusively on them when making funding and resource reallocation decisions. To do so would risk incentivizing a "race to the bottom" in terms of quality.

In some ways, the situation has not changed significantly in 100 years. A 1910 Carnegie Foundation report attempted to develop a time-use accounting formula to estimate the costs and outputs of higher education in order to "measure the efficiency and productivity of educational institutions in a manner similar to that of industrial factories." The authors of that volume struggled with measuring quality and, while forced to confine their observation largely to quantity, did strive "to make quality a background for everything that may appear to have only a quantitative value" (cited in Barrow, 1990:67). A century later, we agree: measuring quality is difficult, which explains why adequate productivity measures, as well as the data and methodologies on which they rest, have yet to be constructed for the sector.

Because the productivity measure developed in this report expresses outputs in terms of quantities of credits and degrees, it does not explicitly take account of changing quality of outputs or inputs. An effect will be captured to the extent that higher quality inputs lead to higher graduation rates, but this effect is indirect. For example, if small classes or better teaching (inputs of different quality) lead to higher graduation rates, this will figure in the output total (the numerator) as a greater sheepskin effect—that is, an added value assigned for degree completion. Similarly, high student and teacher quality at selective private institutions may offset high input costs by creating an environment conducive to high throughput (graduation) rates.

This modest step notwithstanding, continued research to improve measurement of the quality dimension of higher education is essential. For output quality, researchers should aim to identify and quantify student learning outcomes, readiness for subsequent coursework and employment, degree- and credit-related income effects, and the social value of education. Similarly, adjustments should be estimated to reflect the quality of inputs, most notably the mix of students (along such dimensions as preparedness and socioeconomic background) and the effectiveness of faculty instruction. A conventional approach, widely applied in the empirical literature, is to use SAT scores and other indicators of student quality (e.g., high school rank, ethnicity, socioeconomic variables such as educational status and income of parents) to statistically impose the needed adjustments. For this reason, much could be learned from more complete school-wide censuses capturing demographic and preparedness measures for incoming students. In the spirit of monitoring quality (in this case, of the student input) in parallel with the proposed productivity statistic, student distributions could be reported at the quartile or quintile level so as not to make reporting excessively costly.

Nonmarket Production

Further complicating accurate valuation of higher education is that some of the benefits of schooling are nonpecuniary and nonmarket in nature—they are not bought and sold and do not have prices. Additionally, externalities arise, in that not all of the benefits of an educated citizenry accrue to those paying for or receiving education. Nonetheless, policy makers should be concerned with social value, not just the private or market value of the outcomes generated by higher education. For this reason, valuing degrees solely by salaries that graduates earn is misleading. Investment in citizens' careers is not the only objective, from a societal perspective, of supporting and participating in higher education. The nonpecuniary and public goods aspects of higher education output, such as those linked to research, are also important; even the consumption component of college, including student enjoyment of the experience, is quite clearly significant.

Segmentation by Institution Type

The measurement complications identified above can be dampened by recognizing the diversity of missions across the range of colleges and universities and then segmenting institutions into more homogeneous categories along the lines of the Carnegie Classification system, or perhaps using even more detail. For many purposes, it is unwise to compare performance measures across institutions that have different missions. The first implication of this principle is that productivity measures must be designed to register outcomes that can be taken as equivalent to a degree or a fractional portion of a degree-equivalent. This may be especially important for community colleges, where outcomes include successful transfer to four-year institutions, completion of certificates, or attainment of specific skills by students who have no intention of pursuing a degree.

Additionally, for purposes of making comparisons across institutions, states, or nations, it is essential to take into account incoming student ability and preparation. Highly selective institutions typically have higher completion rates than open-access institutions. This may reflect more on the prior learning, preparation, and motivation of the entrants than on the productivity of the institution they enter. Therefore, in the context of resource allocation or other high stakes decisions, the marginal success effect attributable to this input quality effect should ideally be taken into consideration in performance assessments.

Because heterogeneity leads to measurement complications even within institutional categories, it is also important to account for differences in factors such as the mix of degrees and majors. Institution-level cost data indicate that the resources required to produce an undergraduate degree vary, sometimes significantly, by major. Variation in degree cost is linked to, among other things, systematic differences in the amount of time needed to complete a degree. Uninformed comparisons will result in some institutions appearing less efficient in terms of degree production (i.e., exhibiting longer time values), yet they may be functioning reasonably well, given their mission and student characteristics. Therefore, productivity models should include an adjustment for field of study that reflects, among other things, different course requirements, pass rates, and labor input costs.

IMPLICATIONS OF COMPLEXITIES FOR MEASUREMENT PROSPECTS

It is possible, and perhaps even likely, that critics of this report will rebuke the idea of measuring instructional productivity because of the complications noted above and throughout this report. Our view is that this would be a mistake. Failure to implement a credible measure may indefinitely defer the benefits achievable from a better understanding of quantitative productivity, even in the absence of a viable method of quality adjustment. We emphasize again the essential idea that effective and transparent quality assurance systems should be maintained to supplement productivity and other performance measures. This will allow progress to be made in measuring the quantitative aspects of productivity while containing the risk of triggering institutional competition that results in lowering educational quality. Progress on the development of quantitative productivity measures may also boost the priority for developing a serviceable quality adjustment index.

DEVELOPING THE DATA INFRASTRUCTURE

While progress can be made to develop and implement productivity measures using existing information, full implementation of the recommendations in this report will require new or improved data capabilities as well. One significant change required for enhancement of the baseline model involves standardizing the capacity to link credit hours to degree or field. To move in this direction, institutions should collect credit-hour data in a way that follows students, and not only the departments that teach them. Indeed, the necessary information already exists in many institutions' student registration files. To fully exploit the potential from this kind of information, the Integrated Postsecondary Education Data System (IPEDS) produced by the National Center for Education Statistics could report these data along with the numbers of degrees awarded.

Detailed productivity measurement will require other kinds of information as well, such as comprehensive longitudinal student databases (to better calculate graduation rates and estimate the cost and value of degrees) and more accessible administrative sources. The potential of administrative data sources—maintained at various levels, ranging from institutions' accounting and management systems to those of the federal statistical agencies—depends heavily on the ability of researchers and policy analysts to link records across state boundaries and across elementary, secondary, postsecondary, and workforce boundaries (Prescott and Ewell, 2009). Standardization and coordinated linkage of states' student record databases should be a priority. Another example of useful administrative data is unemployment insurance records kept by all states. As with individual state unit record data resources for postsecondary education, it is now often difficult to assemble multi-state or national datasets. This makes it difficult to track cohorts of graduates (or nongraduates) across state lines. The Bureau of Labor Statistics should continue to do what it can to facilitate multi-state links of unemployment insurance wage records and education data which would create new opportunities for research on issues such as return on investment from postsecondary training or placement rates in various occupations.

1

The Importance of Measuring Productivity in Higher Education

This study has two major objectives: to present an analytically well-defined concept of productivity in higher education and to recommend empirically valid and operationally practical guidelines for measuring it. In addition to its obvious policy and research value, improved measures of productivity may generate insights that potentially lead to enhanced departmental, institutional, or system educational processes. In pursuit of these objectives, we address a series of questions: What is productivity and how can the concept of productivity be applied to higher education? What limitations and complexities are confronted when attempting to do so? Why is the measurement of productivity important to education policy? Who should care about measuring productivity? And, how can the measurement of productivity be improved?

These questions are not new. Indeed, 2010 marked the 100th anniversary of the Carnegie Foundation Report (Cooke, 1910), which developed a time-use accounting formula to estimate the costs and outputs of higher education for both teaching and research. Essentially, the Carnegie Foundation Report sought "to measure the efficiency and productivity of educational institutions in a manner similar to that of industrial factories" (Barrow, 1990:67). One goal of this earlier effort was to create a method for measuring productivity so that higher education would be subject to and benefit from competitive market pressures akin to those in private industry. To accomplish this, the Carnegie Foundation Report created a key unit of measure called the *student hour,* defined as "one hour of lectures, of lab work, or recitation room work, for a single pupil" (Barrow, 1990:70). The motivation behind the initiative was to facilitate calculation of relative faculty workloads, the cost of instruction per student hour, and, ultimately, the rate of educational efficiency for individual professors, fields, departments, and universities (Shedd, 2003). These are the essentially the same things we want to know

9

today and which this report again addresses. Additionally, the difficult measurement issues limiting completeness of the analysis 100 years ago are still very much in play, as we detail in Chapter 3.

While productivity measurement in many service sectors is fraught with conceptual and data difficulties, nowhere are the challenges—such as accounting for input differences, wide quality variation of outputs, and opaque or regulated pricing—more imposing than for higher education. Compounding the challenge is that many members of the panel (and many reading the report) are being asked to consider the same measurement tools to analyze their own industry as they would use in analyzing any other. And, from up close, the complexities are much more apparent than when dissecting productivity from a distance.

One lesson drawn from this effort is that we may be too sanguine about the accuracy or relevance of measures of productivity in other sectors, having seen how daunting they can be in a setting with which we are more intimately familiar. The conceptual and practical problems surrounding this effort raise additional concerns because it is known that measurements create incentives, incentives change practices, and those practices have the potential to affect people and institutions we care deeply about. Yet the current higher education environment is not without incentives, many of which have flaws that are at least as profound and distorting as those associated with economic measurement, and are sometimes much worse. Readers of the report will have to make the up their minds whether the potential disadvantages of this approach, as well as the costs of implementing the specific recommendations, are worth the potential benefit. While we understand how some might come to a different conclusion, we believe the advantages outweigh the disadvantages.

1.1. SOCIAL AND POLICY CONTEXT

> Not everything that counts can be counted, and not everything that can be
> counted counts.   —*William Bruce Cameron*

While this observation is broadly profound, it seems exceptionally applicable to the case of higher education. At the same time, a better understanding of the workings and nature of the sector is necessary, given its prominent role in the economy and impact on the future of our society. Higher education is part of the essential fabric of American experience, one in which many citizens spend a significant fraction of their adult lives. For many individuals, higher education is the largest or second-largest consumer decision.

On an aggregate level, colleges and universities employ around 3.6 million individuals, 2.6 million of those in professional positions.[1] The sector accounts

---

[1]From Bureau of Labor Statistics, see http://www.bls.gov/spotlight/2010/college/ [June 2012]. This source also includes data on teacher salaries by field, earnings by graduates, etc.

(directly) for about 3.3 percent of gross domestic product (Soete, Guy, and Praest Knudsen, 2009), which makes it larger than a number of industries for which productivity data are routinely collected. It also accounts for about 10 percent of state budgets in recent fiscal years (National Association of State Budget Officers State Expenditure Report, 2011).

Beyond the production of credentialed citizens, academic institutions also perform much of the nation's research and development. In 2008, colleges and universities spent $52 billion on research and development, with 60 percent of this funding derived from the federal government. Academic institutions performed 55 percent of basic research and 31 percent of total research (basic plus applied) in the United States (National Science Board, 2010:5-4). Although nonacademic organizations conduct research in select functional fields such as health, defense, space, energy, and agriculture, the general prominence of academic research and the established funding patterns reflect a post–World War II political consensus that federally funded basic research is most effectively performed in academic institutions. This contrasts with patterns observed elsewhere in the world, where there is greater reliance on government-operated laboratories, other forms of public research organizations, or industry to conduct research.

In the current global economic and fiscal climate, the attention being paid by policy makers to the competitiveness and general state of higher education in the United States continues to heighten. Recent research (e.g., Carnevale, Smith, and Strohl, 2010) indicates that the economy's expanding sectors and industries rely disproportionately on workers with higher education credentials. During the current recession, characterized by high and persistent unemployment, analyses of evidence such as online job postings and real-time jobs data reveal a mismatch between job openings and the educational credentials of the workforce. Higher education institutions themselves have become increasingly concerned about improving their own performance, competing with peer institutions on cost and quality, and providing a degree of public accountability.

In this environment of strong policy maker and institutional interest in the performance of higher education, stakeholders have used whatever data and measures are available in an attempt to understand trends and perceived problems; for better or worse, some version of productivity *will* be measured. Therefore, it is crucial to develop coherent measurement tools that make the best possible use of available and potentially available data. Failure to do so will keep the door open for an ever-expanding profusion of measures, many of them unnecessarily distortive, and endless debates about measurement as opposed to productivity itself.

Currently in policy debates, administration discussions, and media coverage, attention tends to focus on the soaring sticker price of college (overall costs have remained more or less in line with general inflation). Cost per degree, graduation rates, and retention metrics have been used as though they measured efficiency or overall productivity. What is often ignored in these discussions is the quality of higher education instruction. When attention is overwhelmingly focused on completions or similar metrics, the risk is heightened that the stated goal will be pursued at the expense of quality.[2] If the aim is to know whether increased spending is resulting in commensurate returns, the quantity *and quality* of the sector's inputs and outputs must be reliably tracked, which, for the latter, requires developing assessment tools for quantifying the outcomes of higher education.

Used without a solid understanding of their meaning in divergent contexts, simple metrics such as graduation rates and costs per degree can distort and confuse as much as they inform. In the absence of more rigorous alternatives, however, they will continue to be used—and, at times, misused. In this report, we take a closer look at some of the unidimensional performance metrics to understand better what exactly they reveal. We then develop a more appropriate approach to productivity measurement—one that can serve as a key component in the set of information from which to base resource and other policy decisions. However, even the productivity measure developed in this report, which expresses outputs in terms of quantities of credits and degrees, cannot explicitly take account of quality variation and change. As detailed in Chapter 4, an effect will be captured by the proposed measure to the extent that higher quality inputs, such as better teachers, lead to higher percentages of students completing degrees; but this effect is indirect. Thus, a single metric—even a well-conceived productivity measure—will rarely be sufficient, on its own, to adequately serve as a comprehensive assessment of institutional, system, or even sector-wide performance. Other factors—most notably the quality dimension—must be monitored through parallel tracking of information that will often have to be processed independently from the productivity metric.

Finally, there are aspects of human and, more narrowly, productive enterprise that create social value but that statisical measures do not and indeed do not presume to capture. From a societal perspective, investment in citizens' work careers is not the only motivation for supporting and participating in higher education. Nonpecuniary components of the sector's output assoicated with instruction, research, and other public goods are also important. Like a policeman who brings extraordinary passion to protection of fellow-citizens, a technology entrepreneur whose vision ultimately changes the way people live, or an artist who is appreciated long after creating the art, the passion and dynamism of a master teacher who is truly interested in a student who, in turn, is truly interested in learning cannot be richly portrayed in a number. In this context, some very real elements of the value of experiencing life-changing learning cannot be fully quantified within a (still very important) statistical infrastructure.

---

[2]Similar tendencies to focus on the easily quantifiable hamper discussions of medical care. The increase in costs is known; the value gained from these expenditures, in terms of health benefits to the population, frequently is not.

1.2. CHARGE TO THE PANEL

The statement of task for this project—co-developed by the Lumina Foundation for Education and the National Research Council's Committee on National Statistics at a planning meeting held February 20, 2009—reads as follows:

> The Panel on Improving the Measurement of Productivity in Higher Education will develop a conceptual framework for measuring higher education productivity and describe the data needs for that framework. The framework will address productivity at different levels of aggregation, including the institution, system, and sector levels.
>
> An overarching goal of the study is to catalogue the complexities of measuring productivity and monitoring accountability in higher education. In particular, the study will take into account the great variety of types and missions of higher education institutions in the United States, ranging from open admission colleges to major research universities that compete on an international scale. The study will also address the necessity to consider quality issues when attempting to measure productivity. Since the quality of inputs to and outputs from higher education varies greatly across institution types and, indeed, within them, the study will highlight the pitfalls of using simplistic metrics based on insufficient data for evaluating the performance of higher education.
>
> One objective of the study will be to provide guidance to institutions and policy makers about practical measures that can be developed for the purposes of institutional improvement and accountability. However, to the extent that the differences in inputs, outputs, and institution types within higher education (along with inadequate data) make the development of comprehensive productivity measures impossible, the panel will assess the strengths and weaknesses of the various alternatives in providing evidence on different aspects of the input-output relationship.
>
> At the conclusion of its study, the panel will issue a report with findings and recommendations for developing the conceptual framework and data infrastructure and that provides an assessment of the strengths and limitations of alternative approaches to productivity measurement in higher education. The report will be written for a broad audience that includes national and state policy makers, system and institution administrators, and higher education faculty.

An important aspect of this report is to highlight the complexity of measuring productivity in higher education. A deeper understanding of this complexity reduces the chances that decision makers will misuse measures—for example, by incentivizing "diploma mills" through overemphasis of graduation rate or time-to-degree statistics in accountability policies. While attempting to provide novel insights into productivity measurement, we are cognizant that it is easy to find fault with approaches that policy makers, administrators, and other practitioners have relied upon to do their jobs. It is much more difficult to envision and implement new methods that could become broadly endorsed. Recognizing that funding and personnel decisions, as well as plans to improve resource allocation are sometimes based at least in part on these measures, our intent is to encourage those attempting to improve and apply them in real policy settings.

Due to the sheer breadth of activities associated with higher education in the United States, this report cannot be exhaustive. The scope of the study and the recommendations herein reflect policy information needs as well as feasibility-of-measurement constraints. The report's purview includes all types of higher education institutions (public, private, for-profit), but not all missions. Our measurement prescriptions focus on instruction, which includes all taught programs, regardless of level (e.g., associate, bachelors, taught terminal masters).[3] Joint production of instruction, research, and public service is discussed in detail, though it is recognized that measurement of the latter two is largely beyond the scope of the panel's charge. Other missions, such as health care and athletics, which sometimes are budgeted separately, are also excluded from our measurement proposals, which mean that any synergies that exist between these activities and conventional resident instruction programs are missed. To include them at this point in the development of productivity measurement for the sector would hopelessly complicate the task.

In developing a model of productivity (Chapter 4), the panel recognizes that this is only a starting point for what promises to be a long-term research agenda. It is worth pointing out that no industry is without its complexities, and no productivity measure currently in use is permanently fixed. The extensive and impressive research by the Bureau of Labor Statistics (BLS) into the concepts and techniques of productivity measurement is indicative of the ongoing process and continuing progress but also of the fact that measurement and conceptual barriers remain.[4] Additionally, as described in the next chapter, more than one paradigm exists for constructing productivity models.[5] It is especially worth distinguishing between aggregate models of the kind developed here, which are designed to measure long-term trends, and structural models aimed more specifically at operational improvement and accountability concerns. Aggregate and sector-level productivity models have proved to be important for economic and policy analysis. In higher education, for example, they reveal whether resource usage per unit of output in particular institutional segments

---

[3]Application of the model developed in Chapter 4 uses IPEDS data that do not exclude Ph.D. and research degrees (though they clearly have a quite different teaching production function). Due to the way universities categorize instructional expenses, it is not possible to subdivide these activities on the input side and, therefore, these degrees are not excluded from the output side either (they are also included in the student credit-hour production figures). However, it is doubtful that the small number of degrees and enrollments involved will have much effect on the actual productivity statistics.

[4]For details of the BLS work, see http://www.bls.gov/lpc/lprarch.htm#Concepts_and_Techniques_of_Productivity [June 2012].

[5]OECD (2001) provides a thorough overview of aggregate and industry-level productivity measures.

has been increasing or declining. The model may not reveal why this is so, but at the very least it pushes us to ask additional, useful questions. However, these kinds of models are not typically intended to be used for accountability or incentivizing purposes—especially for applications such as higher education where output prices do not necessarily reflect quality. In contrast, the structural models involve a fairly detailed representation of an entity's internal structure, and thus require more granular data. Such models also generally focus on marginal revenues and marginal costs, as opposed to the average revenues and costs considered in the aggregate models. As noted above, the panel was not charged with developing a structural model and has not attempted to do so.

At a conceptual level, this report dedicates considerable attention to productivity measurement at different levels of aggregation, including the institution, system, and sector levels. For most purposes, it is necessary to segment the sector by institution type to avoid inappropriate comparisons. However, the measure developed in Chapter 4 is focused on productivity of the sort typically applied to aggregate economic sectors (e.g., autos, steel, higher education), which rests on the methodology used by the BLS. While one can imagine aggregating institution-level data to produce a macro productivity measure, such an approach is not practical at the present time for the higher education sector. As a technical matter, there is nothing to prevent the model developed here from being applied at the level of a state, system, or individual institution, but this opens the way for it to be exploited for performance measurement without the proper support of additional quality measures. The panel generally believes that this risk associated with pushing forward with productivity measurment is worth taking, and that to maintain the "know-nothing" status quo would perpetuate dysfunctional behavior.

It is noteworthy that the panel was not charged with recommending processes to improve productivity, for example, through innovative new methods for designing courses or through online education. Similarly, the panel was not asked to develop models for monitoring departmental, institutional, or system activity; these are applications. One stumbling block to productivity measurement—and indeed, to productivity *improvement*—has been the widely-held view that, because learning is a service and its production is labor-intensive, colleges and universities suffer from a condition known as Baumol's cost disease. The underlying theory, which breaks from the notion in classical economics that wage changes are closely tied to labor productivity changes, is that labor costs in some sectors of the economy are affected by productivity gains in other unrelated sectors. Those productivity gains drive an increase in wages across the entire economy. Sectors without productivity gains are nonetheless faced with a higher wage bill, making them appear less efficient.[6] Archibald and Feldman (2011) subscribe to

---

[6]In their landmark book, *Performing Arts: The Economic Dilemma*, Baumol and Bowen (1966) use as an example a Mozart string quintet composed in 1787. More than two centuries later, it still requires five musicians and the same amount of time to perform the piece.

this view, noting that the production processes for colleges and universities rely on human interaction (at least traditionally), nearly fixed amounts of time inputs from faculty and students, and a key role for highly educated, highly compensated employees.

Even when steps can be taken to increase throughput, questions rightfully arise about the effect of the changes on quality. Archibald and Feldman write (2011:40):

> An institution can increase class size to raise measured output (students taught per faculty per year) or it can use an increasing number of less expensive adjunct teachers to deliver the service, but these examples of productivity gain are likely to be perceived as decreases in quality, both in the quality rankings and in the minds of the students.

However, the evidence on the potential of higher education to benefit from new models of production, such as online courses, is not conclusive. Harris and Goldrick-Rab (2011) argue that "researchers and institutions themselves have rarely paid much attention to whether policies and practices are cost-effective. How would you know whether you're spending money effectively if you've never even asked the question?" They conclude that colleges "can conceivably become more productive by leveraging technology, reallocating resources, and searching for cost-effective policies that promote student success." Indeed, many industries that formerly were believed to be stagnant have been able to improve productivity dramatically. Even in the quintessential example of Baumol's cost disease (noted above), string quartets have improved "productivity" dramatically through the capability to simulcast a performance to theaters or, more obviously, by recording their music and earning money while the musicians sleep (Massy, 2010:39). Other examples can be found in medical care, legal services, and elsewhere.

Work by the National Center for Academic Transformation (NCAT) on course redesign provides a contemporary example of what can be accomplished in this area (see Chapter 2 for a description of some of this work; see also Appendix B on NCAT's methods). The organization's clients analyze measures to determine new ways to combine inputs so as to produce student credit hours of the same or better quality than with traditional methods. Quality assurance also enters the process. Indeed, the changes that have been made following such analyses are the classic ones used in essentially all industries: shifts from high-cost to lower-cost labor, more intensive use of and better technology, and elimination of waste in resource utilization.

The idea that instructional productivity may potentially be increased by altering the way inputs in the production function are combined highlights why improved measurement is so important. Potential improvement in productivity also justifies requirements that colleges and universities systematize collection of data on expenditures and the volume and quality of inputs and outputs. Routine generation and collection of such data is a prerequisite for wider efforts to improve productivity and enable external stakeholders to hold institutions accountable.

1.3. AUDIENCE AND REPORT STRUCTURE

In the face of the observations laid out above, we take the following premises as the starting point for our assertion that improved information regarding the functioning of higher education is needed: (1) Those who fund higher education have a legitimate interest in meaningfully measuring productivity, both in order to make the best possible allocations and spending decisions within the sector, and to assess the value of higher education against other compelling demands on scarce resources; (2) Institutions, individuals, and communities whose economic well-being is most directly at stake when funding decisions are made have a legitimate interest in ensuring that measurements of productivity are accurate and appropriate. The analysis and recommendations in this study attempt to balance these interests.

This report has been written for a broad audience including national and state policy makers, system and institution administrators, higher education faculty, and the general public.

- *State and federal legislators*: Policy makers benefit from discussion that identifies important questions, explains the need for particular data programs, and clarifies the meaning of different performance metrics.
- *College and university administrators*: These decision makers are under increasing pressure to address accountability and productivity concerns. This report may provide authoritative backing to resist pressure to impose inadequate assessment systems just so as to be seen to be doing something. These groups may also benefit from guidance about what data to collect to support proposed evaluations of programs.
- *Faculty*: College and university professors need to understand the interaction between their own interests and society's interests in the education enterprise. They need to be informed about innovative approaches to increasing mission efficiency through use of technology and other means. And they need quality information to guide them in the context of shared governance that prevails in most colleges and universities.
- *General public*: We hope that this report will promote a greater understanding of societal interests in higher education and of how the interests of stakeholders (students, faculty, administrators, trustees, parents, taxpayers) fit into that broader picture. The arguments herein may also promote a fuller understanding of the complexity of colleges and universities and how they benefit the economy and society.

The remainder of the report is organized as follows: In Chapter 2, we define productivity and then characterize the activities of higher education in terms of inputs or outputs. We pay particular attention to the heterogeneity of the sector, including the great range of its products and the changes and variation in the quality of its inputs and outputs. Accounting for all outputs of higher education is particularly daunting, as they range from research findings and production of credentialed citizens to community services and entertainment. Although the panel's recommendations focus on degree output, research and other scholarly and creative activities must be acknowledged because they are part of the joint product generated by universities, and because they may affect the quality and quantity of teaching. We also contrast productivity with other measurements that have been used as proxies for it and discuss the merits and limitations of proxies currently in use.

In Chapter 3, we articulate why measurement of higher education productivity is uniquely difficult. Colleges and universities produce a variety of services simultaneously. Additionally, the inputs and outputs of higher education production processes are heterogeneous, mix market prices and intangibles, vary in quality, and change over time. Measurement is further impeded by conceptual uncertainties and data gaps. While none of these difficulties is unique to higher education, their severity and number may be. We detail the complexities—not to argue that productivity measurement in higher education is impossible, but rather to indicate the problems that must be overcome or mitigated to make accurate measurements.

This report will be instructive to the extent that it charts a way forward for productivity measurement. Toward this end, in Chapter 4, we provide a prototype productivity measure intended to advance the conceptual framework. The objective here is not to claim a fully specified, ideal measure of productivity, for such does not exist. Rather, we aim to provide a starting point to which wrinkles and qualifications can be added to reflect the complexity of the task, and to suggest a set of factors for analysts and policy makers to consider when using productivity measures or other metrics to inform policy.

In Chapter 5, we offer practical recommendations designed to advance measurement tools and the dialogue surrounding their use. We provide guidance for developing the basic productivity measure proposed in Chapter 4, targeting specific recommendations for the measurement of inputs and outputs of higher education, and discuss how changes in the quality of the range of variables could be better detected. A major requirement for improved measurement is better data. Thus, identifying data needs demanded by the conceptual framework, with due attention to what is practical, is a key part of the panel's charge. This is addressed in Chapter 6. In some cases, the most useful measures would require data that do not now exist but that could feasibly be collected.

2

Defining Productivity for Higher Education

The importance of productivity growth to an economy is widely recognized because the extent to which living standards can be improved over time depends almost entirely on the ability to raise the output of its workers.[1] From the perspectives of individual industries and enterprises, gains in productivity are a primary means of offsetting increases in the costs of inputs, such as hourly wages or raw materials. Likewise, in higher education, productivity improvement is seen as the most promising strategy for containing costs in the continuing effort to keep college education as affordable as possible. Without technology-driven and other production process improvements in the delivery of service, either the price of a college degree will be beyond the reach of a growing proportion of potential students or the quality of education will erode under pressures to reduce costs.

In this environment, such concepts as productivity, efficiency, and accountability are central to discussions of the sustainability, costs, and quality of higher education. The discussion should begin with a clear understanding of productivity measures and their appropriate application, while recognizing that other related concepts (such as unit cost, efficiency measures, and the like) are also important and inform key policy questions.

At the most basic level, productivity is defined as the quantity of outputs delivered per unit of input utilized (labor, capital services, and purchased inputs).

---

[1]Average annual GDP growth for the United States, 1995-2005, was 3.3 percent. Estimates of the contributions of the various components of this growth (Jorgenson and Vu, 2009) are as follows: Labor quantity, 0.63; labor quality, 0.19; noninformation and communications (ICT) capital, 1.37; ICT capital, 0.48; total factor productivity (TFP) growth, 0.63. These figures indicate the importance of input quality and technology in per capita productivity gains.

The number of pints of blueberries picked or boxes assembled using an hour of labor are simple examples. Productivity, used as a physical concept, inherently adjusts for differences in prices of inputs and outputs across space and over time. While productivity measures are cast in terms of physical units that vary over time and across situations, efficiency connotes maximizing outputs for a given set of fixed resources.[2] Maximizing efficiency should be the same as maximizing productivity if prices are set by the market (which is not the case for all aspects of higher education). Accountability is a managerial or political term addressing the need for responsibility and transparency to stakeholders, constituents, or to the public generally.

Application of a productivity metric to a specific industry or enterprise can be complex, particularly for education and certain other service sectors of the economy. Applied to higher education, a productivity metric might track the various kinds of worker-hours that go into producing a student credit hour or degree. The limitation of this approach is that, because higher education uses a wide variety of operational approaches, which in turn depend on an even wider variety of inputs (many of them not routinely measured), it may not be practical to build a model based explicitly and exclusively on physical quantities. Of even greater significance is the fact that the quality of inputs (students, teachers, facilities) and outputs (degrees) varies greatly across contexts.

A primary objective of industries, enterprises, or institutions is to optimize the efficiency of production processes: that is, to maximize the amount of output that is physically achievable with a fixed amount of inputs. Productivity improvements are frequently identified with technological change, but may also be associated with a movement toward best practice or the elimination of inefficiencies. The measurement of productivity presumes an ability to construct reliable and valid measures of the volume of an industry's (or firm's) output and the different inputs. Though productivity improvements have a close affinity to cost savings, the concepts are not the same. Cost savings can occur as a result of reduction in input prices, so that the same physical quantity of inputs can be purchased at a lower total cost; they are also attainable by reducing the quantity or quality of output produced. But, by focusing on output and input volumes alone, it becomes difficult to distinguish efficiency gains from quality changes. To illustrate, consider homework and studying. Babcock and Marks (2011) report that college students currently study less than previously. Assuming studying is an input to learning, does this mean that students have become more productive or now

---

[2]Kokkelenberg et al. (2008:2) write that: "Economists describe efficiency to have three aspects; allocative efficiency which means the use of inputs in the correct proportions reflecting their marginal costs; scale efficiency which considers the optimal size of the establishment to minimize long-run costs; and technical efficiency which means that given the establishment size and the proper mix of inputs, the maximal output for given inputs under the current technology is achieved." It should be noted that that the productivity index approach, on its own, is unlikely to say much about optimal size and scale efficiency.

shirk more? Arum and Roksa (2010) argue that college students are learning less, implying the latter. But, without robust time series data on test results to verify student learning, the question remains unanswered.

2.1. BASIC CONCEPTS

Several different productivity measures are used to evaluate the performance or efficiency of an industry, firm, or institution. These can be classified as single-factor productivity measures, such as labor productivity (the ratio of output per labor-hour), or multi-factor productivity, which relates output to a bundle of inputs (e.g., labor, capital, and purchased materials). In addition, productivity can be evaluated on the basis of either gross output or value added. Gross output is closest to the concept of total revenue and is the simplest to calculate because it does not attempt to adjust for purchased inputs. Value added subtracts the purchased inputs to focus on the roles of labor, capital, and technology within the entity itself.

For most goods, labor is the single largest factor of production as measured by relative expenditures. Labor productivity is thus a commonly used measure. Labor productivity, however, is a partial productivity measure that does not distinguish between improvements in technology and the contributions of other productive factors. Thus, a measure of labor productivity based on gross output might rise due to the outsourcing of some activities or the improvement of capital used in the production process. In this instance, labor productivity would rise at the expense of additional purchased services or other inputs.

Conceptually, a multi-factor productivity measure based on gross output and changes in the volumes of all individual inputs provides greater insight into the drivers of output growth. It shows how much of an industry's or firm's output growth can be explained by the combined changes in all its inputs. Relative to labor productivity, construction of a multi-factor productivity measure imposes substantially greater requirements on data and estimation methods.

The construction of productivity measures requires quantitative estimates of the volume of outputs and inputs, excluding the effects of pure price changes while capturing improvements in quality. As a simple illustration, total revenues provide a measure of the value to consumers of an industry's production, and the revenues of the individual types of good or services produced by the industry are deflated by price indexes and weighted together by their shares in total revenues to construct an index of output volume. Similar indexes are constructed for the volumes of the inputs. The volume indexes of the inputs are combined using as weights their shares in total income or costs. Alternatively, when feasible, quantities of outputs and inputs may be estimated without deflating expenditure totals when the physical units can be counted directly. The productivity measure is then obtained by dividing the index of output by the composite index of inputs.

After decades of discussion, research and debate, the concepts and methods used to compute productivity within the market-based private economy have achieved widespread agreement and acceptance among economists, policy analysts, and industry specialists. However, comparable progress has not been made with respect to the measurement of productivity in education, and higher education in particular. Progress also has been slow—although perhaps not quite as slow—in a few other service sector industries, such as finance and health care, where outputs are also difficult to define and measure (Triplett and Bosworth, 2002). It is possible to count and assign value to goods such as cars and carrots because they are tangible and sold in markets; it is harder to tabulate abstractions like knowledge and health because they are neither tangible nor sold in markets.

Standard methods for measuring productivity were developed for profit- or shareholder value-maximizing firms engaged in the production of tangible goods. These methods may not be applicable, valid, or accurate for higher education, which is a very different enterprise. Traditional private and public colleges and universities are not motivated by or rewarded by a profit margin. Neither their output nor their prices are determined within a fully competitive market, and thus their revenues or prices (essentially tuition) are not indicative of the value of the industry's output to society.[3] The inputs to education are substantially similar to those of other productive sectors: labor, capital, and purchased inputs. Higher education is distinct, however, in the nature of its outputs and their prices. The student arrives at a university with some knowledge and capacities that are enhanced on the way to graduation. In this instance, the consumer collaborates in producing the product.

Second, institutions of higher education are typically multi-product firms, producing a mixture of instructional programs and research as well as entertainment, medical care, community services, and so on. For market-based enterprises, the production of multiple products raises manageable estimation problems. Outputs are combined on the basis of their relative contributions to revenue shares. This is a common feature of productivity analysis.

However, because research and classroom instruction are both nonmarket activities, there is no equivalent concept of revenue shares to combine the two functions. This greatly complicates the analysis and the possibility of deriving an overall valuation of an institution's output. We have chosen to separate instruction from research (and other outputs), acknowledging the practical reality that an institution's allocation of resources among its multiple functions is in part the result of forces and influences that are quite complex. For example, the value of research universities cannot be fully measured by their instructional contribution alone. Important interactions exist, both positive and negative, between research activities and the productivity of undergraduate instruction. On the positive side,

---

[3]Discounts for financial aid also complicate an institution's value function. The interaction between institutional and consumer value upsets the association of price with value to consumers. Other price distortions are discussed throughout the report.

there is the opportunity for promising undergraduates to work alongside experienced faculty. On the negative side, there is the possibility that the growth of graduate programs detracts from commitments to undergraduate education. While these difficulties in allocating some inputs and outputs by function are very real, and clearly warrant investigation, a separate analyses of instruction and research seems most practical for now and is the approach pursued in Chapter 4.

In Chapter 3, we explore in more detail this and other complexities of measuring productivity in higher education.

2.1.1. Outputs

Estimating productivity presumes an ability to define and measure an industry's (or institution's, or nation's) output. Most systems of output measurement are estimated by deflating the revenues of individual product categories by indexes of price change. As noted above, if the products are sold in open competitive markets, producers will expand output to the point where the marginal revenues of individual products are roughly equal to their marginal costs. Thus, their revenue shares can be used as measures of relative consumer value or weights to combine the various product categories to yield an index of overall output. By focusing on the price trends for identical models, or by making adjustments to account for changing characteristics of products, price indexes can differentiate the price and quality change components of observed changes in overall prices.[4]

In some cases, the output of an industry might be based on physical or volume indicators such as ton miles moved by trucks or, in the case of education, the number of students in a course. Physical measures of output are difficult to aggregate if they differ in their basic measurement units, but methods have been devised to mitigate this problem.[5] A greater challenge is that physical indicators generally miss quality change. While explicit quality adjustments can be included in the construction of a physical output index, it is difficult to know the weight to place on changes in quantities versus changes in quality. The role of quality change and other complications in defining and measuring output of higher education are addressed in detail in Chapters 3 and 4.

Higher education qualifies graduates for jobs or additional training as well as increasing their knowledge and analytic capacities. These benefits of undergraduate, graduate and professional education manifest as direct income effects, increased social mobility, and health and other indirect effects. Measures have been created to monitor changes in these outputs, narrowly defined: numbers

---

[4]The complete separation of price and quality change continues to be a major challenge for the creation of price and output indexes. It is difficult to incorporate new products into the price indexes in a timely fashion, and price and quality changes are often intermingled in the introduction of new models. See National Research Council (2002).

[5]The Törnqvist index used in Chapter 4 uses percentage changes, which takes care of the dimensionality problem.

of degrees, time to degree, degree mix, and the like. Attempts have also been made to estimate the benefits of education using broader concepts such as the accumulation of human capital. For estimating the economic returns to education, a starting point is to examine income differentials across educational attainment categories and institution types, attempting to correct for other student characteristics. Researchers since at least Griliches (1977), Griliches and Mason (1972), and Weisbrod and Karpoff (1968) have estimated the returns to education, controlling for students' cognitive ability by including test score variables in their wage regressions.

Researchers have also examined the impact of socioeconomic status (SES) variables on the returns to education, but the results are somewhat ambiguous. Carneiro, Heckman, and Vytlacil (2010) show that marginal returns to more college degrees are lower than average returns due to selection bias. That is, returns are higher for individuals with characteristics making them more likely to attend college than for those for whom the decision is less clear or predictable. This carries obvious implications for policies designed to increase the number of college degrees produced by a system, region, or nation. On the other hand, Brand and Xie (2010) predict that the marginal earnings increase attributable to holding a degree is actually higher for those born into low socioeconomic status (relative to the higher SES group more likely to select into college) because of their lower initial earnings potential with or without a degree. Dale and Krueger (2002:1491) also found that the "payoff to attending an elite college appears to be greater for students from more disadvantaged family backgrounds." Davies and Guppy (1997) found that socioeconomic factors do not affect chances of entry into lucrative fields net of other background factors, but SES predicts entry into selective colleges and lucrative fields within selective colleges. Establishing the values of degrees generally or of degrees in specific fields—as done by Carnevale, Smith, and Strohl (2010) and Trent and Medsker (1968)—involves estimating the discounted career cost (controlling for selection effects) of not attending college at all. To some extent this line of research has been stunted by the characteristics of available data; many cohort studies have been flawed in not properly including aging effects, not asking about attainment, or not extending for a long enough time period. Such features are important for estimating returns.[6] As a result, the evidence for evaluating the magnitude of differences in outcomes of those who attain higher education and those who do not is surprisingly mixed.

One limitation of the above-described approaches is that the rate of return on various degrees, and college in general, varies over time with labor market

---

[6]For example, the National Center for Education Statistics (NCES) "High School and Beyond" study looked at a large number of students (more than 30,000 sophomores and 28,000 seniors enrolled in 1,015 public and private high schools across the country participated in the base year survey), but did not follow individuals long enough. The NCES National Education Longitudinal Study (NELS) repeated the error by not asking about final degree attainment; the Education Longitudinal Study (ELS) is still following cohorts and may offer a very useful data source.

conditions, independent of the quality of the degree or credits earned. Adding to the supply of graduates tends to lead to a reduction in the wage gap between more and less educated workers, an effect that may be strengthened if the expansion causes educational quality to fall. Another modeling consideration is that, due to market pressures, students may enroll in majors with high projected returns. An increased supply of graduates in those fields should lead to downward pressure on wages. The ebb and flow in the demand for and starting wages paid to nurses is a good example.[7] Nonetheless, wages do provide at least one quantifiable measure, but one that needs regular updating.

Even when research on wages relative to educational attainment is conducted properly, it cannot tell the whole story. The overall returns to instruction (learning) and production of degrees are broader than just the pecuniary benefits that accrue to the degreed individuals. It is a mistake to view the purpose of higher education as solely to increase gross domestic product (GDP) and individual incomes.[8] Some of the nation's most important social needs (e.g., teaching, nursing) are in fields that are relatively low paying. When the focus is on incomes after graduation, a system or institution that produces more credentialed individuals in these socially important but low-paying fields will appear less productive than an institution that produces many highly paid business majors. This would be a false conclusion. Moreover, using lifetime earnings as a measure of productivity and then tying public support for institutions to this measure in effect restricts the educational and career choices of individuals who, capable of entering either, knowingly choose lower paying over higher paying occupations. In Chapter 3, we examine the implications of looking more broadly at the benefits—private and public, market and nonmarket, productive and consumption—produced by higher education.

2.1.2. Inputs

Having established that productivity relates the quantity of output to the inputs required to produce it, it is evident that correct measurement requires identifying all inputs and outputs in the production process. Economists frequently categorize inputs into the factors of production:

- Labor (e.g., professors, administrators)
- Physical and financial capital (e.g., university buildings, endowments)
- Energy (utilities)
- Materials (e.g., paper, pens, computers if not capitalized)

---

[7]Data on graduates' wages do allow students to make informed decisions, so would be useful to students as a resource, and to administrators for resource allocation.

[8]That said, one of the most carefully studied "externalities" of higher education is its role in economic growth—see Card (1999) and Hanushek and Kimko (2000).

- Service inputs (e.g., use of outside payroll, accounting, or information technology [IT] firms)

Here, we review the role of each of these inputs.

Labor Inputs

In most simple measures of labor productivity, the quantity of labor is defined by the number of hours or full-time equivalent workers. Left at this, the measure suffers from the assumption that all workers have the same skills and are paid equivalent wages. This is clearly not true, and can only be maintained in situations where changes and variation in the skill level of the workforce are known to be small.

One means of adjusting for quality is to disaggregate the workforce by various characteristics, such as age or experience, education, occupation, and gender. In competitive labor markets, it is assumed that workers of each skill characteristic will be hired up to the point where their wage equals their contribution to marginal revenue. The price of labor is measured by compensation per hour; hence, labor inputs of different quality are aggregated using as weights their relative wage rates or, alternatively, using the share of each type of labor in total labor compensation. In this respect, the aggregation of the labor input is comparable to the aggregation of individual product lines to arrive at an estimate of total output.

Relative to other sectors, the problem of measuring labor inputs differs only marginally for higher education since, even if higher education is largely a nonmarket activity, its workforce must be drawn from a competitive market in which faculty and other employees have a range of alternatives. Some faculty members are protected by tenure; however, similar issues of seniority and job protection arise in other industries and the differences are generally ones of degree.[9] Despite these similarities, however, it may be desirable to differentiate among the labor categories of teachers as discussed in Chapters 3 and 4.

Another complication arises at research-based institutions. For these institutions, the time and cost of faculty and administrative personnel must be divided between research and instruction.[10] One approach might rely on time-use studies to develop general guidelines on the number of instructional hours that accompany an hour of classroom time, although time required for student consultations and grading may vary with class size. Furthermore, there are so many different kinds of classes and teaching methods that it is not practical to associate hours for

---

[9]The role of tenure in education is often comparable to various union pressures for seniority and other forms of job protection.

[10]Some problems of using wage rates to adjust for the quality of faculty teaching may arise in research-based institutions where the primary criteria for promotion and tenure reflect research rather than teaching skills.

BOX 2.1
A Note on Student Time Inputs

A fully specified production function for higher education might include student time as an input. Given the panel's charge, this area of measurement is not a high priority; however, the student time input, if defined as the number of hours spent in school-related activities multiplied by an opportunity cost wage rate, would be substantial (see National Research Council, 2005, for a discussion of how to deal with nonmarket time valuations within an economic accounting framework). It can be difficult to establish opportunity cost wages when students are subsidized. For example, during periods or in places characterized by high unemployment, a federal Pell grant is a good substitute for a job.

For our purposes, we acknowledge that unpaid student time is a relevant input to the production function (though Babcock and Marks, 2011, find students are studying less). Nonetheless, little would be gained for policy purposes by including it in productivity measures. For applications where this kind of information is important, researchers can turn to the Bureau of Labor Statistics' American Time Use Survey, which includes data on study time by students.

---

specific labor categories with credit hours, even if variation in class size could be handled. As discussed below, we therefore believe the best approach is to allocate inputs among output categories using a more aggregate approach.

Finally, the student's own time and effort is a significant input to the educational process (see Box 2.1). While there has been debate about whether student effort should be treated as an input or an output, the emergent field of service science moots the question by recognizing that the process of consuming any service (including education) requires the recipient to interact with the provider *during* the production process and not only after the process has been completed as in the production of goods.[11] This phenomenon is called coproduction. As applied to higher education, it means student effort is *both* an input and an output. This is consistent with the view that a primary objective of a university is to encourage strong engagement of students in their own education. Equally fundamental, institutions of higher education service a highly diverse student population, and many institutions and programs within those institutions have devoted great effort to sorting students by ability. In the absence of information about the aptitude levels of incoming students, comparing outcomes across institutions and programs may not provide a useful indication of performance.

---

[11]See, for example, Sampson in Maglio, Kieliszewski, and Spohrer (2010:112).

Capital Inputs

The major feature of capital is that it is durable and generates a stream or flow of services over an extended period. Thus, the contribution of capital to production is best measured as a service or rental flow (the cost of using it for one period) and not by its purchase price. Because many forms of capital cannot be rented for a single production period, the rental or service price must be imputed. This is done by assuming that a unit of capital must earn enough to cover its depreciation and a real rate of return comparable to similar investments. The depreciation rate is inversely proportionate to the asset's expected useful life, and the rate of return is normally constant across different types of capital.[12] Short-lived capital assets can be expected to have a higher rental or service price because their cost must be recovered in a shorter period. These rental rates are comparable to a wage rate and can be used in the same way to aggregate across different types of capital services and as a measure of capital income in aggregating the various inputs to production.

The role of capital in the measurement of productivity in higher education is virtually identical to that for a profit-making enterprise. Assets are either purchased in markets or valued in a fashion similar to that in the for-profit sector. Thus, the standard measurement of capital services should be appropriate for higher education. The education sector may exhibit a particular emphasis on information and communications capital because of the potential to use such tools to redesign the education process and by doing so to achieve significant productivity gains. The more significant problem at the industry level is that there is very little information on the purchases and use of capital in higher education. The sector is exempt from the economic census of the U.S. Census Bureau, which is the primary source of information for other industries. However, the Internal Revenue Service Form 990 returns filed by nonprofit organizations do contain substantial financial information for these organizations, including data on capital expenditures and depreciation.

Energy, Materials, and Other Purchased Inputs

Productivity measures require information on intermediate inputs either as one of the inputs to the calculation of multi-factor productivity or as a building block in the measurement of value added. In some measures, energy, materials, and services are identified separately. Such a disaggregation is particularly useful in the calculation of meaningful price indexes for purchased materials. In the past, the lack of significant information on the composition of intermediate inputs was a significant barrier to the calculation of productivity measures for many

---

[12]The rental rate is measured as a proportion of the replacement cost of a unit of capital or P_k $(r + d)$, where P_k is the replacement cost, r is the real rate of return, and d is the depreciation rate.

service industries. Lack of relevant information on purchased inputs continues to be a major shortfall for estimating productivity in higher education. This kind of data is particularly important for analyses attempting to control for the effects of the outsourcing of some service activities. As with capital, the primary problem in measuring the role of purchased inputs in higher education is the lack of a consistent reporting system. The information is known at the level of individual institutions, but there is no system for collecting and aggregating the data at the national level for the purpose of establishing performance norms.

2.1.3. Instructional and Noninstructional Elements of the Higher Education Production Function

For the purposes of this report, it is essential to distinguish inputs and outputs along functional lines. In particular, an effort should be made to identify the inputs that go into each of the multiple outputs produced by the sector. These inputs can be designated:

- Instructional, including regular faculty, adjunct faculty, and graduate student instructors.
- Noninstructional and indirect costs including, for example, administration, athletics, entertainment, student amenities, services, hospital operation, research and development, student housing, transportation, etc.[13] Some of these are budgeted separately.
- Mixed, including other capital such as instructional facilities, laboratory space and equipment, and IT. The best way to distribute the cost of such inputs across instructional, administrative, and research categories is not often clear.

In the model presented in Chapter 4, we attempt to identify all the inputs associated with the instruction function, while recognizing the difficulty of separating instructional and noninstructional costs or inputs. The main concern is to distinguish inputs associated with instruction from those designated for research. As faculty are involved in a range of activities, it is difficult to assign their wages to one category or another.

Instructional costs can also vary greatly. On the faculty side, per unit (e.g., course taught) instructional costs vary by field, institution, and type of instructor. On the student side, per-unit instructional costs vary by student level—undergraduate, taught postgraduate, and research students; mode of attendance—full- versus part-time students (the cost of student services varies by

---

[13]See Webber and Ehrenberg (2010).

mode of attendance even if the teaching cost per credit hour does not[14]); and field of study, with business and the humanities costing less than science and engineering, which in turn cost less than medicine. At the institutional level, costs can be subject to large-scale activity-based costing studies. Costs can also be disaggregated to the department level. Because the panel's interests and charge focus primarily on groups of institutions of different types and within different states, our recommendations do not emphasize detailed breakdowns of costs at the student level. Nevertheless, some way of controlling for these variations will be essential to ameliorate significant distortions and criticisms.

For administrative and other purposes, universities typically track inputs along other dimensions, such as by revenue source. For our purposes, the only reason for classifying inputs according to revenue source is to separate the inputs associated with organized research and public service as described in Chapter 4. University accounting systems assign costs to funds. This practice tends to differentiate among payers, but obfuscates productivity unless specific outputs also are assigned to the fund. Differentiating inputs among payers departs from the idea of productivity as an engineering concept relating physical inputs and outputs. Further, not all revenues are fungible; they cannot all be used to increase production of undergraduate degrees (Nerlove, 1972).

Higher education costs may also be identified and categorized according to their source:

- institutional funds such as gifts and endowments;
- public-sector appropriations, including state, local, and federal government subsidies and financial aid;
- tuition and fees from students and their families (and note that some factors affect costs to specific payers but not overall cost; cost to university may also differ from total cost); and
- sponsored research.

For some policy purposes it is important to distinguish between trends in tuition and trends in cost per full-time equivalent (FTE) student. Some analyses dispute the common notion that the cost of higher education is rising faster than consumer prices broadly; rather, the composition of who pays is changing. Even when the total cost of a college education is relatively stable, shifts occur in the proportions paid by different players and what activities the revenues support.

McPherson and Shulenburger (2010) highlight the important difference between cost and price. In simple economics terms, the cost, or supply schedule, is based on an underlying production function. Productivity improvements shift the

---

[14]Mode of attendance may affect the relationship between transcript and catalog cost measures. For example, part-time students may take more courses or repeat courses because of scheduling problems or less efficient sequencing and thus learning (Nerlove, 1972).

cost schedule downward, with (other things being equal) attendant reductions in price and increases in quantity demanded for a given demand schedule. The full price of undergraduate education (determined by both the demand and supply functions) is the sum of tuition charges, campus subsidies, and state subsidies. Affordability and access thus depend on state appropriations as much as they depend on changes in productivity. For example, if an increase in productivity occurs simultaneously with a reduction in state appropriations, price to student (tuition) may not fall; it may even rise depending on relative magnitudes.

In the same vein, it is important to highlight differences between public and private higher education, as has been done by the Delta Cost Project (2009). Tuition increases in private higher education invariably are associated with increased expenditures per student.[15] In marked contrast, tuition increases in public higher education often are associated with decreases in expenditures per student as the tuition increases often only partially offset cutbacks in state support.

2.2. PRODUCTIVITY CONTRASTED WITH OTHER MEASUREMENT OBJECTIVES

Dozens of metrics have been created to serve as proxies for productivity or as indicators to inform accountability programs and to track costs and outcomes.[16] Beyond productivity as defined above, measures of efficiency and cost are other performance metrics with policy value. While there are certainly appropriate uses for a variety of measures, there are also dangers of misuse, such as the creation of perverse incentives. For example, if degrees granted per freshman enrolled was used to track performance, then institutions could enroll large numbers of transfer students to improve their standing. Our review of various measures below informs our recommendations for developing new measures and for modifying existing ones. New, improved, and properly applied performance measures will begin filling information gaps and allow multiple stakeholders to better understand performance trends in higher education.

2.2.1. Productivity and Cost

An alternative approach to measuring productivity—one typically used in cost studies—is to estimate the expenditures incurred for instructional activity

---

[15]Pell grants, state need-based scholarships, and other sources of student aid can, in principle, offset tuition hikes.

[16]See Measuring Quality in Higher Education (http://applications.airweb.org/surveys/Organization. aspx [February 2012]), a database developed by the National Institute for Learning Outcomes Assessment, which describes four categories: assessment instruments; software tools and platforms; benchmarking systems and other extant data resources; and assessment initiatives, collaborations, and custom services. The database can be searched by unit of analysis and aggregation level. These are categorized not too differently from our matrix (i.e., student, course, institution, and state or system).

(including allocated overheads), then divide by a volume measure of output to produce a ratio such as cost per degree. Under tightly specified conditions, this would produce the same result as a productivity measure. These conditions, however, are rarely if ever realized. The problem is that simple ratios like cost per student or degree does not take into consideration quality and the multiple outputs produced by higher education institutions. Hence, this approach conveys too little information to be able to attribute productivity differences to differences (over time or between institutions) in price and quality.

Efficiency is improved when cheaper inputs are substituted for more expensive ones without damaging quality proportionately. For example, it has become a common trend for institutions to substitute adjunct instructors for tenure-track faculty. Whether this move toward lower-priced inputs has a proportionately negative impact on output quantity and quality (e.g., numbers of degrees and amount learned) is not yet fully known, and surely varies from situation to situation (e.g., introduction and survey classes versus advanced seminars). In reviewing evidence from the emerging literature, Ehrenberg (2012:200-201) concludes that, in a wide variety of circumstances, the substitution of adjuncts and full-time nontenure-track faculty for tenure-track faculty has resulted in a decline in persistence and graduation rates.

Without data tying changes in faculty composition to student outcomes, efforts to implement accountability systems will be made with only partial information and will lead to problematic policy conclusions. For example, in 2010 the office of the chancellor of Texas A&M University published what amounted to a "a profit-and-loss statement for each faculty member, weighing annual salary against students taught, tuition generated, and research grants obtained … the number of classes that they teach, the tuition that they bring in and research grants that they generate" (*Wall Street Journal*, October 22, 2010). When a metric as simple as faculty salary divided by the number of students taught is used, many relevant factors are omitted. An instructor teaching large survey courses will always come out ahead of instructors who must teach small upper-level courses or who are using a year to establish a laboratory and apply for grants, as is the case in many scientific disciplines.[17] These metrics do not account for systematic and sometimes necessary variations in the way courses at different levels and in different disciplines are taught; and they certainly do not account for differences in the educational experience across faculty members and across different course designs.

The value of productivity and efficiency analysis for planning purposes is that it keeps a focus on both the input and output sides of the process in a way

---

[17]In recognition of these limitations, administrators did pull the report from a public website to review the data and the university president promised faculty that the data would not be used to "assess the overall productivity" of individual faculty members (see http://online.wsj.com/article/SB10 001424052748703735804575536322093520994.html [June 2012]).

that potentially creates a more thorough and balanced accounting framework. If costs were the only concern, the obvious solution would be to substitute cheap teachers for expensive ones, to increase class sizes, and to eliminate departments that serve small numbers of students unless they offset their boutique major with a substantial grant-generating enterprise.[18] Valid productivity and efficiency measures needed for accountability require integration of additional information—for example, the extent to which use of nontenure track faculty affects learning, pass rates, and preparation for later courses relative to the use of expensive tenured professors. The implication is that analysts should be concerned about quality when analyzing statistics that purport to measure productivity and efficiency. Different input-output ratios and unit costs at differing quality levels simply are not comparable.

Finally, it is important to remember that even valid measures of cost and productivity are designed to answer different questions. A productivity metric, for example, is needed to assess whether changes in production methods are enabling more quality-adjusted output to be generated per quality-adjusted unit of input. That this is an important question can be seen by asking whether higher education is indeed subject to Baumol's cost disease (see Chapter 1)—the question of whether, in the long run, it is a "stagnant industry" where new technologies cannot be substituted for increasingly expensive labor inputs to gain efficiencies. Unit cost data cannot answer this question directly, but they are needed for other purposes, such as when legislatures attempt to invest incremental resources in different types of institutions to get the most return in terms of numbers of degrees or graduation rates. This kind of resource-based short-run decision making responds to funding issues and institutional accountability, but addresses productivity only indirectly and inadequately.

A critical asymmetry also exists in the way productivity and cost-based measures are constructed. Current period price data can be combined with the physical (quantity) data to calculate unit costs, but it is impossible to unpack the unit cost data to obtain productivity measures. The fact that most measurement effort in higher education is aimed at the generation of unit cost data has inhibited the sector's ability to assess and improve its productivity.

2.2.2. Other Performance Metrics

Many other performance measures have been proposed for higher education. The most prominent of these are graduation rates, completion and enrollment ratios, time to degree, costs per credit or degree, and student-faculty ratios. These kinds of metrics are undeniably useful for certain purposes and if applied correctly. For example, Turner (2004) uses time-to-degree data to demonstrate the

---

[18]To the credit of Texas A&M University, it did not respond to the findings of its faculty assessment in any of the above-mentioned ways.

relative impact on student outcomes of changing incoming student credentials versus effectiveness in the allocation of resources within public higher education. She finds that the former has a smaller impact than the latter. Similarly, studies have usefully shown how tuition and aid policies affect student performance as measured partially by these statistics. The range of performance metrics, including a discussion of the meaning of graduation rates as calculated by the Integrated Postsecondary Education Data System (IPEDS), is described in detail in Appendix A.

While their role is accepted, the measures identified above should not be confused with productivity as defined in this report. Used as accountability tools, one-dimensional measures such as graduation rates and time-to-degree statistics can be abused to support misleading conclusions (e.g., in making comparisons between institutions with very different missions). Also, because graduation rates are strongly affected by incoming student ability, using them in a high-stakes context may induce institutions to abandon an assigned and appropriate mission of broad access. Use of these kinds of ratio measures may similarly induce institutions to enroll large numbers of transfer students who are much closer to earning a degree than are students entering college for the first time, whether that is the supposed mission or not.

To illustrate the ambiguity created by various metrics, student-faculty ratio levels can be linked to any combination of the following outcomes:

Low Student-Faculty Ratio	*High Student-Faculty Ratio*
low productivity	high productivity
high quality	low quality
high research	low research
resource diversion	unsustainable workload

The ability to distinguish among these outcomes is crucial both for interpreting student-faculty ratios and for policy making (both inside and outside an institution).

Time to degree, graduation rate, and similar statistics can be improved and their misuse reduced when institutional heterogeneity—the mix of full- and part-time students, the numbers of students who enter at times other than the fall semester, and the proportion of transfer students—is taken into account. Additional refinements involve things like adjusting for systemic time-frame differences among classes of institutions or students. A ratio measure such as a graduation rates that is lagged (allowing for longer time periods to completion) is an example. To avoid the kinds of overly simple comparisons that lead to misguided conclusions—or, worse, actions—responsible use of performance metrics (including productivity if it is used for such purposes) should at the very least be used only to compare outcomes among like types of institutions or a given institution's actual performance with expected levels. The institutional segmentation approach has been used by College Results Online,[19] a Web site that allows users to view graduation rates for peer institutions with similar characteristics and student profiles. The second method is exemplified by Oklahoma's "Brain Gain"[20] performance funding approach that rewards institutions for exceeding expected graduation rates. These existing measures and programs with good track records could serve as models or pilots for other institutions, systems, or states.

While the panel is in no way attempting to design an accountability system, it is still important to think about incentives that measures create. Because institutional behavior is dynamic and directly related to the incentives embedded within the measurement system, it is important to (1) ensure that the incentives in the measurement system genuinely support the behaviors that society wants from higher education institutions, and (2) attempt to maximize the likelihood that measured performance is the result of authentic success rather than manipulative behaviors.

The evidence of distortionary and productive roles of school accountability is fairly extensive in K-12 education research, and there may be parallel lessons for higher education.[21] Numerous studies have found that the incentives introduced by the No Child Left Behind Act of 2001 (P.L. 107-110) lead to substantial gains in at least some subjects (Ballou and Springer, 2008; Ladd and Lauen, 2010; Reback, Rockoff, and Schwartz, 2011; Wong, Cook, and Steiner, 2010), and others have found that accountability systems implemented by states and localities also improve average student test performance (Chakrabarti, 2007; Chiang, 2009; Figlio and Rouse, 2006; Hanushek and Raymond, 2004; Neal and Schanzenbach, 2010; Rockoff and Turner, 2010; Rouse et al., 2007). However, these findings have been treated with some skepticism because, while Rouse and colleagues (2007) show that schools respond to accountability pressures in productive ways, there is also evidence that schools respond in ways that do not lead to generalized improvements. For example, many quantitative and qualitative studies indicate that schools respond to accountability systems by differentially allocating resources to the subjects and students most central to their accountability ratings. These authors (e.g., Booher-Jennings, 2005; Hamilton et al., 2007; Haney, 2000; Krieg, 2008; Neal and Schanzenbach, 2010; Ozek, 2010; Reback, Rockoff, and Schwartz, 2011; White and Rosenbaum, 2008) indicate that schools under accountability pressure focus their attention more on high-stakes subjects, teach skills that are valuable for the high-stakes test but less so for other assessments, and concentrate their attention on students most likely to help them satisfy the accountability requirements.

Schools may attempt to artificially boost standardized test scores (Figlio and Winicki, 2005) or even manipulate test scores through outright cheating (Jacob

---

[19]See http://www.collegeresults.org/ [June 2012].

[20]See http://www.okhighered.org/studies-reports/brain-gain/ [June 2012].

[21]The panel thanks an anonymous reviewer for the following discussion of incentive effects associated with accountability initiatives in the K-12 context.

and Levitt, 2003). These types of behaviors may be the reason that the recent National Research Council (2011) panel on school accountability expressed a skeptical view about accountability while recognizing the positive gains associated with these policies.

One potential solution emerging from the K-12 literature is that "value added" measures of outcomes tend to be less manipulable than are measures based on average levels of performance or proficiency counts. The rationale is that when schools are evaluated based on their gains from year to year, any behaviors generating artificial improvements would need to be accelerated in order for the school to continue to show gains the next year. In higher education, however, this year's post-test is not next year's pre-test, so there remains the very real possibility that institutions could manipulate their outcomes (or their inputs) in order to look better according to the accountability system; and while value added measures might allow for more apples-to-apples comparisons among institutions, they will not reduce the strategic behavior problem by as much as they might in K-12 education.

One example of how higher education institutions respond strategically to the incentives embedded within an evaluation system is observable in relation to the *U.S. News & World Report* rankings. Grewal, Dearden, and Lilien (2008) document ways in which universities strategically deploy resources in an attempt to maximize their rankings. Avery, Fairbanks, and Zeckhauser (2003) and Ehrenberg and Monks (1999) find that the ranking system distorts university admissions and financial aid decisions.

If institutions make failure more difficult by implementing systems of support to help struggling students improve, this is a desired outcome of the accountability system. If instead they act in ways that dilute a curriculum, or select students who are likely to help improve the institution's ranking, this could be a counterproductive consequence of the system. The more background characteristics are used to predict graduation rates, the harder this manipulation would become, but on the other hand, only a small number of background factors are currently available on a large scale.

To sum up, many proxy measures of productivity have been constructed over the years. They have some utility in comparing institutions and programs, if used cautiously and with knowledge of their drawbacks. But experience has shown that they can result in major misunderstandings and the creation of perverse incentives if applied indiscriminately. As with productivity measurement itself, these proxies are significantly affected by context. Among the most important contextual variables that must be controlled for are institutional selectivity, program mix, size, and student demographics. The model outlined in Chapter 4 suggests approaches for dealing with some of the shortcomings of traditionally used performance measures. Part-time students are treated as partial FTEs; semester of entry does not create distortions; and successful transfers are accounted for through awarding bonus points analogous to the sheepskin effect for bachelor's degrees.

3

Why Measurement of Higher Education Productivity Is Difficult

Productivity measurement involves a conceptually simple framework. However, for the case of higher education, complexities are created by a number of factors, the following among them:

- Institutions of higher education are multi-product firms (that is, they produce multiple kinds of services);
- Inputs and outputs of the productive process are heterogeneous, involve nonmarket variables, and are subject to quality variation and temporal change; and
- Measurement is impeded by gaps in needed data.

None of these complexities is completely unique to higher education, but their severity and number may be.[1] In this chapter, we examine each of these complexities because it is essential to be aware of their existence, even while recognizing that practical first steps toward measurement of productivity cannot fully account for them.

---

[1] A wise tempering of this assertion is offered in the Carnegie Foundation report (Cooke, 1910:5):

It is usual in the industrial world to find manufacturers and business men who look upon their own undertakings as being essentially different from every other seemingly like undertaking. This could not be otherwise, because every one knows the difficulties of his own work better than those of his neighbor. So I was not surprised to learn that every college feels that it has problems unlike, and of greater difficulty of solution than, those to be encountered at other colleges. As a matter of fact, from the standpoint of organization, uniformity in collegiate management is a much easier problem than it is in most industries, because in any industry which I know about, the individual plants vary considerably more than do the colleges.

3.1. BEYOND THE DEGREE FACTORY—MULTIPLE OUTPUTS AND JOINT PRODUCTION

The greatest barriers to estimating the output of higher education derive from the fact that most institutions are multi-product firms.[2] Large research universities produce undergraduate, professional and graduate degrees, research (including patents and pharmaceutical development), medical care, public service activities (especially at land grant universities), entertainment (such as cultural and athletic events), and other goods and services from a vector of capital, labor, and other inputs. Community colleges produce remedial education, degree, and certificate programs designed for graduates entering directly into careers, academic degree programs that create opportunities for transfer to four-year institutions, and programs designed to meet the needs of the local labor market and specific employers. It is admittedly extremely difficult to develop accounting structures that capture the full value of these outputs which accrue to both private and public entities.[3]

Firms and sectors in other areas of the economy produce multiple goods and services as well. An automobile manufacturer, for example, may produce cars, trucks, and airplane parts; a bank may offer loans as well as an automatic teller machine, checking accounts, and a range of other services. While it can be difficult to specify a functional form that represents the technological input-output relationships that exists for multi-product producers, it has been done (Christensen, Jorgensen, and Lau, 1973; Diewert, 1971). The range and nature of outputs produced by higher education, however, makes such estimation much more complex than for most other industries.

Though the panel's recommendations in Chapters 5 and 6 focus on improving measurement of instructional inputs and outputs, research, and other scholarly and creative activities should be acknowledged in a comprehensive accounting because they are part of the joint product generated by universities. Among the difficult analytical problems created by joint production are how to separate research and development (R&D) production costs from degree production costs; how to compare the relative value of research and degree output; and how to assign faculty and staff time inputs into each (which raises the problem of separating different kinds of research, whether done at a faculty member's initiative or with outside sponsorship). Judgments must be made in the process of separat-

---

[2]Triplett (2009:9) writes:

Measuring medical care output is difficult. Measuring the output of education is *really* hard.... The fundamental difficulty in education has little to do with test scores, class sizes and similar attributes that have figured so intensively in the discussion so far, though those measurement problems deserve the attention they are getting. More crucially, the output of educational establishments is difficult to measure *because they are multi-product firms*. They do not produce *only* education, they produce other things as well.

[3]McPherson and Shulenburger (2010) provide an excellent description of the multi-product nature of higher education institutions, plus a sensible first attempt to separate these into educational and other components. On the regional impact of universities, see Lester (2005).

ing the instructional and noninstructional components of the higher education production function.

Additionally, the linkage of research and research training coupled with responsibility for baccalaureate and professional education is relevant to the instructional component of output, and a defining and internationally distinctive characteristic of the U.S. system of higher education.[4] Statistics on degrees and research activity document the central place of research universities in the generation of advanced degrees in scientific and engineering fields. Research universities—defined here, using the Carnegie Classification of Academic Institutions, as doctorate-granting institutions—are few in number (approximately 283) relative to the total number of U.S. colleges and universities (estimated at 4,200). Nonetheless, they awarded 70 percent of doctorates, 40 percent of master's degrees, and 36 percent of bachelor's degrees in science and engineering in 2007.[5] The connection between research and graduate instruction in America's universities is well understood and indeed is a core rationale for their substantial role in the national R&D system.[6]

While fully appreciating the value and variety of higher education outputs, the panel decided to focus on instruction. This decision entails analytical consequences. Specifically, a productivity measure of instruction can provide only a partial assessment of the sector's aggregate contributions to national and regional objectives. In particular, the omission of some kinds of research creates a truncated view not only of what colleges and universities do but also of their critical role in national research innovation and postbaccalaureate educational systems. And, just as there should be measures of performance and progress for the instructional capabilities of educational institutions, measures should also be developed for assessing the value of and returns to the nation's investments in research (especially the publicly funded portion). As outlined in the next chapter, we believe it is useful to assess and track changes in instructional productivity as a separate output.

---

[4]In his comparative study of national higher education systems, Burton Clark describes U.S graduate education as a "tower of strength," adding: "This advanced tier has made American higher education the world's leading magnet system, drawing advanced students from around the world who seek high-quality training and attracting faculty who want to work at the forefront of their fields" (Clark, 1995:116). Jonathan Cole (2009) cites a host of inventions that have fundamentally altered the way Americans live, contributed to U.S. economic competitiveness and raised the U.S. standard of living. He describes the United States as being "blessed with an abundance of first-rate research universities, institutions that are envied around the round," further calling them "national treasures, the jewels in our nation's crown, and worthy of our continued and expanded support" (Cole, 2009:x-xi).

[5]Estimates are from National Science Board (2010:2ff-7ff).

[6]Less well understood is how the coupling of instruction and research serves to attract high-performing researchers to faculty positions and to then provide incentives to undertake high-risk, frontier research.

3.2. HETEROGENEITY OF INPUTS AND OUTPUTS

The inputs and outputs of higher education display widely varying character-istics. The talents of students and teachers vary, as do their levels of preparedness and effectiveness in teaching and learning. At community colleges, for example, the student mix and to some extent instructor qualifications are typically quite unlike those for four-year research universities. In the composition of a student body, the following characteristics are widely acknowledged to affect educational outcomes and thus, the relationship between inputs and outputs:

- Economic inequality and mix of low-income and minority students.[7]
- Student preparedness. College preparedness affects the efficiency with which graduates can be produced. The link between academic prepara-tion and performance in college is extremely strong (Astin, 1993; Horn and Kojaku, 2001; Martinez and Klopott, 2003).[8] Remedial courses (those not part of the required total for graduation) also add to the cost of degree completion.
- Student engagement. Education is a service where the recipient must be an active partner in the process of creating value ("coproduction").[9] Variation in student motivation as well as ability strongly affects the learning process and, therefore, productivity.
- Peer effects. Student interaction affects both higher education outputs and inputs, and is difficult to measure. If the performance of a less pre-pared student is raised by being surrounded by better prepared students, this enhances learning and is part of the value of the higher education experience.[10]

The composition of an institution's student body will influence how that institu-tion will score in a performance metric. If the measure of interest is graduation rates, lower levels of student preparation will likely translate into lower produc-tivity. If the metric is value added or marginal benefit, lower levels of student

---

[7]Two perennial policy goals are the promotion of productivity and equity, which, in different situ-ations, can be complementary or conflicting. See Immerwahr et al. (2008) to get a sense of the views of college presidents regarding costs and equity.

[8]Adelman (1999) found completing high-level mathematics classes such as algebra II, trigonometry, and calculus in high school to be the best single predictor of academic success in college.

[9]Coproduction, introduced in Chapter 2, is recognized as a defining feature of service operations including education. See, for example, Sampson (2010:112). The complexity introduced by copro-duction should be taken into account when developing productivity models. Notice, however, that issues of coproduction arise in the handling of input heterogeneity, and that there is no suggestion that student time should be priced into the productivity formula.

[10]Zimmerman (2003) shows students' grades being modestly but significantly affected by living with high, medium, or low SAT score roommates.

preparation may lead to higher measured gains because the learning gap that can be closed is larger.[11]

In the same vein, faculty characteristics, skills, and sets of responsibilities will impact the quality of outputs produced by an institution. At the simplest level, college faculty can be categorized into two groups: tenure-track faculty and adjunct faculty. Tenure-track faculty are involved in teaching, research, and public service, with time allocation to each dependent on the type of institution they are associated with. At research universities, some time is obviously directed toward research, while at community colleges efforts are concentrated almost exclusively on teaching courses. Adjunct (nontenure track) faculty at all types of institutions are assigned to teach specific courses and may not have a long-term affiliation with an institution. In the current economic downturn, with universities facing budget cuts, the utilization of adjunct faculty has become increasingly prominent.[12] This situation raises the need for analyses of the quality of instruction adjunct faculty provide. In the section on inputs, below, and again in Chapter 5, we return to the topic of variable student and instructor quality, and its implications for productivity measurement.

On the output side, the mix of degrees by level and subject varies across institutions. These differences affect both the production process and the labor market value of graduates. Institutions serve diverse student communities and pursue very different missions. While all aim to produce better educated and credentialed citizens, some institutions produce two-year degrees, certificates, and students equipped to transfer to four-year schools, while others produce bachelor's and graduate degrees in a wide range of disciplines. Some of these outputs are inherently more expensive to produce than others. This heterogeneity means that production functions for institutions with different output mixes will display different characteristics.

Adjusting for the distribution of degrees requires data on the course-taking patterns of majors in different fields. The cost of a degree in chemistry, for example, depends on the number of math classes, laboratory classes, and general studies classes that such majors must take and the average cost of each type of class. Regression analyses using data at the state level have been used to produce estimates of the cost of degrees in different majors. In their models, Blose, Porter, and Kokkelenberg (2006) found that carefully adjusting per-student expenditures to account for the distribution of majors and the average costs to produce each

---

[11]See Carey (2011) on the relationship between student quality and the cost of obtaining educational outcomes.

[12]Even in the period before the recession, the trend was well established: According to data from the American Federation of Teachers, in the mid-1970s, adjuncts—both part-timers and full-timers not on a tenure track—represented just over 40 percent of professors; 30 years later, they accounted for nearly 70 percent of professors at colleges and universities, both public and private (see http://www.nytimes.com/2007/11/20/education/20adjunct.html?pagewanted=all [June 2012]).

major improved estimates of the impact of measured instructional expenditures on graduation and persistence rates.

Another approach to determining the cost of degrees in different fields involves working back from the level and field coefficients in the funding models used by various jurisdictions to adjust an institution's total instructional cost on the basis of its data in the Integrated Postsecondary Education Data System (IPEDS). Data on degrees may not be robust enough for regression analysis, but they ought to be sufficient for this approach based on an assumed set of coefficients. In our data recommendations in Chapter 6, we advise that credit-hour data for productivity analyses be collected in a way that follows students in order to better control for differences in degree level and field. This manner of collecting data, discussed in Chapter 4, will be a big step forward in productivity and cost analysis.

The problem of heterogeneity can be at least partially addressed by cross-classifying institutions that enroll different kinds of students and offer various degree levels and subjects. One cell in the classification might be chemistry Ph.D. programs in research universities, for example, while another might be undergraduate business majors in comprehensive or two-year institutions. While measuring the relation between inputs and outputs for each cell separately would significantly limit variations in the educational production function, and also would help control for differences due to the joint production of research and public service, it would not eliminate the problem.[13] Variation in student inputs will still be present to some extent since no institution caters specifically to only one kind of student, and students do not always enroll in school with a definite idea of what their major will be. Students also frequently change majors.

Such a multi-fold classification is most likely impractical for any kind of nationally based productivity measure. Two strategies exist for overcoming this problem. First, certain cells could be combined in the cross-classification by aggregating to the campus level and then creating categories for the standard institutional type classifications used elsewhere in higher education (e.g., research, master's, bachelor's, and two-year institutions). In addition to reducing the number of cells, aggregation to the campus level subsumes course-level issues that occur, for example, when engineering majors enroll in English courses. While compiling data at the campus level introduces a significant degree of approximation, this is no worse than would likely occur in many if not most industries elsewhere in the economy. Individual institutions can and should analyze productivity at the level of degree and subject, just as manufacturers should analyze productivity at the level of individual production processes. The techniques required to do so are beyond the panel's purview.

An alternative is to control for key variations within the productivity model

---

[13]Of course, too much disaggregation could also be harmful, by reducing sample size too much to be useful for some analyses, for example.

itself. This might entail tracking the number of degrees and credits separately by level and subject for each institutional category. Cross-classification is carried as far as practical and then formulas are constructed to control for the variation in key remaining variables. The two approaches are analogous to poverty measures that combine cross classification and formulaic adjustment to allow for differences in wealth, in-kind benefits, or cost of living differences. The baseline model described in Chapter 4 employs both of these strategies.

3.3. NONMARKET VARIABLES AND EXTERNALITIES

Further complicating the accounting of inputs and outputs of higher education is that some, such as student time and nonpecuniary benefits of schooling, are nonmarket in nature—these factors are not bought and sold, do not have prices, and are not easily monetized. Additionally, not all of the benefits of an educated citizenry accrue to those paying for education. Such characteristics make these factors difficult to measure and, as a result, they are often ignored in productivity analyses. In this sense, higher education (and education in general) is analogous to activities in other areas, such as health care, home production, and volunteerism.[14]

Policy makers concerned with, say, a state's returns on its investment in education should be interested in the full private *and* social benefits generated by their institutions. A truly comprehensive accounting would include the sector's impact on outcomes related to social capital, crime, population health, and other correlates of education that society values. Much of this social value is intangible and highly variable; for example, social capital creation attributable to higher education may be greater at residential colleges and universities than at commuter colleges due to peer effects. These kinds of nonmarket quality dimensions are no doubt important parts of the production function, although they cannot yet be measured well. The policy implication is that the fullest possible accounting of higher education should be pursued if it is to be used for prioritizing public spending.[15]

That positive externalities are created by higher education is implicitly acknowledged as college tuition (public and private) is deliberately set below the

---

[14]See National Research Council (2005) for difficulties and approaches to measuring nonmarket inputs and outputs in an accounting framework.

[15]According to Brady et al. (2005), Texas generates $4.00 of economic output per each dollar put into higher education; California generates $3.85 for each dollar invested. The issue of states' returns on education is complex. Bound et al. (2004) have shown that the amount that states spend on their public education systems is only very weakly related to the share of workers in the state with college degrees. Intuitively, this is because educated labor is mobile and can move to where the jobs are. Because of mobility, some social benefits of higher education accrue to the nation as a whole, not just to individual states. This may create an incentive for states to underinvest in their public higher education systems.

equilibrium market-clearing price, and institutions engage in various forms of rationing and subsidies to manage demand. Financial aid and other forms of cross-subsidization provide mechanisms to increase enrollment. Thus, because the resulting marginal cost does not align with price, total revenues do not equate with the value of an institution's output; the distribution of revenues across different activities also cannot be used to construct a combined index of output that reflects relative consumer value.[16]

At the most aggregate level, Jorgenson and Fraumeni (1992) circumvented the problem of defining a measure of output by assuming that the value of education can be equated with the discounted value of students' future incomes. They assess the contribution of education to human capital based on lifetime earning streams of graduates. Without additional assumptions, however, such a measure cannot be related back to a specific educational episode. The focus on outcomes may also subsume the role of education as a sorting mechanism to distinguish individuals of differing abilities, potentially overstating the contribution of education alone.[17]

3.4. QUALITY CHANGE AND VARIATION

A fully specified measure of higher education productivity would account for quality changes over time and quality variation across inputs and outputs by individual and institution. However, the kind of sophisticated data and analysis that would be required for accurate and sensitive quality measurement is very much in the long-term research phase. Nonetheless, it is important to conceptualize what is needed in order to make progress in the future.

Many sectors of the economy are characterized by wide variety of quality in outputs. Computers vary in processing speed, reliability and data storage capacities; luxury cars are built to higher standards than economy models; and the local hardware store may have superior customer service relative to superstores. Quality also changes over time—computers become faster, cars become safer, and power tools more powerful. What is unique about higher education is the lack of generally accepted measures of quality change or variation. And indeed, consumers may not be aware of the measures that do exist. This reinforces the conclusion of the previous section: variations in the demand for higher education cannot be taken as reflecting quality.

Many aspects of measuring quality change have been explored for other difficult-to-measure service sectors and progress has been made. In its price

---

[16]Within the framework of the national accounts, nonmarket activities such as education have been valued on the basis of the cost of their inputs. That approach rules out the possibility of productivity change.

[17]Spence (1973) developed models to identify these kinds of sorting effects, such as those whereby employers use credentials to identify workers with desirable, but not directly observable, traits.

measurement program, the Bureau of Labor Statistics (BLS) employs a number of methods for separating pure price and quality effects as it monitors products in its market basket over time. Methods for addressing some of the more generic issues (e.g., defining output in service sectors, adjusting for changing product characteristics) may translate to the education case.[18] As described in Box 3.1, lessons from work on productivity and accounting in the medical care sector may exhibit the closest parallels to the education sector.[19]

3.4.1. Inputs

Quality variations exist for nearly the full range of higher education inputs: students, faculty, staff, library, and physical facilities. Some dimensions of student quality can potentially be adjusted for using standardized test scores, high school grade point averages (GPAs), parents' education, socioeconomic status, or other metrics. For comparing institutions, additional adjustments may be made to reflect variation in the student population characteristics such as full-time or part-time status, type of degrees pursued, and preparation levels, as well as the differing missions of institutions. Institutions with a high percentage of remedial or disadvantaged students need longer time-horizons to bring students to a given level of competency. They are often further burdened by smaller endowments, lower subsidies, and fewer support resources, all of which can lengthen time to degree for their students. Students select into institutions with different missions, according to their objectives. Institutional mission and character of student body should be considered when interpreting graduation rates, cost statistics, or productivity measures as part of a policy analysis.

Measures of student engagement generated from major student surveys such as the National Survey of Student Engagement (NSSE), the Community College Survey of Student Engagement (CCSSE), the Student Experience in the Research University (SERU), and the Cooperative Institutional Research Program (CIRP) can provide additional insight about the experiences of students enrolled in a given institution. This is important because the extent to which students devote effort to educationally purposeful activities is a critical element in the learning process. However, engagement statistics require careful interpretation because— beyond student attributes—they may also reflect actions by an institution and its faculty. For example, effective educational approaches or inspiring teachers can sometimes induce less well-prepared or -motivated students to achieve at higher levels. Thus, measures of student engagement can be instructive in understanding an institution's capacity to enhance learning. Limitations of student surveys, such

---

[18]See National Research Council (2002) for a full description of the statistical techniques developed by BLS, the Bureau of Economic Analysis, and others for adjusting price indexes to reflect quality change.

[19]For more information, see National Research Council (2005, 2010a).

BOX 3.1
Higher Education and Medical Care

An analogy exists between higher education—specifically the production of individuals with degrees—and health care—specifically the production of completed medical treatments. Lessons for measuring the former can possibly be gleaned from the latter. Nearly all the complications making productivity measurement difficult can be found in both sectors:

- In both cases, additional outputs beyond degrees and treatments are produced.
- Product categories exhibit a wide variety—different kinds of degrees and different kinds of treatments are produced. Some of the products have more value than others, depending on how value is calculated. For example, an engineering degree may generate more income than a philosophy degree, and cardiovascular surgery produces greater health benefits (in terms of quality-adjusted life years, for instance) than does cosmetic surgery.
- Outcomes vary substantially such that some students or patients enjoy more successful outcomes than others. Some students get a great education and find worthwhile employment while others do not; some patients recover fully, while others die.
- Inputs are heterogeneous. Some students are better prepared and therefore enter college with a higher chance of graduation. Some patients are more fit than others and therefore have a greater probability of successful outcomes from medical treatment.
- Institutional missions also vary. Institutions of higher education range from small locally oriented colleges to large universities with national and international influence. Similarly, medical care treatments are administered in a variety of institutions with different missions, ranging from doctors' offices to small local hospitals to large regional hospitals (which also jointly produce medical students).

as those noted above, are debated in Arum and Roksa (2010) who point out that, while data focused on "social engagement" are important for questions related to student retention and satisfaction outcomes, data on academic engagement are also needed if the goal is improved information about learning and academic performance. While NSSE does include a few questions related to social engagement (e.g., nonacademic interactions outside the classroom with peers), many more questions address areas of academic engagement such as writing, discussing ideas or doing research with faculty, integrative learning activities, and so forth.

In looking at any measure of student characteristics, it must be remembered that between-institution variance is almost always smaller than within-institution

- Varying production technologies are possible in both sectors. Educational institutions vary in their student/faculty ratios, their reliance on graduate student instructors and adjunct faculty, and their use of technology. Similarly, hospitals vary in doctors, nurse, and staff-to-patient ratios, in their reliance on interns and residents, and in their use of technology.
- Pricing and payment schemes also vary in the education and health sectors. Students can pay very different prices for apparently similar English degrees, just as patients can pay very different prices for apparently equivalent medical treatments. Also, in both sectors, payments are made not only by the primary purchaser but by a variety of third-party payers, such as the government or insurance companies. This complicates price estimation and costing exercises.

National Research Council (2010a) provides guidance on how to deal with the complexities associated with estimating inputs, outputs, and prices for medical care. Essentially, outputs are defined so as to reflect completed treatments for which outcomes can be quantified and thus quality of the output adjusted.

For performance assessment purposes, hospital mortality rates have been adjusted to reflect the complexity of the case mix that each deals with. For example, a tertiary care hospital with relatively high numbers of deaths may receive "credit" for the fact that its patients are sicker and hence at a greater likelihood of death. An analogous risk adjustment approach exists for higher education wherein schools that enroll less well-prepared students would be assigned additional points for producing graduates because the job is more difficult. One effect of such an adjustment is that the highly selective schools would be adjusted downward because more of their students are expected to graduate. Regression models have been used to attempt to make these adjustments using institutional resources and student characteristics to estimate relative performance. For example, the ranking system of the *U.S. News & World Report* takes into account characteristics of both the institution (wealth) and of the students (both entry test scores and socioeconomic background). In this system, SAT results essentially predict the rank order of the top 50 schools.

variance on proxy measures of quality (Kuh, 2003). This is because individual student performance typically varies much more *within* institutions than average performance does *between* institutions. This appears to be true at every level of education. Results from the NSSE reveal that for all but 1 of the 14 NSSE scales for both first-year and senior students, less than 10 percent of the total variance in student engagement is between institutions. The remaining variance—in several instances more than 95 percent—exists *at the student level* within a college or university. Thus, using only an institutional level measure of quality when estimating productivity can be misleading.

Beyond students—the "raw material" for learning[20]—many of the variations in inputs are no different in principle from those encountered in other industries. However, teacher quality bears special mention. The central role of teachers has long been reflected by the separation of faculty from other kinds of staff in the human resource policies of educational institutions and in government data collection. The distinction between tenure-track and nontenure-track faculty is also common. A recent trend has been to use inexpensive adjunct teachers who receive no benefits and lack job stability. Adjunct teachers may be of the same quality as tenure-track faculty member in terms of their ability to teach the material for a given course, but they tend to be less well integrated into the institution's departmental structure. This, plus the fact that adjuncts do less (or no) research and do not participate comparably in departmental administration means that productivity improvements arising from shifts toward greater use of them may be more apparent than real.

Whether adjuncts are better or worse in motivation and ability than tenure-track faculty is an empirical question; indeed, it is these kinds of questions that highlight the need for better productivity measurement. And the answer is likely to differ depending on circumstances: in some settings, research and administrative responsibilities may improve teaching quality; in others, publication pressures may be such that tenure-track faculty are not selected for teaching quality and have strong incentives to neglect their teaching. These possibly significant factors are one reason why the model presented in Chapter 4 includes adjunct usage as an explicit factor.

A survey of the chief financial officers (CFOs) of 500 colleges by *The Chronicle of Higher Education* revealed their view that the most effective cost-cutting or revenue-raising strategies are to raise teaching loads and increase tuition.[21] Another favored strategy is to reallocate tenure and adjunct faculty positions and, as a result, universities and colleges are increasingly scrutinizing faculty productivity. An example of this is the recent initiatives by the University of Texas and Texas A&M University. These initiatives resulted in the release of performance data identifying faculty teaching loads versus the cost to keep faculty members employed. The basic idea was to examine the number of students taught by an individual faculty member relative to the cost borne by the university in faculty salaries, benefits, and overhead. In the current atmosphere of accountability for public funds, this kind of measure of faculty performance will be used synonymously with faculty productivity, even though William Powers, president of the

---

[20]See Rothschild and White (1995) for a discussion of higher education and other services in which customers are inputs.

[21]See "Economic Conditions in Higher Education: A Survey of College CFOs" at http://chronicle. com/article/Economic-Conditions-in-Higher/128131/ [June 2012].

University of Texas at Austin, said that "there is no attempt to measure the quality, and therefore the true productivity, of the learning experience."[22]

Faculty quality is often measured by grades and student evaluations. However, these outcomes can be heavily influenced by external factors which make it difficult for institutions to ascertain the contribution of faculty quality toward student success. In a controlled study by Carrell and West (2010), U.S. Air Force Academy students were randomly assigned to a permanent or a part-time instructor. Student grades over a course sequence were analyzed to evaluate teacher quality. The study found that the students taught by part-time instructors (more specifically, less experienced instructors who did not possess terminal degrees) received better grades in the lower level course taught (Calculus I). However, "the pattern reversed" for higher division courses (e.g., Calculus II), where the same students performed worse relative to those taught by the experienced professors in the introductory course. The study concluded that part-time instructors were more likely to teach the introductory course to improve students' test performance for that course, while the permanent instructors were more likely to teach to improve students' knowledge of the subject.[23] Even though the study provides a useful direction for measuring faculty quality, it is not possible for all universities and colleges to conduct such controlled studies—though more could do so than actually do—and therefore such rich data may not typically be available for analysis.

The OECD and Institutional Management in Higher Education (IMHE) conducted a joint study on quality teaching practices in institutions of higher education around the world.[24] The study pointed out that to understand fully the causal link between teaching and quality of learning, pioneering and in-depth evaluation methods and instruments are necessary. The National Research Council (2010b) report on measuring quality of research doctoral programs also outlined assessment methods for the quality of faculty involved in Ph.D. programs. The assessment utilized a broad data-based methodology that included more specific items than were included in previous years' assessments, such as number of publications, citations, receipt of extramural grants for research, involvement in interdisciplinary work, demographic information, and number of awards and honors. Even though the NRC report addressed a complicated issue, it emphasized measuring faculty quality as it pertains to research-doctoral programs in four-year research universities. The absence of guidelines on measuring quality of instructional faculty in four-year universities and community colleges was attributed to the trend of relying on wages earned as a proxy of faculty quality. The

---

[22]Powers (2011), see http://www.statesman.com/opinion/powers-how-to-measure-the-learning-experience-at-1525080.html [June 2012].

[23]The Carrell and West finding is consistent with research by Bettinger and Long (2006), who found that the use of adjunct professors has a positive effect on subsequent course interest, and Ehrenberg and Zhang (2005), who found a negative effect on student graduation.

[24]OECD (2009), see http://www.oecd.org/dataoecd/31/2/43136035.pdf [June 2012].

series of models presented in the next chapter uses faculty salaries to distinguish across labor categories.

3.4.2. Outputs (and Outcomes)

We have made the point that higher education produces multiple outputs. Even for those concerned primarily with the instructional component, looking narrowly at the production of four-year degrees may be inadequate because degrees are far from homogeneous.[25] Ideally, for valuing outputs, it would be possible to identify quality dimensions and make adjustments integrating relevant indicators of learning, preparation for subsequent course work, job readiness, and income effects. Even with full information, weights that would be applied to these characteristics would still entail subjective assessments. We emphasize, explicitly and unapologetically, that adjusting degrees or otherwise defined units of higher education output by a quantitative quality index is not feasible at the present time. However, it is possible to begin dealing with the problem through classification of institutions by type and mission and then, as described in Chapter 4, by seeking to assure that quality within each segment is being regularly assessed and at least roughly maintained.

When considering a productivity metric focusing on instruction, objectively measurable outputs such as credit hours earned and number of degrees granted represent the logical starting point; however, the quality problem arises almost immediately since these can be expected to differ across courses, programs, and institutions. While universities often use credit hours as a measure of the importance and difficulty of each course, these quality adjustments are incomplete because they do not reflect the full course value to students (and to society).

---

[25]Ehrenberg (2012) finds the presence of differential tuition by major or year in a program to be quite widespread in American public higher education, reflecting differences in the cost of providing education in different fields (or levels) or the expected private return to education in the field or year in the program. For example, among four-year public institutions offering primarily bachelor's degrees, 23 percent have differential tuition by college or major. The University of Toronto has a differential tuition price policy that makes the expected relative public to private benefit of the degree one of the criteria for determining the level of public subsidy vs. private tuition (see http://www.governingcouncil.utoronto.ca/policies/tuitfee.htm [June 2012]). From an economic perspective, it makes sense to base tuition on the expected value of the major and the costs. One practical problem is that lower income students may be excluded from majors with high costs but high return. In addition, the needs of states may call for training students in areas that are high cost but provide limited economic return to students. Another problem is that the policy could lead to the production of the wrong kind of degrees over different time frames (for example, swings in demand for nurses). It is understandable why states may do this, but the policy may emphasize costs of degrees over students' interests. On the other hand, if infinite cross-subsidization is not endorsed or feasible, and if cross subsidies have gone beyond what is seen as a reasonable level, then students may be required to bear a larger portion of costs.

Economic Returns

Market-oriented assessments of educational output, with attention to how salary effects vary by area of study and by institutional quality, have been explored in the economics literature.[26] Some studies attempt to assess evidence on the relationship between college cost and quality in terms of student and institutional performance. Beyond wage outcomes, indicators have reflected number of graduates who find a job within a given period after graduation; surveys of alumni satisfaction with their education; surveys of local business communities' satisfaction with the university's role in providing skilled workers; percentage of students taking classes that require advanced work; and number of graduates going on to receive advanced degrees.

Despite work in this area, many tough issues remain even if the goal is to estimate only the economic returns to education. How can wage data best be used for such calculations, and what is most important: first job, salary five years out, or discounted lifetime earnings?[27] Furthermore, intergenerational and business cycle effects and changing labor market conditions cause relative wages to be in constant flux. Perhaps most importantly, student characteristics, demographic heterogeneity, accessibility and opportunities, and other factors affecting earnings must be controlled for in these kinds of economic studies. The reason full quality adjustment of the output measure is still a futuristic idea is that much research is still needed to make headway on these issues. The literature certainly offers evidence of the effects of these variables, but using precise coefficients in a productivity measure requires a higher level of confidence than can be gleaned from this research.

Student Learning

Beyond measures of credits and degrees produced, and their associated wage effects, is the goal of measuring the value added of student learning.[28] The motivation to measure learning is that the number of degrees or credit hours completed is not, by itself, a complete indicator of what higher education produces. That is, earning a baccalaureate degree without acquiring the knowledge, skills, and competencies required to function effectively in the labor market and in society is a hollow accomplishment. Indicators are thus needed of the *quality* of the degree represented by, for example, the amount of learning that has taken

---

[26]See, for example, Pascarella and Terenzini (2005), Shavelson (2010), and Zhang (2005).

[27]Estimating lifetime earnings would introduce long lags in the assessments as some evidence suggests that the most quantitatively significant wage effects do not take effect until 8 to 10 years after undergraduate degree.

[28]Not only is learning difficult to measure in its own right, it would be challenging to avoid double counting with wage effects (assuming those who learn most do best in the job market).

place and of its post-college value (represented by income, occupational status, or other measure) beyond that attributable to the certificate or degree itself.

Ignoring measures of learning outcomes or student engagement (while, perhaps, emphasizing graduation rates) may result in misleading conclusions about institutional performance and ill-informed policy prescriptions. Is it acceptable for a school to have a high graduation rate but low engagement and outcomes scores? Or are individual and public interests both better served by institutions where students are academically challenged and demonstrate skills and competencies at a high level, even if fewer graduate? Strong performance in the areas of engagement, achievement, and graduation are certainly not mutually exclusive, but each says something different about institutional performance and student development. One conclusion from Pascarella and Terenzini's (1991, 2005) syntheses is that the impact of college is largely determined by individual student effort and involvement in the academic, interpersonal, and extracurricular offerings on a campus. That is, students bear a major responsibility for any gains derived from their postsecondary experience. Motivation is also a nontrivial factor in accounting for post-college differences in income once institutional variables such as selectivity are controlled (Pascarella and Terenzini, 2005).

A number of value-added tests have been developed over the years: the Measure of Academic Proficiency and Progress (MAPP) produced by the Educational Testing Service, Collegiate Assessment of Academic Proficiency (CAAP) produced by the ACT Corporation, and the Collegiate Learning Assessment (CLA) designed by RAND and the Council for Aid to Education. The CLA is most specifically designed to measure valued added at the institutional level between the freshman and senior years.[29] This kind of quality adjustment is desirable at the level of the institution or campus for purposes of course and program improvement, but is unlikely to be practical anytime soon for the national measurement of productivity in higher education. It is beyond the scope of this panel's charge to resolve various longstanding controversies, such as using degrees and grades as proxies for student learning versus direct measures of learning as represented by MAPP, CAPP, and CLA. Nonetheless, it is important to work through the logic of which kinds of measures are relevant to which kinds of questions.[30]

The above kinds of assessments show that even identical degrees may represent different quantities of education produced if, for example, one engineering graduate started having already completed Advanced Placement calculus and physics while another entered with a remedial math placement. Modeling approaches have been developed to estimate time to degree and other potentially

---

[29]The Voluntary System of Accountability (VSA), which has been put forth by a group of public universities, is a complementary program aimed at supplying a range of comparable information about university performance, but it is less explicitly linked to a notion of value added by the institution. Useful discussions of the merits of assessment tests are provided in Carpenter and Bach (2010) and Ewell (2009a).

[30]See Feller (2009) and Gates et al. (2002).

relevant indicators of value-added learning outcomes and student engagement (Kuh et al., 2008). These take into account entering student ability as represented by pre-college achievement scores (ACT, SAT) and prior academic performance, other student characteristics such as enrollment status (full- or part-time), transfer status, and financial need (Wellman, 2010).

Popular proxies for institutional quality such as rankings are flawed for the purpose of estimating educational productivity. The major limitation of most rankings and especially that of *U.S. News & World Report* is they say almost nothing about what students do during college or what happens to them as a result of their attendance. As an illustration of the limitations of most ranking systems, only one number is needed to accurately predict where an institution ranks in *U.S. News & World Report*: the average SAT/ACT score of its enrolled students (Webster, 2001). The correlation between *U.S. News & World Report*'s rankings (1 = highest and 50 = lowest) and institutional average SAT/ACT score of the top 50 ranked national universities was –0.89 (Kuh and Pascarella, 2004). After taking into account the average SAT/ACT score, the other indices included in its algorithm have little meaningful influence on where an institution appears on the list.

This is not to say that selectivity is unrelated to college quality. Peers substantially influence students' attitudes, values, and other dimensions of personal and social development. Being in the company of highly able people has salutary direct effects on how students spend their time and what they talk about. Hoxby (1997, 2000, 2009) has quantified the returns to education and shown that the setting of highly selective schools contributes to the undergraduate education of at least some subsets of students. More recently, Bowen, Chingos, and McPherson (2009) present evidence that institutional selectivity is strongly correlated with completion rates, controlling for differences in the quality and demographics of enrolled students as well as factors such as per student educational expenditures. The authors argue that students do best, in terms of completion rates, when they attend the most selective schools that will accept them, due in part to peer effects. A related point, also documented in Bowen, Chingos, and McPherson (2009:198ff), is that productivity is harmed greatly by "undermatching"—the frequent failure of well-prepared students, especially those from poor families, to go to institutions that will challenge them properly. Hoxby (1997, 2009) also shows that improved communications and other factors creating national markets for undergraduate education have improved the "matching" of students to institutions and thereby improved outcomes.[31]

At the same time, research shows that other factors are important to desired outcomes of college. These include working collaboratively with peers

---

[31]López Turley, Santos, and Ceja (2007) have also studied "neighborhood effects," such as the impact on education outcomes of low-income Hispanics locked into local areas due to family or work concerns.

to solve problems, study abroad opportunities, service learning, doing research with a faculty member, and participating in learning communities (Pascarella and Terenzini, 2005). Longitudinal data from the National Study of Student Learning and cross-sectional results from the NSSE show that institutional selectivity is a weak indicator of student exposure to good practices in undergraduate education—practices such as whether faculty members clearly articulate course objectives, use relevant examples, identify key points, and provide class outlines (Kuh and Pascarella, 2004). These kinds of practices and experiences are arguably much more important to college quality than enrolled student ability alone.

In other words, selectivity and effective educational practices are largely independent, given that between 80 to 100 percent of the institution-level variance and 95 to 100 percent of the student-level variance in engagement in the effective educational practices measured by NSSE and other tools cannot be explained by an institution's selectivity. This is consistent with the substantial body of evidence showing that the selectivity of the institution contributes minimally to learning and cognitive growth during college (Pascarella and Terenzini, 2005). As Pascarella (2001:21) concluded,

> Since their measures of what constitutes "the best" in undergraduate education are based primarily on resources and reputation, and not on the within-college experiences that we know really make a difference, a more accurate, if less marketable, title for [the national magazine rankings] enterprise might be "America's Most Advantaged Colleges."

Other measures of educational quality are worth considering, given the increasing diversity of college students and their multiple, winding pathways to a baccalaureate degree. These could include goal attainment, course retention, transfer rates and success, success in subsequent course work, year-to-year persistence, degree or certificate completion, student and alumni satisfaction with the college experience, student personal and professional development, student involvement and citizenship, and postcollegiate outcomes, such as graduate school participation, employment, and a capacity for lifelong learning. Measures of success in subsequent coursework are especially important for students who have been historically underrepresented in specific majors and for institutions that provide remedial education. Participation in high-impact activities—such as first-year seminars, learning communities, writing-intensive courses, common intellectual experiences, service learning, diversity experiences, student-faculty research, study abroad, internships and other field placements, and senior capstone experiences—might also be useful indicators of quality, as they tend to be associated with high levels of student effort and deep learning (Kuh, 2008; Swaner and Brownell, 2009).

The two most relevant points for thinking about how to introduce explicit quality adjustment into higher education output measures may be summarized as follows:

1. Research on student engagement and learning outcomes is promising. This area of research has established a number of high-impact educational practices and experiences. Even where direct measures of student learning are not available, the existence of these practices could be used as proxies in evaluating the quality of educational experience reflected in a given set of degrees or credit hours. This kind of evidence, even if it cannot currently be directly included in a productivity measure (such as that developed in Chapter 4) due to data or conceptual limitations, can be considered in a comprehensive performance evaluation of an institution, department, or system.

2. Even the best statistical models that show institutional differences in the quality and quantity of education produced rarely allow for meaningful discrimination between one institution and another. Studies by Astin (1993), Kuh and Pascarella (2004), and Pascarella and Terenzini (2005) show that institutions do matter, but individual student differences matter more. Once student characteristics are taken into account, significant effects for institutions still exist, though the difference between any two given institutions, except for those at the extreme ends of the distribution, will often be small.

3.5. MEASUREMENT AT DIFFERENT LEVELS OF AGGREGATION

Adding to the complexity of productivity measurement is the fact that various policy and administrative actions require information aggregated at a number of different levels. Institution and state level measures are frequently needed for policy and are relevant to the development of administrative strategies. A major motivation for analyzing performance at these levels is that policy makers and the public want to know which institutions and which systems are performing better and how their processes can be replicated. Prospective students (and their parents) also want to know which institutions are good values. As we have repeatedly pointed out, for many purposes, it is best to compare institutions of the same type.

3.5.1. Course and Department Level

A course can be envisioned as the atomistic element of learning production, and the basic building block of productivity measurement at the micro level. For example, this may be expressed as the number of semester credits produced from a given number of faculty hours teaching. However, increasingly, courses themselves can be broken down further to examine quantitative and qualitative aspects within the course or classroom unit (Twigg, 2005). Classroom technology is changing rapidly. The introduction of scalable technologies is important, as are the effects of class size and technology. The technology of how education is delivered across and within categories (disciplines, institutions, etc.) varies widely.

Flagship state universities often have big classes while private colleges often have smaller ones. The latter is almost certainly more expensive on a per unit of output basis; less is known about the quality of the outcome. Those students that can make college choices based on tradeoffs in price and perceived quality offered by the range of options. Adding to the complexity is the faculty mix, including the use of graduate student instructors or adjunct faculty. This may also affect cost and quality of delivering credit hours.

A growing body of research and an increasing number of programs assess efficiencies at the course level seeking cost, quality tradeoffs that can be exploited. For example, the National Center for Academic Transformation (NCAT) develops programs for institutions to improve efficiency in production of higher education through course redesign.[32] In the NCAT model, the redesign addresses whole courses (rather than individual classes or sections) to achieve better learning outcomes at a lower cost by taking advantage of information technologies. Course redesign is not just about putting courses online, but rather rethinking the way instruction is delivered in light of the possibilities that technology offers. NCAT reports that, on average, costs were reduced by 37 percent in redesigned courses with a range of 9 to 77 percent. Meanwhile, learning outcomes improved in 72 percent of the redesigned courses, with the remaining 28 percent producing learning equivalent to traditional formats. Appendix B to this volume provides a description of how NCAT measures comparative quality and cost of competing course design models.

For some purposes, an academic department or program is a more appropriate unit of analysis.[33] This is because input costs as well as output valuations that markets, societies, and individuals place on various degrees vary by majors or academic field.[34] Collecting physical input and output data that can be associated with specific departments or fields of study within an institution provides maximum flexibility as to how the production function will actually be organized, and also provides the data needed for productivity measurement.

Despite these advantages, department-based analysis is inappropriate for determining sector-based productivity statistics. One difficulty is that it is not easy to compare institutions based on their departmental structures. What counts

---

[32]NCAT is an independent, not-for-profit organization dedicated to the effective use of information technology to improve student learning outcomes and reduce costs in higher education. Since 1999, NCAT has conducted four national programs and five state-based course redesign programs, producing about 120 large-scale redesigns. In each program, colleges and universities redesigned large-enrollment courses using technology to achieve quality enhancements as well as cost savings. Participating institutions include research universities, comprehensive universities, private colleges, and community colleges in all regions of the United States.

[33]Massy (2010) presents one effort to systematize the course substructure (using physical rather than simply financial quantities) for purposes of aggregation.

[34]See DeGroot et al. (1991) and Hare and Wyatt (1988) for estimates of cost/production functions for university research-graduate education.

as a department in one institution may be two departments in another or simply a program in a third. This is one reason why IPEDS does not require institutions to specify faculty inputs and other expenditures by department.

A framework that tracks students through fields of study has an analytical advantage over a framework that uses department as the unit of analysis when the concern is interactive effects. For example, the quality (and possibly quantity) of output associated with a labor economics class (in which students must write empirical research papers) clearly depends upon what they learn in their introductory statistics classes. Thus, one department's productivity is inherently linked to another's. While institutions allocate resources at the department level, productivity analysis can be enhanced by creating a representative student in various majors that captures all coursework in all departments. As discussed in Chapter 6, such an approach would require an extension of data collection capabilities, which possibly could be integrated with the IPEDS data system.[35]

3.5.2. Campus Level

A major source of demand for performance measures is to inform rankings and provide accountability, generally at the campus level. This aggregation level is analogous to productive units, such as automobile plants or hospitals, frequently monitored in other sectors. It is a logical starting place for many key applications of productivity measurement as it is easier to think of the practical value (ideas for improving efficiency) at this level than at the state or higher levels of aggregation—at least in terms of production processes. Certainly there is value for a university to track its productivity over time.

Of course, campus level productivity measurement invites inter-institution comparisons as well. We discussed earlier how heterogeneity of inputs and outputs requires segmentation by institutional type. It is not obvious exactly how many categories are needed to make groups of institutions sufficiently homogeneous so that productivity calculations are meaningful. As a starting point for defining and classifying institutional types, we can use basic categories consistent with the Carnegie Classification of Academic Institutions:

- credit hours not resulting in a degree (continuing education);
- community colleges providing associate's degrees certificates and the possibility of transferring to a four-year college;
- colleges granting bachelor's degrees;
- colleges and universities granting master's degrees; and
- universities granting doctorates.

---

[35]The UK's Higher Education Funding Council for England collects cost and output data by field of study.

Within an institutional category, it makes more sense to compare costs and outcomes across campuses. Measurement problems associated with heterogeneity of inputs and outputs are dampened when factors such as percentages of students in particular programs remain constant over time. However, even within categories of higher education institutions, characteristics vary and multiple functions are performed. For example, a university system (such as Florida's) may enjoy high four-year graduation rates in part due to strict requirement that less well-prepared students attend two-year institutions. Even so, segmenting the analysis by institutional type seems to be a prerequisite to accurate interpretation of various performance and cost metrics.

It is also worth noting that data collection at the campus level is simpler than it is at the course or department level. Aggregation at the campus level consolidates the effects of out-of-major courses and does not require allocating central services and overheads among departments. Reporting data at the campus level that is potentially useful for productivity measurement does not require weighting departmental inputs and outputs. Estimating total labor hours for the campus as a whole is equivalent to summing the hours for the individual departments, but the data collection process is much simpler. Summing student credit hours and awards also is straightforward although, as discussed in Chapter 4, a complication arises when linking enrollments to degrees by field.

3.5.3. State or System Level

For some purposes, it is useful to have productivity statistics at state, multi-campus system, or even national levels (see Box 3.2). For example, there have been efforts to develop state-by state "report cards" for tracking higher education outcomes, such as those reflected in student learning or skills assessments (Ewell, 2009). Additionally, as we discuss in the recommendations chapters, sometimes it makes sense to follow students at the state level so that events such as inter-institution transfers and measures such as system wide completion rates can be tracked.

One approach for generating state-level data is to aggregate the campus-level productivity measures described earlier. For example, if a system has a research-university campus, several baccalaureate campuses, and a two-year campus, productivity statistics could be calculated for each campus and compared with the averages for the segment into which the campus falls. An overall figure for the system or state could be obtained by aggregating the campus statistics. Thought will need to be given to the weights used in the aggregation but, in principle, the problem does not appear to be unsolvable.

BOX 3.2
Macro or Sector Level Accounting

The U.S. statistical agencies do not currently produce a measure of education sector productivity, although some components of such a measure are available. The Bureau of Economic Analysis (BEA) produces several nominal and real higher education consumption measures. The National and Income and Product Accounts (from which the nation's gross domestic product statistics are estimated) include real and nominal measures for education personal consumption expenditures (PCE) and for education consumption expenditures aross all government levels. The PCE tables include expenditures for books, higher education school lunches, and two other expenditure categories: (1) nonprofit private higher education services to households and (2) proprietary and public education. The nominal value of these two components is deflated by the BLS CPI-U college tuition and fees price index to produce an inflation-adjusted measure. The nominal value for gross output of nonprofit private higher education services to households is deflated by an input cost-based measure, which is a fixed weight index. This input cost-based deflator is constructed from BLS Quarterly Census of Employment and Wages, PPI, and CPI data. Although BEA measures the nominal value of education national income components such as wages and salaries and gross operating surplus (profits, rents, net interest, etc.), it does not produce real measures of these education input income components. Accordingly, BEA data would have to be supplemented with other data to create a measure of education productivity.

Beyond the United States, a mandate from Eurostat motivated European Union members and others to undertake research on how to measure education output and inputs. In the United States, most of this kind of research has focused on elementary and secondary education. In the United Kingdom, debate about how to measure government output, including education, resulted in the formation of the Atkinson Commission. However, though there have been calls to do so, no consensus has been reached about how to measure the real output of education independently from inputs.

A different approach to understanding higher education productivity would be to look at more indirect measures. One possibility is to use information such as that slated to be released in 2013 by the Programme for the International Assessment of Adult Competencies (PIAAC) of the OECD. PIAAC will assess adults' literacy and numeracy skills and their ability to solve problems in technology-rich environments. It will also collect a broad range of information from the adults taking the survey, including how their skills are used at work and in other contexts such as in the home and the community. Ideally, in addition to educational attainment, information on college major, previous work experience, and the dates and types of higher education institutions attended is desired to estimate higher education productivity based on PIAAC-collected data. Accordingly, PIAAC and other skill-based surveys might be a better indicator of human capital, rather than higher education output or productivity.

3.6. CONCLUSION

In this chapter, we have described how measuring productivity in higher education is especially challenging relative to the simple textbook model. Joint production of multiple outputs, heterogeneous inputs and outputs, quality change over time, and quality variation across institutions and systems all conspire to add complexity to the task. In order to advance productivity measurement beyond its current nascent state, it is necessary to recognize that not all of the complexities we have catalogued can be adequately accounted for at least at the present time. The panel recognizes the difficulties of moving from the conceptual level of analysis (Chapters 1-3), which is surely the place to start, to empirical measurement recommendations. Like other economic measures in their incipient stages—such as GDP estimates and the national economic accounts on which they rest (particularly early on in their development)—new measures of higher education productivity will be flawed.

Because the performance of the sector cannot be fully organized and summarized in a single measure, it becomes all the more important to bear the complexities in mind and to monitor supporting information, especially regarding the quality of output (e.g., student outcomes). Without this awareness, measures will surely be misused and improper incentives established. For example, the danger of incentivizing a "diploma mill," pointed out earlier, is real. Measuring performance is a precursor to developing reward structures that, in turn, incentivize particular behavior.

Here, we can only reiterate that the productivity measure proposed in Chapter 4—or any single performance metric for that matter—if used in isolation, will be insufficient for most purposes, particularly those linked to accountability demands. For the most part, a productivity measure will not be of great use for improving performance at the institutional level. What is relevant is the question of whether being able to measure higher education productivity in the aggregate will produce a better policy environment, which may in turn lead to indirect productivity improvements over time.

4

Advancing the Conceptual Framework

This chapter presents a framework intended to provide a starting point for measuring productivity in higher education. Chapters 2 and 3 presented arguments for why productivity measurement in higher education is exceedingly difficult and why, in turn, the panel cannot simply prescribe a fully defined metric. Nonetheless, because governments and many other stakeholders insist on, and in fact need, an aggregate measure of productivity change, it is important to begin developing the best measure possible.

The measure proposed involves a number of important assumptions and approximations, which are elaborated below. Chief among these is the lack of an agreed-upon measure of educational quality. Productivity should be defined as the ratio of quality-adjusted outputs to quality-adjusted inputs, but the needed quality adjustments are not currently possible in higher education and are not likely to become possible any time soon. We recognize the problem, but believe it is important to extract as much information as possible from the (quantitative) data that can be measured. We will describe later how the risks associated with the lacuna of measures of quality can be minimized including, for example, how entities can use university and third-party quality assurance methods to ensure that focusing on the quantitative inputs and outputs does not trigger a "race to the bottom" in terms of quality.

4.1. CHAPTER OVERVIEW

The productivity measure proposed here is consistent with the methodology practiced by the Bureau of Labor Statistics (BLS), and offers several significant advantages over the ad hoc approaches that have been used to date. In particular:

- The measure is a multi-factor productivity index. It captures output in physical units (credit hours, degrees) and, unlike cost studies, measures direct labor inputs in terms of full-time equivalents (FTEs). Labor productivity can be derived from the multi-factor results if desired.

- Outputs include credit hour production and degree attainment, both of which have been shown to be important in labor market studies. Most if not all the measures currently in use (e.g., credit hour production alone or graduation rates) depend on one or the other but not both, and therefore miss a critical output dimension.

- The measure does not vary along with the proportion of part-time students, except to the extent that being part-time might require different student services or contributes to wasting credits or dropping out. This feature sidesteps the problem of comparing graduation rates and average times to degree among schools with different numbers of part-time students.

- Credits not on the mainline path to a degree, including those due to changes in major and dropouts, are counted and thus dilute the degree completion effect. In other words, programs with a heavy dropout rate will have more enrollments per completion, which in turn will boost resource usage without commensurate increases in degrees. Productivity could thus increase with the same number of credit hours if more students actually complete their degrees. Credit earned, however, is not treated as entirely wasted just because a degree was not awarded.

- The measure allows differentiation of the labor and output categories, although doing this in a refined way will require significant new data.

- The measure readily lends itself to segmentation by institutional type, which is important given the heterogeneity of the higher education sector.

- The measure can in principle be computed for institutions within a state, or even single institutions. However, the incentives associated with low-aggregation level analyses carry the risk of serious accuracy degradation and misuse unless it is coupled with robust quality assurance procedures. Until quality adjustment measures are developed, the panel advises against using the productivity metric described in this chapter for institution-to-institution comparisons (as opposed to more aggregate level, time series, or perhaps state-by-state or segment analyses).

- Data collection, including data beyond the Integrated Postsecondary Education Data System (IPEDS) and the proposed special studies, appears to be feasible.

We emphasize again that the proposed measure follows the paradigm of aggregate productivity measurement, not the paradigm for provision of institution-level incentives and accountability. As stressed in Chapter 3, institutions should be prepared to resist inappropriate initiatives to improve productivity as measured by applying the formula below to their particular data, *and to buttress their resistance with their own internal data about quality.*

Section 4.2 presents our base model. It is a "multi-factor productivity model" in that it uses output and input quantities and includes all categories of inputs. Section 4.3 proposes a segmentation scheme, which is important because of the heterogeneity of higher education. The section also discusses how the model can be computed at the state and single-institution level but, again, we stress that this will be dangerous without a robust quality assurance system. Section 4.4 enhances the base model by differentiating among labor categories. This is important because of the fundamental difference between academic and nonacademic labor, and the difference between tenure-track and adjunct faculty. Section 4.5 differentiates among output categories, which again is important because of institutional heterogeneity and the fact that production of degrees at different levels and in different fields involves different production functions. Finally, Section 4.6 presents the rationale for using the model in conjunction with quality assurance procedures.

Nearly all the data required for calculating values using the model sketched out here can be obtained from the U.S. Department of Education's IPEDS or other standard public sources (though this would not be the case for the fully specified "ideal"). Adding the model refinements outlined in Section 4.3 requires a modest amount of additional information. Data requirements for the enhancements described in Section 4.4 can be approximated from IPEDS, but proper implementation will require additional data collection. The panel's recommended changes to IPEDS are discussed in detail in Chapter 6. The new data that are called for would break useful ground not only for productivity analysis, but also for institutional planning and resource allocation. This is important because an institution's use of data for its own purposes makes data collection more palatable and improves accuracy.

4.2. A BASELINE MULTI-FACTOR PRODUCTIVITY MODEL FOR HIGHER EDUCATION

Following the concepts defined in Chapter 2, the model calculates the ratio of changes in outputs (credit hours and degrees) to inputs (labor, purchased materials, and capital). The focus is on instructional productivity, with inputs being apportioned among instruction, research, and public services prior to calculating the productivity ratio. As emphasized throughout this report, our model involves only quantitative factors. It will be reliable only to the extent that input and output quality remains approximately constant, or at least does not decline materially. Currently, quality measurement—of both inputs and outputs—is largely beyond the capacity of quantitative modeling; but, because quality should never be taken for granted, we return to the issue at the end of the chapter.

4.2.1. Multi-Factor Productivity Indices

Multi-factor indices relate output to a bundle of inputs; that is, they show how much of an industry's or firm's output growth can be explained by the combined changes in its inputs. The panel has concluded that a multi-factor productivity index is appropriate for measuring higher education productivity at the segment and sectoral levels. Other kinds of productivity models—for example, those which estimate educational production functions—are of course possible and worthwhile. However, the panel was not charged with recommending such models. Nor was it charged with developing strategies for improving productivity.

Our proposed productivity model is based on the methodology for multi-factor productivity indices used by BLS, the OECD, and other U.S. and foreign agencies that produce sectoral productivity statistics (Bureau of Labor Statistics, 2007; Schreyer, 2001). For example, BLS uses this methodology to calculate productivity indices for aggregate manufacturing and some eighteen manufacturing industries.

The BLS method uses what is known as a Törnqvist index. This differs in important ways from the method of simply calculating weighted averages of the variables in the numerator and denominator and then taking the ratio of the two averages. The key ideas behind the Törnqvist index are as follows (from Bureau of Labor Statistics [2007:6-7]):

1. The figures for input and output are calculated as *weighted averages of the growth rates* of their respective components. Weighting average growth rates avoids the assumption, implicit in directly averaging the variables, that the inputs are freely substitutable for one another. It also removes issues having to do with the components' dimensionality. Both attributes are important when comparing variables like adjusted credit hours with labor and other inputs.

2. The *weights are allowed to vary* for each time period in which the index is calculated. This means the index always represents current information about the relative importance of the variable in question while maintaining the requirement (discussed in Chapter 2) that the weights move more slowly than the variables themselves.

3. The weights are defined as *the means of the relative expenditure or revenue shares* of the components for the two data periods on which the current index is based. This method brings relative wages and prices into the equation because they affect total expenditures.

The Törnqvist scheme has often been the indexing structure of choice for describing multi-factor productivity change under fairly broad and representative assumptions about the nature of production: specifically, that the production function can be represented by a translog generalization of the familiar Cobb-Douglas function with mild regularity conditions on the parameters (Caves et al., 1982). A technical description of the Törnqvist methodology is provided in the appendix to this chapter.

Determining appropriate indices embodying the general ideas put forward in Chapters 2 and 3 remains a task for future work. As such, it would be premature for the panel to commit to a specific approach. However, because of its widespread use in other applications—a Törnqvist index is used here for expository purposes. The denominator of our baseline higher education productivity index uses a Törnqvist structure to represent the composite growth rates of labor and capital inputs. The numerator also takes the form of a Törnqvist index, though in this case with only one element. Section 4.4 extends the index in the denominator to include more than one labor category, and Section 4.5 uses multiple output categories in the numerator. The final productivity index is the ratio of the indices in the numerator and the denominator.

4.2.2. Outputs

On the output side, the model uses two data elements that can be obtained from IPEDS:

1. *Credit Hours*: 12-month instructional activity credit hours summed over undergraduates, first-year professional students, and graduate students;
2. *Completions*: awards or degrees conferred, summed over programs, levels, race or ethnicity, and gender.[1]

Illustrative data for a four-year private university are shown in Table 4.1.[2] The data cover three years: 2003, 2006, and 2009 (it is best to aggregate over multiyear periods to reduce volatility associated with noise in the data, but the illustration ignores that refinement). For reasons explained earlier, both credit hours and degrees (or completions) are included as outputs. Whatever their flaws, these are the standard unit measures of instruction in American higher education.

The model uses adjusted credit hours as its measure of output, defined as follows:

Adjusted credit hours = Credit hours + (Sheepskin effect × Completions)

---

[1]For broader use, definitions become more complicated. For example, as discussed in the next chapter and elsewhere in the report, "completions" defined as certificates and successful transfers become relevant in the community college context. Nondegree seekers (e.g., summer transients) also come into play at many kinds of institutions.

[2]The data are based on an actual institution, but certain adjustments were made to make the illustration more coherent.

TABLE 4.1 Illustrative Data from IPEDS for the Base Model

	Period 1	Period 2	Period 3
Enrollments and Completions			
Credit hours	578,815	574,176	602,000
Completions	2,154	2,310	2,500
Adjusted credit hours	*638,435*	*643,476*	*677,000*
Total Number of Staff			
Full time	6,265	6,656	6,826
Part time	683	4,949	2,250
Labor FTEs	*6,493*	*8,306*	*7,576*
Finance: Core Expenditures			
Wages and Fringe Benefits			
Instruction	$421,534	$525,496	$641,749
Research	295,814	531,759	424,075
Public service	5,339	5,500	5,700
Student services	39,178	50,113	62,626
Administration and support services	488,969	563,969	534,924
Intermediate Expenditures			
Instruction	$161,142	$328,987	$427,833
Research	436,824	332,909	424,075
Public service	463	450	450
Student services	19,643	31,374	62,626
Administration and support services	491,953	366,841	534,924
Total Cost			
Instruction	$582,676	$854,483	$1,069,582
Research	732,638	864,668	848,149
Public service	5,802	5,950	6,150
Student services	58,821	81,487	125,251
Administration and support services	980,921	930,810	1,069,847
Finance Balance Sheet Items			
Land improvements; ending balance	$233,698	$238,269	$269,551
Buildings; ending balance	2,370,981	2,455,427	2,940,552
Equipment, including art and library; ending balance	1,150,228	1,191,801	1,372,257
Total Capital	*$3,754,907*	*$3,885,497*	*$4,582,360*

NOTE: FTE = full-time equivalent, IPEDS = Integrated Postsecondary Education Data System.
SOURCE: This, and all other tables in Chapter 4, were calculated by the panel and staff.

The "sheepskin effect" represents the additional value that credit hours have when they are accumulated and organized into a completed degree. The panel believes that a value equal to a year's worth of credits is a reasonable figure to use as a placeholder for undergraduate degrees.[3] Additional research will be needed to determine the sheepskin effect for graduate and first professional programs.

---

[3]Jaeger and Page (1996) suggest something more than an additional year for the sheepskin effect. They conclude "Sheepskin effects explain approximately a quarter of the total return to completing 16

4.2.3. Inputs

Inputs consist of the following variables, which can be calculated mainly from IPEDS data as shown in Section 4.2.4.

a) *Expenditures on Labor* (*LE*): nominal value of salaries and wages plus fringe benefits, used as the weight of L when aggregating the input.

b) *Labor* (*L*): the quantity measure for labor input, approximated by full-time equivalent (FTE) employees. Both academic and nonacademic employees are included in the calculation (this assumption, driven by the limitations in IPEDS data categorization, is relaxed in Section 4.4). FTE figures are calculated from total full- and part-time employees, with a part-time employee counting as one-third of a full-time employee, as assigned in IPEDS (this, too, could be adjusted with empirical justification). Labor is the biggest input into higher education instruction.

c) *Expenditures on Intermediate Inputs* (*IE*): nominal cost of materials and other inputs acquired through purchasing, outsourcing, etc. (the sum of the IPEDS "operations & maintenance" [O&M] and "all other" categories). These nominal values are used in calculating weights for intermediate inputs.

d) *Intermediate Inputs* (*I*): Deflated nominal expenditures (IE) are used to represent the physical quantities.

e) *Expenditures on Capital* (*KE*): opportunity cost for the use of physical capital; also called rental value of capital. Expenditures equal the IPEDS book value of capital stock times an estimated national rate of return on assets, where book value of capital stock equals the sum of land, buildings, and equipment.[4] Overall, the book value reported in IPEDS is likely too low; however, it does include buildings that may not be specifically allocated to teaching, which offsets the total to an unknown degree.[5] These nominal capital values are used in calculating the capital weights.

---

years of education and more than half of the return to completing 16 years relative to 12 years. . . . The marginal effect of completing a Bachelor's degree over attending 'some college' is 33%, conditional on attending school for 16 years." Park (1999) found the sheepskin effect to be somewhat lower. Wood (2009) provides a review of the literature. See also Section 5.1.1.

[4]Book value is typically defined as the original cost of an asset adjusted for depreciation and amortization.

[5]An alternative option was considered: current replacement value, the cost to replace an asset or a utility at current prices. This figure is available in IPEDS estimates of current replacement value for educational institutions and also calculated by Sightlines, a private company (see http://www.sightlines.com/Colleges-Universities_Facilities.html [June 2012]). Sightlines calculates current replacement value based upon the age, function, and technical complexity of each building. Current replacement value is defined as the average cost per gross square foot of replacing a building in kind in today's current dollar value. The Sightlines figures reflect the total project cost, including soft

   f)   *Capital (K)*: For the quantity of capital input, the book value is deflated by the Bureau of Economic Analysis's investment deflator for gross private domestic investment.

The deflators for intermediate expenditures and capital are, respectively, the Producer Price Index (PPI) and the index for Gross Private Domestic Investment: Chain-Type Price Index (GPDICTPI). These figures cannot be obtained from IPEDS but they are available from standard sources.[6]

4.2.4. Allocations to Education

The first step in the allocation process is to isolate inputs for the institutions' educational function from those attributable to the research and public service functions. Because IPEDS does not break out the FTE and capital variables by function,[7] our approach is to allocate these variables proportionally to expenditures by function—which *are* available in IPEDS. Here, "education" means "Education and Related Cost" (E&R), as defined by the Delta Project on Postsecondary Education Costs as "Instruction plus Student Services" (Delta Cost Project, 2009).

The allocation formulas are:

$$L = FTE(EdShAll_{LE} + EdShDir_{LE} \times AdShAll_{LE})$$
$$LE = DLE_I + DLE_S + DLE_A \times EdShDir_{LE}$$
$$I = IE/PPI$$
$$IE = DIE + DIS + DIA \times EdShDir_{IE}$$
$$K = KE/GPDICTPI$$
$$KE = Stock \times ROR(EdShAll_{Tot} + EdShDir_{Tot} \times AdShAll_{Tot})$$

---

costs, and are adjusted for architectural significance and region. Of course there is scope for further exploration and refinements in this estimate which is best left to the judgment of college/university authorities. As per e-mail exchange between one panel member and Jim Kadamus (vice president of Sightlines), the company's staff conducted some preliminary comparisons between current replacement values as calculated by IPEDS and Sightlines. The Sightlines estimates (for comparable space) are 70-100 percent greater than the value reported in IPEDS. The entity charged with implementing the productivity model will have to decide which estimate to use.

[6]The PPI is available at http://www.bls.gov/ppi/ and the GPDICTPI is available from http://www.bea.gov via the GDP and personal income interactive data link.

[7]The IPEDS Human Resources section provides a functional breakdown for direct teaching, research, and public service staff, but only an occupational breakdown for nonteaching staff. This scheme does not map into our model, and in any case the functional breakdown may be unstable due to inconsistencies in institutional classification schemes.

Additional variables (beyond those on p. 67) are defined as:

- DLE_I = "Direct labor expenditures for instruction" as given by IPEDS; notations follows this format for student services (DLE_S) and administration.
- $EdShAll_{LE}$ is "Education's share of all labor expenditures"; $AdShAll_{LE}$ is "Administration and support services' share of all labor expenditures"; notation follows this format for intermediate expenditures and capital. Finally, $EdShDir_{LE}$ is "Education's share of direct labor expenditures," and similarly for all the other shares. The difference between $EdShAll_{LE}$ and $EdShDir_{LE}$ is that the former's denominator includes labor expenditures for administration and support services whereas the latter's does not.
- IE is expenditures on intermediate inputs; DIE is direct nonlabor expenditures on instruction; DIS is direct nonlabor expenditures on student services; DIA is direct nonlabor expenditures on administration; $EdShDir_{IE}$ is education share of direct nonlabor expenditures.
- *Stock* is capital stock as shown on institutional balance sheets, *ROR* is the national rate of return on capital, *PPI* is the producer price index, and *CPDICIPI* is the price index for gross private domestic investment (both price indices are suitably normalized).[8]

Faculty time that is separately budgeted for institutional service is included in administration and support services, and unbudgeted faculty service time (e.g., departmental administration) is included in instruction.

4.2.5. Illustrative Productivity Calculations

Table 4.2 shows the productivity calculation for the institution referred to above. The calculation can be broken down into four steps:

1. *Allocate the quantity and expenditure data to the Education function*: Apply the formulas above. For example, adjusted credit hours in the three periods equal 638,435, 643,476, and 677,000.
2. *Calculate the change in the quantity data from period to period*: The change for adjusted credit hours equals the current value divided by the

---

[8]See Hodge et al. (2011:25, Table 2). The rate of return to the net stock of produced assets for other nonfinancial industries is used as a proxy for the rate of return to higher education land, buildings and equipment. Other industries includes agriculture, forestry, fishing and hunting; transportation and warehousing; information; rental and leasing services and lessors of intangible assets; professional, scientific, and technical services; administrative and waste management services; educational services; health care and social assistance; arts, entertainment, and recreation; accommodation and food services; and other services, except government.

TABLE 4.2 Base Model Productivity Calculations

	Period 1	Period 2	Period 3
Step 1: Allocations to Education			
Outputs			
Adjusted credit hours (ACHs)	638,435	643,476	677,000
Input Quantities			
Labor FTEs (L)	3,926	4,296	4,705
Intermediate expenditures	$324,680	$486,147	$643,599
Rental value of capital (K)	$261,834	$267,507	$348,033
Input Expenditures			
Wages and fringe benefits	$756,399	$867,311	$1,036,594
Intermediate expenditures	$324,680	$550,921	$777,193
Retail value of capital (K)	$261,834	$301,954	$400,791
Total Cost	$1,342,913	$1,720,186	$2,214,578
Step 2: Quantity Changes	**Period 1**	**Period 1 → 2**	**Period 2 → 3**
Output Change			
Adjusted credit hours	1.000	1.008	1.052
Input Change			
Labor FTEs	1.000	1.094	1.095
Real intermediate expenditures	1.000	1.497	1.324
Real capital stock	1.000	1.022	1.301
Step 3: Input Index			
Weights (average)			
Wages and fringe benefits		53.4%	48.6%
Normal intermediate expenditures		28.1%	33.6%
Real capital stock		18.5%	17.8%
Weighted geometric average		1.180	1.204
Step 4: Multi-Factor Productivity			
Productivity index		0.854	0.874
Productivity change			2.3%

NOTE: FTE = full-time equivalent.

previous one, with the first value being initialized at one. The ratios for Periods 2 and 3 are 1.008 and 1.052, for example, which indicate growth rates of 0.8 percent and 5.2 percent.

3. *Calculate the input index*: For inputs, the composite index ("weighted geometric average") is equal to the geometric average of the indices for the individual variables using the arithmetic average of the successive periods' nominal expenditure shares as weights (no averaging is needed for outputs because there is only one output measure).[9] This calculation

---

[9]The index for the more complicated models presented later is based on the geometric average of output changes, the same as for inputs.

BOX 4.1
Productivity and Quality

The productivity measure here does not take account of quality changes. Instead, it depends on the market to police quality erosion. Normally such policing is done through the price mechanism, although sometimes products such as computers whose quality is increasing over time do become cheaper. As argued earlier in this report, higher education prices generally are not set in competitive markets. Hence the conclusion, "Productivity has increased by 'x' percent" must be taken as tentative until the constancy of quality has been verified, for example, through a separate quality assurance procedure. A master artist produces 10 paintings in a month; her student also produces 10 paintings in the same period, for example. We sense that the quality of the artists is different, and that this difference should be reflected in the final product. But we cannot tell the difference in productivity just by counting the hours and the paintings (nor can we quantify the quality difference just by looking at them)—though we may eventually get some evidence by tracking the price that the paintings sell for or whether they sell at all. We return to the question of output quality in Section 4.6.

---

comes from the third equation in the Technical Appendix. The results are 1.180 and 1.204, which indicate average input growths of 18.0 percent and 20.4 percent.

4. *Calculate the productivity index*: This is expressed as the ratio of the index for the change in outputs to the index for the change in inputs— i.e., 1.008/1.180 = 0.854 for the first period and 1.052/1.204 = 0.874 for the second. The last line, "productivity change," is the ratio of the productivity indexes for the two periods: (0.854/0.874 − 1), or 2.3 percent.

An alternative but equivalent calculation illuminates Step 4. Notice that the output index grew by 1.052/1.008 = 1.044 (4.4 percent) and the input index grew by 1.204/1.180 = 1.020 (2.0 percent) between the second and third periods. Dividing the output growth by the input growth yields 1.044/1.020 = 1.023, or 2.3 percent, the same as in the table. Put another way, the output index grew 2.3 percent faster than the input index—which represents productivity improvement (see Box 4.1).

4.3. INSTITUTIONAL SEGMENTATION AND DISAGGREGATIVE INDICES

Having established the basic productivity index, we now present refinements intended to make it more useful. This section describes how indices can be calculated for different segments or subsectors of the postsecondary education universe that have heterogeneous modes of production. Then we build on this description to describe how the index can be calculated for individual institutions or for a subset of institutions (e.g., all institutions in a state's public system). We emphasize again, however, that such disaggregated indices should not be used as accountability measures unless a robust quality assurance system is operating in parallel.

4.3.1. Institutional Segmentation

The reason for segmenting colleges and universities into groups with similar characteristics is to avoid largely meaningless comparisons between highly differentiated institutions. Research universities, for example, differ in their outputs and production methods from master's and bachelor's universities and community colleges. The base model's procedure for allocating costs among teaching, research, and public service handles some of the heterogeneity, but by no means all of it. As discussed earlier, research universities include a substantial amount of departmental research under the rubric of instructional cost, an intermixing that our allocation methodology cannot tease apart. Therefore, a decline in the share of educational output accounted for by research universities would boost the productivity index as production is shifted from higher-cost to lower-cost institutions, even though productivity within each individual institution remains unchanged. This will represent a true increase in overall higher education productivity only if the educational outputs are substantially similar—an assumption that is suspect.

Productivity indices may be calculated for each of a number of institutional segments and then aggregated to the national level using an appropriate indexing methodology. Total Education and General expenditures for the segments might be used as weights, though this suggestion should be reviewed. The alternative, calculating a single national statistic to start with, would eliminate the possibility of comparing productivity trends across segments. Retaining the ability to compare results should indicate whether productivity changes result primarily from shifts in enrollment and completion among segments, or from intra-segment productivity changes. IPEDS data for individual institutions include potentially useful descriptors, making it possible to formulate and test alternative segmentation schemes.

A natural starting point to defining institutional groups is to follow the approach established for the Delta Cost Project, if for no other reason than a considerable amount of experience in working with them has been accumulated. The Delta Cost Project employs six institutional groups: public research, public master's, public community colleges, private nonprofit research, private nonprofit master's, and private nonprofit bachelor's. To these six we would add for-profit institutions, for a total of seven groups.[10] It may be desirable to have more than one for-profit segment and to create separate sub-categories for public and private research universities that do and do not have medical schools, but this is an open questions.

The simplest approach is to base the productivity calculations on aggregate data for all or a sample of institutions in a given segment. Such aggregation is standard practice in sectoral productivity analysis and we see no reason not to use it in higher education. Given that IPEDS reports data for individual institutions, it is almost as easy to do the calculations separately by segment as it is to do them on national aggregates. With the segment indices in hand, it is straightforward to aggregate them to produce a sector-wide index.

Finally, the productivity index for each segment should be normalized to 1.0 in the base period, before the aggregation proceeds. This is a natural step within most any indexing methodology. Moreover, the normalization will emphasize that it is the productivity *trends* that are being measured and not comparisons of absolute productivity across segments.

4.3.2. State-Level and Single-Institution Indices

The panel's charge states that we should consider productivity measures at "different levels of aggregation: including the institution, system, and sector levels." Our proposed model is designed to operate at the sector or subsector (segment) level. Given the IPEDS dataset and the specifics of the calculations, however, there is nothing to prevent researchers or administrators from applying the formulas to individual campuses and, by extension, to any desired set of campuses—say, within a system or state. Indeed, the illustration in Tables 4.1 to 4.4 is based on a single institution.

Two methodological caveats must be noted. First, trend comparisons should be made only with institutions in the same segment as the one being studied. Second, state-level or similar indices should themselves be disaggregated by segment. It makes no more sense to combine the apples and oranges of different segments at the state level than it does at the national level. Aggregation to a single state-level index should use the same methodology as the one described for segment aggregation. However, a question arises regarding the weights to be used for aggregation: should they be the same as for the national aggregation, or

---

[10]We indicate for-profit higher education as a separate category because its production methods often differ substantially from those in the nonprofit sector. The for-profit sector has been growing rapidly; additionally, recent concerns about the performance of these schools—including questions about their heavy revenue reliance on federal student loans and issues of quality—make them well worth consideration as part of any serious appraisal of higher education performance. We are not proposing that the productivity of for-profit higher education be measured differently, but rather that it be placed in its own segment for comparison purposes.

should they reflect expenditure or similar shares at the state level? The question of which weights to use should be examined further through future research.

While we feel obligated by our charge to raise the possibility of single-institution and state-level indices, the panel remains uncomfortable with the prospect that this might invite use of the model for accountability purposes. No such invitation is intended! Single-institution results may exhibit considerable volatility due to short-term variations in key input and output variables and the likelihood of data errors. Such volatility will likely decline as the number of institutions in the set increases. More importantly, as we have already emphasized, is the need to deploy robust quality assurance procedures in any situation where high-stakes quantitative productivity measures are used. In the slightly longer term, these quality assurance procedures should be supplemented by improvement-oriented structural models of the kind discussed in Chapter 2.

4.4. DIFFERENTIATING LABOR CATEGORIES

The first enhancement to the model is to track key labor categories separately from total FTEs. Separate tracking of labor types is typically a feature of sectoral productivity studies, but it is less commonly used to distinguish full-time from part-time employees; clearly, this differentiation is likely to be important in higher education. There are four reasons for this view.

1. One of the critical assumptions of the conventional productivity model is not viable in higher education. The typical productivity study assumes that, because labor is secured in competitive markets, relative compensation approximates relative marginal products. There is, in such a situation, no need to differentiate full-time from part-time employees. Unfortunately, tenure-track faculty labor may not be linked tightly to marginal product in education because such faculty often are valued for research and reputational reasons and/or protected by tenure, or else locked into institutions because of tenure.

2. Another assumption is that the market effectively polices output quality, which is manifestly not the case for higher education. Colleges pursue strategies—larger classes or less costly instructors—that reduce costs per nominal output but could dilute quality when taken to extremes. As noted earlier in this report, for example, it may be attractive to employ less expensive, but also less qualified, personnel who are not well integrated into a department's quality processes. The panel is concerned lest the measurement of productivity add to the already problematic incentives to emphasize quantity over quality in higher education.

3. The distinction between teaching and nonteaching staff is blurring as information technology shifts the modalities of teaching and learning. In some institutions, for example, faculty time is leveraged by modern learning software, a change that may require entirely new kinds of labor inputs. Such technologically driven changes are not unique to higher education, but the pace of change seems unusually brisk at the present time.

4. Productivity statistics are more likely to weigh heavily in policy debates on higher education than in policy debates on other industries. The U.S. public policy environment includes a significant oversight and account-ability component requiring information about productivity. Therefore, it is important that the statistics be as complete as possible on the im-portant issues, including those associated with labor substitution (e.g., between tenure-track and nontenure-track teachers). Of course, proper analysis brings with it the responsibility to monitor and assess the qual-ity of education obtained by students as the mix of inputs change.

These considerations suggest the following three-way labor classification scheme based on IPEDS data.

- Regular faculty FTEs: approximated from IPEDS data for "Number of full-time Instruction/Research/Public Service staff with faculty status."
- Part-time teaching FTEs who are hired on a course-by-course basis: approximated by one-third of the "Number of staff by primary func-tion/occupational activity" listed as "Part-time" and "Primarily instruc-tion" ("PT/PI"). Ideally graduate assistants whose primary function is instruction should be included here. IPEDS contains data on graduate assistants, and they are reported separately under part-time staff.
- All other FTEs: i.e., the base-model value minus the sum of the above.

The Human Resources/Employees by Assigned Position section of the IPEDS survey questionnaire requires institutions to report number of full-time and part-time staff involved in instruction/research/public service. The values reported for staff under this item will vary from one institution to another. Two-year colleges are more likely to report their entire faculty under "primarily instruction." Some four-year institutions may change the way they report; for example, all kinds of faculty (irrespective of how much research they are doing) may be grouped un-der instruction/research/public service, creating biases in period to period trend comparisons.

In Table 4.3, part-time staff are converted to FTEs, and other staff FTEs are obtained by subtracting from total FTEs as used in the base model. Total wages and salaries and fringe benefits for instruction, research, and public service also

TABLE 4.3 Additional IPEDS Data for the Differential Labor Market

	Period 1	Period 2	Period 3
Quantities			
Number of FTEs—instruction, research, and public service staff with faculty status	1,564	1,601	1,1601
Number of PT/PI staff	2	2	2
Number of other staff	4,928	6,704	5,974
Expenditures			
Expenditures on wages and salaries for instruction, research, and public service	$529,572	$701,791	$874,051
Expenditures on fringe benefits for instruction, research, and public service	193,203	361,064	193,373
Expenditures on wages and salaries for other functions	380,610	410,296	482,139
Expenditures on fringe benefits for other functions	147,449	203,686	119,510
Average salary for FT instructional, staff	108,200	114,464	122,508

NOTE: FT = full-time, FTE = full-time equivalent, PT/PI = part-time/primarily instruction.

come directly from IPEDS, with those for other functions obtained by subtraction. Average salary for full-time instructional staff comes from the corresponding table in IPEDS. The very small PT/PI share may be an artifact of the particular data used in the example, but because the number is growing across the sector we believe this variable remains worthy of consideration.

Only one required data element is unavailable in IPEDS: the ratio of PT/PI salaries per FTE to those of regular faculty. It is possible (though perhaps not cost-effective) that IPEDS could be expanded to get this information; absent the change it may be adequate to assume the compensation ratio or determine it by special study.[11] Finally, the expenditures for tenure-track and adjunct faculty expenditures are subtracted from total labor expenditures to get the figure for other labor.

Table 4.4 illustrates the calculations. The first step is to allocate the quantities and expenditures to the Education function. The figures for full-time tenure-track faculty and other staff are portioned using the education share variable computed in the base model. PT/PI staff needs no allocation because they are "primarily instruction" to start with. The FTE figures for Period 3 have been adjusted to demonstrate the effect of substituting PT/PI staff for full-time tenure-track faculty (discussed below): specifically, we subtracted 100 instructional FTEs from tenure-track faculty and added them to PT/PI.

---

[11]One-third may be a reasonable approximation. We obtained this figure by assuming that (a) PT/PI staff get about $5,000 per course with no benefits, (b) average annual faculty salary plus benefits is $90,000, and (c) the average full-time faculty member teaches 6 courses a year. In this case the calculation is $5,000/($90,000/6) = 1/3.

TABLE 4.4 Differentiated Labor Index Calculations

	Period 1	Period 2	Period 3
Allocations to Education			
Quantities			
Regular faculty FTEs	946	828	828
PT/PI staff FTEs	2	2	2
Other staff FTEs	2,978	3,466	3,875
Expenditures			
Effective fringe benefit rate	36.5%	51.4%	22.1%
Regular faculty	$139,667	$143,552	$123,891
PT/PI staff	$28	$32	$30
Other staff	$616,704	$723,726	$912,673
Total expenditures	$756,399	$867,311	$1,036,594
Index Calculations			
Quantities			
FT regular faculty	1.000	0.876	1.000
PT/PI staff	1.000	1.000	1.000
Other staff	1.000	1.164	1.118

		Period 1 → 2	Period 2 → 3
Quantity Change			
FT regular faculty		0.876	1.142
PT/PI staff		1.000	1.000
Other staff		1.164	1.118
Weights			
FT regular faculty		17.5%	14.3%
PT/PI staff		0.00%	0.00%
Other staff		82.5%	85.7%
Labor Index			
Geometric average		1.107	0.985
Change in the average			(0.110)

NOTE: FT = full-time, FTE = full-time equivalent, PT/PI = part-time/primarily instruction.

Calculating the expenditures requires the effective fringe benefits rate to be computed as a preliminary step. (It equals the ratio of fringe benefits to salaries and wages in Table 4.3.) The expenditure figures can be computed as follows:

Expenditures for regular faculty = (1+ Fringe benefits rate) × Average salary for FTE instructional staff × Regular faculty FTEs;

Expenditures for PT/PI staff = (1+ Fringe benefits rate/2) × PT/PI salary ratio × Average salary for FTE instructional staff × PT/PI FTEs; and

Expenditures for other staff = Total wages + fringe benefits − (Expenditures for regular faculty and PT/PI staff).

Total "Wages & fringe benefits" is taken from Table 4.1, and readers may notice that PT/PI staff receive only half the fringe benefits rate.

The final step, calculating the change indices and their weights, proceeds as in the base model. As shown in Table 4.4, resulting geometric averages show more variation than did the labor indices in Table 4.2. This produces larger multifactor productivity indices, and also a larger change in the index, as shown at the bottom of the table. Which approach is more accurate may become more clear during implementation.

4.5. DIFFERENTIATING OUTPUTS

Another potentially key model enhancement is to control for the heterogeneity of educational outputs. Institution-level cost data indicate clearly that the resources required for producing an undergraduate degree vary across fields. Likewise, the resource requirements for producing bachelor degrees differ systematically from those for associate, graduate, and first professional degrees. Failure to control for these differences would risk the kinds of distortions described earlier. For example, a shift of outputs from the more expensive disciplines of science, technology, engineering, and mathematics (STEM) to non-STEM disciplines would falsely boost the productivity index.

IPEDS provides data on degrees by field and award level. A difficulty arises only in differentiating the credit hours associated with degree production. It is not unusual for institutions to track credit hours by the department or broad discipline in which a course is taught (as required to apply the so-called Delaware cost benchmarks for example), but these data cannot be mapped directly to degree production because students take many courses outside their matriculated area. Researchers have made the necessary correspondences by creating course-taking profiles for particular degrees, but these matrices are difficult to manage and maintain on an institution-wide basis. There is a better way, which we outline below—one that feeds directly into the productivity statistics and produces the course-taking profiles as by-products.[12]

For the long run, credit-hour data for productivity analysis should be collected in a way that follows the students, not only the departments that teach them. The necessary information exists in most institutions' student registration files and the needed statistics can be extracted as follows:

- Identify the students matriculated in a given degree program ("output category") as defined by the IPEDS fields and degree levels. Undeclared students and students not matriculated for a degree would be placed in separate ("nonattributable") output categories.

---

[12]Simply applying a sheepskin effect to each degree category and summing the result before adding to aggregate credit hours is insufficient because shifts in degree production will induce shifts in credit-hour production, which will produce the kinds of distortion described in the text.

- For each output category, accumulate the credit hours earned by the students in that category, regardless of the department in which the course was offered or the year in which it was taken.
- Allocate credits earned by matriculated but undeclared students in proportion to the credit-hour fractions of declared students for the given degree. Retain nonmatriculated students in their own separate category, one that has no sheepskin effect but in other respects is treated the same as other categories.

The question arises as to whether these data need to be collected by each institution, or whether generalized weights based on special studies (e.g., using the Postsecondary Educational Transcripts Study, PETS) could be used. The use of generalized weights is not inconceivable, but we worry that the heterogeneity of programs from school to school means that much information would be lost. Further, institutions may find the data on credit hours by degree program useful for internal purposes as well as for reporting—for example, in studying student profiles of course-taking behavior and benchmarking costs per degree program. It seems likely that, once in hand, these data will open significant new opportunities for institutional research.

It may be some time before data on student-based credit hour accumulations can be obtained, but there is a simple interim procedure that can be computed from the available IPEDS data. It is to allocate total enrollments to fields and levels based on fractions of completion. While ignoring differences in the course-taking profiles, the procedure does allow at least some differentiation among output categories.

Aggregation to a single output index is best accomplished by taking a geometric average of the output category indices using their net student revenue shares as weights. A geometric average with weights equal to revenue shares reflects the BLS methodology described earlier. Use of net as opposed to gross shares appears reasonable because revenue based on net prices (which is what the institution can spend on operations) is consistent with the underlying Törnqvist model as presented by Caves, Christensen, and Diewert (1982).

We recognize that getting these data may be problematic for institutions, in which case an alternative based on reported tuition and financial aid rates might well suffice. We also should note that it is not necessary to allocate any inputs across output categories. Such a requirement would disrupt data collection. Like most sectoral productivity indices, ours simply divides the aggregate output index for a segment by its aggregate input index.

4.6. VARIATIONS IN OUTPUT QUALITY

The quality of education is the elephant in the room in all discussions about instructional productivity, and the issue has been raised repeatedly in this report.

The panel would have liked nothing better than to propose an explicit quality adjustment factor for weighted credit hours as part of our conceptual framework. In our model, an effect will be captured to the extent that higher quality inputs lead to higher graduation rates (and, in turn, a larger degree bonus in the numerator), but this effect is indirect. For example, if small classes or better teaching (inputs of different quality) lead to higher graduation rates, this will appear in the output numerator as a greater sheepskin effect. Similarly, high student and teacher quality at selective private institutions may offset high input costs by creating an environment conducive to high throughput rates.

This modest step notwithstanding, full (or even adequate) integration of quality adjustment into a productivity measure will not be possible any time soon. Significant progress on quality assessment has been made, but there is a long way to go before a generally accepted cardinal measure—one that can be used reliably to adjust weighted credit hours—can be agreed upon. It is possible, and perhaps even likely, that critics will call for a moratorium on all efforts to measure instructional productivity until a valid and reliable output quality index can be developed. We believe this would be unwise, for two reasons.

First, the kind of productivity measures proposed in this report is intended to deal primarily with changes over time rather than comparisons across institutions. It is true that an increasing focus on the quantitative aspects of productivity might trigger a "race for the bottom" in educational quality as competing institutions make increasingly larger concessions, seeking to boost the numerator and cut the denominator of the productivity fraction. Pressures on enrollments relative to budgets make this a danger whether quantitative productivity is properly measured or not, but there is no doubt that an increasing emphasis on the quantitative elements of productivity could exacerbate the problem. Normalizing the productivity index for each segment to 1.0, as is done in Section 4.3.1, will help alleviate this danger—though of course it is always possible to manipulate data to achieve desired results. Attention to the limitations of the metric for measuring at low levels of aggregation is also important.

Second, failure to agree on an economically valid and technically robust quantitative productivity measure will only increase proliferation of the weaker measures described in Chapter 2. These are even more susceptible to missing differences in quality than the method proposed here. Furthermore, failure to implement a good measure would indefinitely defer the benefits achievable from a better understanding of quantitative productivity even in the absence of quality adjustment. These considerations suggest a strategy of simply assuming that, absent evidence to the contrary, the quality of outputs is not declining significantly over time. The panel believes, albeit reluctantly given our desire for evidence, that the general approach proposed has much to recommend it.

To broaden the applicability of the measure developed here, additional steps should be taken. The essential idea is that effective and transparent quality assurance systems should be maintained to insure that output quality does not race for the bottom (Massy, 2010). These could be based on extant accreditation systems, on the methods of academic audit being used effectively in Tennessee and certain overseas venues (Massy, Graham, and Short, 2007), or on the other quality-reviewing initiatives now being conducted at the state level. From a modeler's perspective, the approach converts a quantity that would be included in the objective function if a cardinal measure were available to a "yes-no" constraint that needs only binary measurement. The binary constraint amounts to what might be called a "watchdog evaluation": remaining silent if all is well but sounding the alarm if it is not. The watchdog evaluation would be at root subjective, but based upon evidence; we return to this idea in Section 5.3.2.

The approach is by no means perfect. However, it allows progress to be made in measuring the quantitative aspects of productivity while containing the risk of triggering institutional competition that results in lowering educational quality. Progress on the development of quantitative productivity measures may boost the priority for developing a serviceable quality adjustment index.

TECHNICAL APPENDIX

The Törnqvist Productivity Index

This Appendix briefly describes the theoretical basis and calculations for the Törnqvist productivity index used in Chapter 4. The argument follows Caves, Christensen, and Diewert (1982:1393). As noted in the text, the Törnqvist index is used by the Bureau of Labor Statistics in calculating multi-factor productivity change (cf. Bureau of Labor Statistics, 2007). The appendix text is adapted from Section 1 of Massy (2012). Where applicable, the equations are keyed to Steps 2-4 of Table 4.2.

Input Indices, Distance Functions, and Productivity

We define "Firm k" and "Firm l" as two enterprises whose productivity is to be compared. Standard usage takes the two to be the same organization at different time periods, but this is not a requirement of the Törnqvist theory. For example, the two could be separate enterprises operating in the same or different periods.

At their Eq. 6, Caves and colleagues (1982) define the Malmquist input index for Firm k with respect to the inputs of Firm l as:

$$(1) \qquad Q^k(x^l, x^k) = \frac{D^k(y^k, x^l)}{D^k(y^k, x^k)},$$

where y^k is an m-element vector of outputs and x^k is an n-element vector of inputs for firm k. The numerator of the right-hand side, called "Firm k's input *distance function* with respect to the inputs of Firm l," is defined at Eq. 7 as:

$$(2) \qquad D^k(y^k, x^l) = \max_\delta \left\{ \delta : F^k\left(\tilde{y}^k \frac{x^l}{\delta}\right) \geq y_l^k \right\},$$

where $F^k(y^k, x^k) = 0$ is k's production function, $\tilde{y}^k$ is the vector $\{y_2^k, y_3^k, ... y_n^k\}$, and $y_1^k = F^k(\tilde{y}, x^k)$. Maximizing δ determines the "minimum Firm l input mix required to produce Firm k's output using k's production function"—i.e., it "deflates" k^l onto k's production function. From this it can be seen that $D^k(y^k, x^k)$, the denominator in (1), always must equal one because any firm can produce its own output using its own inputs. This means $Q^k(x^l, x^k) = D^k(y^k, x^l) \geq 1$, which implies that "the input vector of firm l, x^l, is 'bigger' than the input vector of firm k (i.e., k, x^k) from the perspective of Firm k's technology" (Caves, Christensen, and Diewert, 1982:1396). A similar argument applies to $Q^l(x^l, x^k)$.

Suppose now that Firms k and l are in fact the same entity, observed at times t_1 and t_2 respectively, and $Q^k(x^l, x^k) \geq 1$. This means the technology used at time would have required more inputs to produce the t_2 outputs than does the technology at t_2 (this conclusion does not require the outputs at t_1 and t_2 to be the same). In other words, there has been a productivity improvement.

A Practical Method of Computation

This is a powerful result, but the calculation cannot be done without detailed knowledge of the production function and its parameters—knowledge that is rarely if ever available. Caves and his co-authors surmount this difficulty by invoking classic profit maximization—an assumption that is dubious when applied to higher education institutions (see below)—together with a modest technical simplification. In their words:

> By making use of a specialized functional form and the assumption of cost-minimizing behavior, it is possible to compute a geometric average of the two Malmquist indices and $Q^k(x^l, x^k)$, using only observed information on input processes and quantities. We demonstrate this fact for the case in which each firm has a translog distance function, but the properties of the two translog functions are allowed to differ substantially. In this case the geometric average of the two Malmquist indices turns out to be a Törnqvist index. (Caves, Christensen, and Diewert, 1982:1397).

The technical simplification is that the production functions' cross-product parameters for inputs and outputs be equal within and across firms. The authors point out that these restrictions are not onerous because "The translog distance function is capable of providing a second-order approximation to an arbitrary distance function. Thus the technologies in the two firms can be virtually arbitrary (to the second-order) except for the restrictions" [Caves, Christensen, and Diewert, 1982:1398]. Nonetheless, research will be needed to assess whether or not these restrictions are reasonable in the higher education context.

The resulting theorem, Caves Equation (15) reproduced below, shows how one can compute the geometric average of the two input indices using only observable data. This is all that's needed to estimate productivity change.

$$(3) \quad \frac{1}{2}\ln Q^k(x^l, x^k) + \frac{1}{2}\ln Q^l(x^l, x^k) = \frac{1}{2}\sum_{j=1}^{n} \left[\frac{w_j^k \times w_n^k}{w^k \odot x^k} + \frac{w_j^l \times w_n^l}{w^l \odot x^l}\right]\left[\ln x_j^l - \ln x_j^k\right].$$

The new symbols w^k and w^l are vectors of input prices and $w^k \bullet x^k$ is total expenditure, the dot-product of price and quantity. This means the fractions represent shares of input expenditure. Hence the right-hand side defines the log of a Törnqvist index, denoted by: namely, the geometric average of physical inputs using expenditure shares as weights.

The quantity $Q(w^l, w^k, x^l, x^k)$ is shown for the transitions from Period 1 to Period 2 and Period 2 to Period 3, in the second-to-last line of Table 4.2 (the first line of step 4). Step 2 of Table 4.2 shows the inputs for the quantity-change (i.e., the last) term in the right-hand side of (3): i.e., in x^l_j. Step 3 shows the weights and the resulting geometric averages of the quantity changes. Notice that the weights are themselves an average of the weights in the two periods being considered.

The Overall Productivity Measure

Section 4 of Caves, Christensen, and Diewert (1982:1401), points out that there are "two natural approaches" to the measurement of productivity changes: differences in maximum output conditional on a given level of inputs ("output-based" indices) and those based on minimum input requirements conditional on a given level of output ("input-based" indices). Furthermore, the two approaches "differ from each other by a factor that reflects the returns to scale of the production structure." Without going into the details, it is intuitively reasonable that a geometric average of the output-based and input-based indices represents a good overall measure of productivity.[13] Therefore, the desired productivity index is the ratio of the output-based and input-based Törnqvist indices. Changes in productivity are obtained by taking the ratios of the indices in successive periods.

Step 4 of Table 4.2 performs these final calculations. The first line is the productivity index itself: the ratio of the output to the input indices. The second line shows productivity change: the ratio of the indices in the two successive periods, minus one.

Applying the Index to Nonprofit Enterprises

The proof of optimality for the Törnqvist index depends on the assumption of profit maximization. As noted above, this assumption is dubious when applied to traditional universities (it applies perfectly well to for-profit universities, however). This leads to two questions that need to be addressed by further research: (1) Will application of the index to nonprofits produce misleading results? (2) What modifications to the Törnqvist (or perhaps an entirely different approach) will likely be better than the traditional index?

Regarding the first question, we note that a lack of optimality is not equivalent to a lack of efficacy. Many algorithms and measures are used, in economics

---

[13]Adjustments for decreasing and increasing returns to scale are described in later sections of the Caves paper. They are interesting but, we believe, not of particular concern to productivity measurement in colleges and universities. While scale economies in higher education are intuitively plausible, it appears that significant size increases are likely to trigger institutional responses (e.g., scope or support service increases) that tend to drive up costs (cf., Brinkman, 1990:120). Our model does not adjust for scale effects.

and elsewhere, whose optimality cannot be proved or that have even been shown to be suboptimal. The question is an open one which calls for additional research.

Regarding the second question, Massy (2012) has proposed a modification to Equation (3) to achieve optimality in the nonprofit case. Still, additional research will be needed to determine how the required new parameters can be estimated and to identify the conditions under which the new model produces results that differ materially from the traditional one. The question of material differences will, in turn, shed light on the answer to question (1).

5

Recommendations for Creating and Extending the Measurement Framework

No method of measuring a societal phenomenon satisfying certain minimal conditions exists that can't be second-guessed, deconstructed, cheated, rejected or replaced. This doesn't mean we shouldn't be counting—but it does mean we should so do with as much care and wisdom as we can muster.
　　　　—*John Paulos, New York Times Sunday Magazine*, May 16, 2010

Educational leaders and critics around the country are increasingly calling for greater accountability in higher education. This call creates new demands for reliable performance metrics and data infrastructure to support them. This report attempts to advance the conversation about how best to proceed in response to these demands by identifying promising approaches to productivity measurement that would supplement the statistical information needed by policy makers and administrators to guide resource allocation decisions and assess the value of higher education against other compelling demands on scarce resources; in the process, insights may also be generated that, at least indirectly, lead to improved performance of higher education over the long run.

In sorting through the wide variety of potential applications and contexts—differentiated by characteristics of student populations, institution types and missions, and relevant level of aggregation—it is immediately clear that no single metric can suit all purposes. An appropriately constructed productivity measure for open-admission locally-based colleges will differ from that for major research universities that compete for students, faculty, funds, and recognition on an international scale. Regarding mission, operations such as university hospitals, museums, or athletic programs—for which costs can often be separated out—are typically less central to the pressing policy and public information needs with which this report is concerned.[1] Regarding aggregation, productivity can be measured at increments from the micro level (for example, course and departmental units of analysis, which are important for assessing institutional efficiency) to the macro level (relevant in itself for policy, and also because national accounting offers principles for assembling data used in productivity analysis).

Even as we attempt to advance the discussion of measurement in higher education, we recognize that methodologies and data collection will continue to develop. The measure proposed in Chapter 4, while more promising than simpler metrics, still represents only a partial accounting of the output of the higher education sector. As a first approximation for estimating the value of degrees in various fields, researchers have looked at the associated earnings profiles of those who have earned them. The members of this panel have a range of views on the validity and usefulness of this approach. Some argue that there are legitimate reasons for policy makers to look at market wages, such as when assessing the contribution of college graduates or institutions to economic growth in their regions. Others on the panel argue that such analyses unjustifiably devalue liberal arts education (and fields such as education and social work), and may be particularly harmful when undertaken under pressures created by tightening state budgets.

The panel does agree that policy makers should be concerned with social value, not just market value generated by higher education, and that, for many purposes, emphasis on the latter is a mistake. Earlier chapters include discussion of why current salary differentials (by degree and field) are not necessarily good predictors of future differentials and, thus, why valuing degrees by salaries that graduates earn may be misleading. Some socially important fields pay relatively low salaries which do not reflect their full social value. Furthermore, investment in citizens' careers is not the only objective, from a societal perspective, of supporting and participating in higher education. The nonpecuniary components of higher education output, such as research and other public goods, are also important; even the consumption component of college, including student enjoyment of the experience, is quite clearly significant.

While acknowledging inherent limitations in our ability to comprehensively and coherently account for such a multi-dimensional and diverse productive activity, our view is that simplified, practical approaches that can be implemented by administrators and policy makers can add analytic value. Our recommendations provide guidance for establishing and building on the model of productivity measurement presented in Chapter 4, predicated on the notion that acknowledging the quantitative aspects of productivity is reasonable as a first step.

---

[1] Of course, just because a cost can be separated does not mean that it always should be. A museum, for example, may provide classes and a cultural center. A portion of the museum's cost would then be attributed to the educational mission and a portion to student services.

5.1. THE BASIC PRODUCTIVITY MEASURE

Measuring productivity for higher education begins with the collection of data for quantifying the relationships between units of inputs and outputs, expressed either as volume measures or inflation-adjusted monetary measures. This is the same approach used in productivity measurement for other categories of services and goods produced in the economy. As with higher education, other kinds of firms and sectors produce multiple products and services at quality levels that are difficult or impossible to measure objectively. What is different about higher education is the scale and interconnectedness of these complexities, as examined in Chapter 3. Nevertheless, the basic principles of productivity measurement, appropriately adjusted (or qualified to acknowledge lack of adjustment) for the sector's heterogeneities, can be applied in higher education.

Applying these basic principles leads to Recommendation (1), below. We emphasize that this is only a starting point—that additional research, such as that on the measurement of both the quantity and quality of inputs and outputs, is urgently needed.[2] Nonetheless, it is not premature to propose a basic form as a starting point for productivity measurement. Indeed, having such a form in view will help set the research agenda.

Recommendation (1): The baseline productivity measure for the instructional component of higher education—baseline because it does not capture important quality dimensions of all inputs and outputs— should be estimated as the ratio of (a) the quantity of output, expressed to capture both degrees or completions and passed credit hours, to (b) the quantity of inputs, expressed to capture both labor and nonlabor factors of production.

The model is experimental and should not be adopted without scrutiny, modifications, and a trial period. As we describe in Chapter 6, the model presented will also help motivate and guide data collection and survey design by institutions and by the federal statistical agencies such as the National Center for Education Statistics (NCES), which produces the Integrated Postsecondary Education Data System (IPEDS). Data collection should also be organized so that measures can be aggregated for different purposes. Ideally, estimation of the productivity measure would proceed by first compiling institution-level data for creation of measures for institutional segments, which can then be further aggregated to state and national levels.

---

[2]Dealing with the output of two-year institutions—specifically the production of transfers and nonfour-year degrees—is another complication, which we discuss later in the chapter.

5.1.1. Instructional Outputs and Benefits

To accurately and meaningfully assess the higher education sector's contributions to society and individuals, graduation rates and other uni-dimensional statistics alone are insufficient, and should be avoided. Even a well specified measure, while a considerable step in the right direction, does not offer a full portrait of all that is important, even if a practical way to adjust outputs and inputs for quality were at hand.[3] With this caveat, the panel recommends—for constructing the baseline measurement of instructional output—a formula that sums *student credit hours* and a multiplier that captures the added benefit of achieving *academic credentials* (degrees or certificates).

> **Recommendation (2): The metric used for instructional output (numerator of the productivity ratio) should be a weighted mix of total credits plus additional points for graduation (degree or equivalent) such that:**
>
> **Adjusted credit hours = Credit hours + Sheepskin effect × Completions.**

The underlying theme here, consistent with the economics literature of human capital accumulation, is that even education that does not result in a degree adds to a student's knowledge and skill base, and thus has value. Bailey, Kienzl, and Marcott (2004), Barro and Lee (2010a), and others have concluded that the appropriate unit of measurement for estimating costs and benefits is neither per credit hour nor cost per completion exclusively—and that a hybrid scheme is required. Appropriate data on enrollments and completions are obtainable from IPEDS. The two positive outputs can be combined into a single quantity by weighting the student credit hours with the added value of the degree or certificate over and above the equivalent years of schooling (the "sheepskin effect").

Labor market studies indicate that, due to a combination of credentialing and other effects, starting salaries are consistently higher for those with a bachelor's degree relative to those with similar characteristics and an equivalent number of credit hours but lacking a degree. Estimates of the size of the sheepskin effect to be applied in the model must be empirically based, as in the work of Card (1999) and Jaeger and Page (1996). At this point, a single national weighting scheme for the value of credits versus completions could be applied for all institutions; in Chapter 4, we suggest a degree bonus (for four-year institutions) equivalent to an additional year of credits, pending further empirical investigation. In time,

---

[3]The criticism that a measure is not useful when incomplete is analogous to the criticism of GDP as a measure of societal welfare or progress. GDP is important, but statistics on poverty, income/wealth distribution, mental and physical health, well-being, etc. are also needed to form a full picture of whether or not social and economic conditions are improving. Likewise, a productivity measure is one element of a complete picture of the sector's performance.

with sufficient information, a more granular adjustment factor could be devised that allows for variation by academic field, institution, and possibly region.[4] Estimates of the market value of degrees should be adjusted as warranted by ongoing research, and regularly updated as the values change with labor market trends. Longitudinal surveys (e.g., the Wisconsin Longitudinal Study) designed to determine the average salary for degree and nondegree earners at various points after graduation (starting, after five years, etc.) are essential for this kind of research and may serve as a model.[5]

Adjusting Output Measures to Reflect Institution Type and Mission

Appropriate specification of a productivity measure varies by context and by intended use. For many purposes, it is misleading to compare performance measures across institutional types unless adjustments are made.[6] Community colleges, which are likely to continue to contribute to any increases in the nation's production of postsecondary education, provide a clear example of the need for flexibility in the measurement concept. In this case, the unit of output should be defined to reflect a student body mix dominated by individuals pursuing (at least as a first step) an objective other than a four-year degree. The method of establishing point totals in the numerator of the productivity measure for community colleges can use the baseline framework presented in Chapter 4; however, it will have to be modified to reflect different mission objectives. Specifically, certifi-

---

[4]At this point, it may be asking too much to provide the differentials by field, but it warrants further research along the lines of Arum and Roksa (2010). Credit hours for students who have not declared a major would be prorated over the declared majors for that degree level. There may be credit hours that cannot be assigned to specific majors. If a residual category of "nonmatriculated students" is needed, a weighting procedure could be devised. Also, in some fields, such as nursing, the credentialing effect is strong and credits themselves less so; in other cases, such as the student with two years in liberal arts at a prestigious institution, credits themselves may be quite valuable. One possible benefit of applying a single degree bonus to all degrees is that it may avoid unhelpful attacks on academic areas (such as the humanities) for which social benefits are less fully captured by current salary data.

[5]In addition to the longitudinal data, modeling techniques must control for student characteristics that may affect both the probability of graduating and subsequent earnings levels. Thus far, the literature has mainly addressed earnings differentials between those who attend or do not attend college (see Dale and Krueger, 2002), but the methods would be similar. Techniques should also ensure that the marginal earnings effect of an advanced degree is not attributed to the undergraduate degree. Eliminating those with advanced degrees from the study may introduce a selection bias in either direction. That is, those with the highest earning potential may have a tendency either to enter the labor market directly with a bachelor's degree or to pursue a graduate degree.

[6]A good example is the "Brain Gain" initiative of the Oklahoma Board of Regents, which employs a statistical methodology that estimates the amount an institution deviates from model-predicted graduation rates that takes into account such variables as average admissions test scores, gender, race, and enrollment factors such as full- versus part-time status.

cates, associate's degrees, or successful transfers will have to enter the equation. This will create new data needs (see next chapter).[7]

> **Recommendation (3): Definitions should be established for outcomes at institutions other than traditional four-year colleges and universities with low transfer-out rates, and appropriate bonus figures estimated and assigned to those outcomes. This is especially important for community colleges where, in contrast to B.A. and B.S. degrees, outcomes might be successful transfers to four-year colleges, completion of certificates, or acquisition of specific skills by students with no intention of pursuing a degree.**

If supported by empirical research on the added value of these milestones, the same methodology that is used for the four-year institutions (analogous to the sheepskin effect) could be applied.[8] In the short run, a proxy could be developed using data from the Beginning Postsecondary Study (BPS, which includes information on transfers) to determine profiles of community college students whereby an outcome measure indicating a given number of credit hours earned counts as a success (see Bailey and Kienzl, 1999).

Additional empirical work will be needed since the salary premium—that is, the salary bump for someone with two years of postsecondary schooling and an associate's degree relative to someone with similar schooling but no degree—is likely to be quite different from the four-year counterpart. The bonus will also vary by degree type. An associate of arts degree may lead to only a small sheepskin effect; a technical associate's degree, on the other hand, may be quite valuable in the labor market.[9] These are empirical questions.

To study salary effects for transfers, these students must be distinguished from nontransfers (transfers typically can only be identified by the receiving institutions). For transfers, in cases where the degree is ultimately earned, the degree bonus could be allocated by percentage of time spent—or, probably better, credits earned—at each institution. For institutions at which a significant proportion of

---

[7]This more flexible kind of accounting creates virtuous incentives such as encouraging community colleges to produce student transfers to four-year institutions.

[8]It is noteworthy that the Gates Foundation has stated as a program objective establishing these kinds of metrics for grantees. Lots of data are being generated through these projects but the definitions and methods are still in flux.

[9]Additionally, state systems have different policies that affect the need for an associate's degree. In some, a student may automatically matriculate to a four-year institution with full credits; a degree is not needed to transfer. It is also unclear whether there is any significant sheepskin effect associated with a two-year degree for individuals who go on to get a four-year degree.

new students enter as transfers, new additional measures of incoming class level may be needed.[10]

The multiplicity of institutions again points to the need to develop data tools designed to follow students rather than institutions so as to accurately assign output quantities in the accounting system. Longitudinal data also would add considerable analytic capacity for estimating education outcomes of transfer students. Without this kind of data, it will be impossible to differentiate between transfer students who ultimately receive degrees and students who begin at four-year institutions and receive the same degree. Additionally, much of the discussion about tracking student outcomes along with student characteristics suggests the need for student unit record systems that are different from cohort graduation rate record datasets. We discuss these data implications in more detail in Chapter 6.

5.1.2. Instructional Inputs and Costs

Ideally, for many monitoring and assessment purposes, separate productivity measures should be developed for direct instructional activities and for the various noninstructional activities that take place at higher education institutions. As with outputs, expenditures on inputs attributable to some kinds of research, public service, hospitals and the like should be excluded from the instructional production function. Proportionate shares of various overhead functions such as academic support, institutional support, operations and maintenance, and other core expenses should be included.

As detailed in Chapter 4, the most quantitatively significant input to higher education instruction is labor, represented as units of FTE employees. Some portion of nonlabor inputs—specifically, the cost of materials and other inputs acquired through purchase or outsourcing and the rental value of physical capital—must also be accounted for. The Bureau of Labor Statistics (BLS) recommends a methodology based on percentage changes for the various categories of physical inputs, with weightings based on total category expenditures, for combining the various inputs.[11] Following this approach:

Recommendation (4): The metric used for instructional input (denominator of the productivity ratio) should be a composite index based on the instructional components of (a) full-time equivalent labor hours,

---

[10]Another question is how to weight the outputs of institutions at which students begin accumulating credit for transfer (e.g., a community college that produces a significant percentage of students who eventually attend a four-year college) against those with a terminal degree focus, such as community colleges that specialize in technical training and that produce a small percentage of transfers to four-year schools.

[11]The BLS method assumes that the entities for which productivity is being measured are profit-maximizers, an assumption that does not strictly apply to traditional colleges and universities. Massy (2012) extends the BLS methodology to the nonprofit case.

perhaps broken down by labor category, (b) intermediate inputs, and (c) the rental value of capital.

The first challenge here is to correctly allocate the quantities of various inputs to the different categories of outputs produced. Accounting systems vary in their classification and treatment of costs (which is more likely to affect disaggregated than aggregated data). Any proposed approach should assess the available options in terms of their capability to capture the desired information.[12]

A second challenge involves differentiating among the various categories of labor inputs. Chapter 4 suggests grouping labor categories with similar marginal productivities and which operate in similar markets. The starting point is to allocate labor FTEs into categories differentiating tenure-track (mainly but not exclusively full-time) and adjunct (mostly part-time), faculty. Ultimately, if empirical evidence justifies treating them as fundamentally different types of labor, it may be desirable to differentiate full-time faculty by seniority, permanent/temporary status, tenure status, or teaching load assignment. This basic approach can be modified as necessary pending more thorough study:

Recommendation (5): The National Center for Education Statistics (NCES) or a designee should examine the feasibility of (a) modifying university accounting systems and IPEDS submissions to identify FTEs by labor category, as ultimately specified for the model, according to the function to which they are charged; and (b) calculating total compensation for each category and function.

As discussed in the next chapter, the eventual scheme may involve modest changes to IPEDS to fully account for the small number of tenure-track faculty members with part-time status. The change to IPEDS in regard to part-time faculty suggested in Chapter 4 is one such modest change. If additional elements are added to IPEDS, NCES should consider ways to limit the total reporting burden, such as eliminating little-used or inconsistently reported disaggregations of personnel data.

To complete the baseline model, it is necessary to account for *nonlabor expenditures* such as the cost of materials and other inputs acquired through purchasing and outsourcing. This can be done by summing expenditures on "operations & maintenance" and "all other" categories (most of these data can be obtained in IPEDS). Deflated (real) values are used to represent the physical quantities (N) and nominal values as the weights (NE). Additionally, a portion of the *rental value of capital* attributable to instruction—estimated as the opportunity cost for the use of physical capital—must be included in the aggregation of inputs. The rental value of capital is estimated as the book value of capital stock

---

[12]The cost allocation algorithm developed for the Delta Cost Project is an example of a logical and well-considered basis for allocating costs.

multiplied by an estimated national rate of return on assets, where capital stock equals the sum of land, buildings, and equipment. In the Base Model (Table 4.2) developed in Chapter 4, rental value of capital is calculated as the instructional capital stock times the rate of return.

5.2. ADJUSTING FOR RESEARCH PRODUCTION

The most methodologically complicated "mixed" input, at least for one large subset of institutions, is faculty time spent in research and service, including public service. In Chapter 2, we describe the complications associated with distinguishing faculty labor associated with research and service from that for other functions. Accounting for institutions' intermediate inputs and capital usage is more straightforward, and standard allocation techniques from cost accounting can be used to good advantage. Even here, however, there are differences in methodology that complicate our ability to achieve comparable productivity measures. These methodological assumptions need to be reviewed and perhaps revised.

Recommendation (6): The National Center for Education Statistics or a designee should develop an algorithm for adjusting labor and other inputs to account for joint production of research and service. Faculty labor hours associated with instruction should exclude hours spent on sponsored research and public service, for example, and the algorithm should provide an operational basis for adjusting other inputs on the basis of expenditures.

Commentators such as Jonathan Cole have argued that research capacity is in fact the primary factor distinguishing U.S. universities from those in the rest of the world (Cole, 2010). Cole argues convincingly that America's future depends strongly on the continued nurturing of its research-intensive universities. Indeed, that is why the federal government and state governments have invested and continue to invest billions of dollars in university-based research. Thus, in not fully accounting for research activities, the baseline model omits a central mission of research oriented universities.

The decision to limit the report's focus to measurement of undergraduate instruction was made for pragmatic reasons and is not intended as a comment on the relative importance of teaching, research, and public service for institutions with multiple missions. Even if the sole objective was in measuring instruction, understanding of faculty time spent in research should be improved because it is substantial, not fully separable, and may affect the quality of teaching. For example, Webber and Ehrenberg (2010) show that increases in sponsored research expenditures per student were associated with lower graduation rates after holding instructional expenditures per student constant—perhaps because regular faculty spend less time on optional tasks and rely more on adjuncts. The authors hypothesized that institutions with high levels of sponsored research probably

---

BOX 5.1
The Case Study Afforded by For-Profit Universities

Though separating the cost of departmental research and instructional costs is clearly important, it involves a fundamental issue that relates to the growing for-profit sector. The for-profit sector is exclusively focused on providing instruction, and the curriculum is based on the knowledge that is produced in the rest of the higher education sector. This means that for-profit higher education, which will not have departmental research, operates on a lower cost schedule than the rest of higher education. If state policy makers reduce funding of departmental research, the growth of the knowledge base will slow and thus, in the long run, gains from attending college will diminish. Trying to minimize the current costs of producing degrees *for all types of institutions* may not be in the best interest of either research or teaching efficiency and quality. Conceptually, there is a great distance between this perspective and that underlying state legislators' preoccupation with performance indicators for undergraduates. It is the distance between the largely autonomous operating environment of an internationally prominent private university and the resource-dependent environments of the larger number of public institutions.

---

also had higher levels of departmental research (discussed below), but this could not be demonstrated. On the positive side, what a professor does in the classroom may depend in part on whether he or she stays current with skills and the issues in the field.[13] Without an active research program, professors risk falling behind the state of knowledge in their fields and thus being unable to teach material at the frontier. Additionally, active researchers may be versed in new knowledge that will not reach journals for a year or two and textbooks for much longer.

In earlier chapters, it was argued that instructional program data should exclude sponsored research and organized public service activities because these outputs are distinct from the undergraduate educational mission. When and where these activities are separately budgeted and involve little joint production (i.e., are far removed from the instructional mission), they are easy to parse. For sponsored research, the practice of being released from teaching duties by grants puts a natural price on the time spent in the activity. Other kinds of research, such as unsponsored faculty research, are more difficult to account for. The question of how to account for research is even relevant to the for-profit university and community college cases—where the mission is almost exclusively instruction—because, in the long run, these institutions ultimately rely on the knowledge base developed by the research (Box 5.1).

---

[13]A related issue is the need to deal with undergraduate and other taught programs when graduate-research programs play a role as inputs (i.e., supplying teachers).

5.2.1. Project-Driven Departmental Research

The recommendations in this report about the appropriate treatment of departmental research differ in important respects from those contained in the costing study conducted in 2002 by the National Association of College and University Business Officers (NACUBO). The NACUBO costing study asserts that all departmental research should be combined with instructional costs because, "The integration of research and education is a major strength of the nation's colleges and universities and directly benefits undergraduates" (National Association of College and University Business Officers, 2002:28). However, the tendency to report cost study results in terms of the difference between unit costs and the tuition and fees paid by students has led some commentators to argue that at least some of these costs should be separated (assuming that a means of separation can be found). Massy (2010) asks why the cost of faculty research—pursued for its own sake and often with only tenuous links to the educational mission—should be described as a subsidy to students. NACUBO's approach carries the perverse implication that the lower a department's apparent productivity (for example, because it pursues objectives not desired by students or stakeholders and/or fails to manage teaching loads effectively), the greater is the apparent subsidy to students—an incentive system that fails to drive improvement and undermines the credibility of higher education.

Departmental research (DR) falls into two categories: project-driven and discretionary. Each has different implications for the measurement of instructional productivity. Project-driven departmental research involves work required to fulfill the terms of a sponsored research project, and may involve some cost sharing. For example, principal investigators on a grant from the National Science Foundation (NSF) may not receive academic-year salary offsets, yet the considerable amounts of time they spend on their projects often necessitates reduced teaching loads (reductions that count as departmental research). Arrangements made between colleges or departments and faculty members to seed proposal writing or provide bridge support between sponsored projects also fall comfortably under project-driven DR even if they are not separately budgeted.

The direct link between project-driven DR and sponsored research provides a strong argument for excluding the former from instructional costs. Only the idiosyncrasies of university accounting and the market power of sponsoring agencies enable those agencies to enforce cost-sharing on academic-year effort in order to spread their funds further. Arguing on principle for inclusion of research costs in instructional cost is tantamount to arguing that the sponsored research itself be included—which, in addition to being intrinsically illogical, would hugely distort the productivity measures.[14]

---

[14]A study by Webber and Ehrenberg (2010) supports the idea that project-driven DR may lower graduation rates and lengthen time to degree (presumably because of its demands on faculty effort).

Fortunately, the association of project-driven DR with sponsored research opens the way to a statistical adjustment for instructional cost based on the amount of sponsored research extant in the department. Objection to basing the adjustment on sponsored research because it is unequally distributed across fields will be mooted by the partition of DR into project-driven and discretionary components.

Recommendation (7): An estimate of the departmental research (DR) directly associated with sponsored research projects (project-driven DR, now typically considered part of the instructional cost in universities' accounts) should be excluded from faculty instructional labor. The algorithm for doing this will have to be developed through a special study, since it appears impractical to capture the data directly in university accounting systems.

Some ideas about how the special study might be conducted are presented in Appendix D.

Once an empirically based aggregate estimate (the default for each institutional type) is established, institutions might be allowed to report their own percentage of DR, either higher or lower than the default, based on local data (the same percentage would have to be reported to all audiences). This would have a balanced effect on incentives: selecting a higher percentage would boost the university's reported productivity, but it also would raise research expectations and expose the institution to criticism from stakeholders. Regardless, the percentage figure (and the evidence put forward to justify the difference from the default) will stimulate a needed dialog which will improve the understanding of departmental research as well as the calculation itself.

5.2.2. Discretionary Departmental Research

Discretionary departmental research refers to work initiated by a faculty member without outside support. Like all departmental research, discretionary research and scholarship is done on the departmental budget—that is, without being separately accounted for. Separately budgeted research may be sponsored or unsponsored, but departmental research is paid for by the university. The largest element of departmental research expense arises from reduced teaching loads for faculty. Teaching load reductions may be defended on the grounds that they enable: (a) research and scholarship for fields where sponsored research is not typically available—for example, the humanities; (b) research and scholarship for faculty who are less successful in obtaining sponsored projects than their peers or who are at departments or institutions that typically do not attract sponsored research funds but who, for various reasons, are deserving of dedicated research time; (c) time to be directed toward seed efforts to reorient research agendas or to lay the foundation for large, complex proposals; or (d) "education research" to spur teaching improvement and course and curriculum development.

Good arguments exist for including at least a part of discretionary departmental research in the cost base for instruction, especially if one can escape the subsidy notion discussed in the previous section. For one thing, it is difficult or impossible to separate the effects of educational research and development (R&D) from the other motivators of low teaching loads (other than those associated with sponsored research projects), and there is no doubt that educational R&D should be included in the instructional cost base. Meaningful educational R&D expenses and work that sustains the life of disciplines (and that are not sponsored research) should be defendable to stakeholders. Additionally, some allocation of faculty time entails service that is required to keep institutions running. Other time commitments, such as those to public service and administrative work related to sponsored research, do not contribute directly to instruction.

Recommendation (8): Discretionary departmental research and service should be included in the instructional cost base for purposes of measuring productivity.

Because of the variation in intensity of departmental research across institutions, productivity comparisons across categories should be avoided. For example, departmental research that enhances the knowledge base in disciplines provides much of the intellectual content for classes taught by both four-year research and for-profit institutions. However, since instructors at for-profit institutions spend little time doing this research, they will appear more efficient (because of the time faculty at other institutions spend producing new knowledge, which eventually is used by the for-profits).

5.3. DEALING WITH HETEROGENEITY AND QUALITY ISSUES

Ideally, input and output quantities would be adjusted for quality, but this is difficult; developing data and methods for doing so is a very long-term project, especially if the goal is systematic quality adjustment such as that routinely performed by BLS for product categories like computers and automobiles. Incomplete accounting of quality variation or change in a given measure makes it all the more essential to monitor when apparent increases in measurable output arise as a result of quality reduction. This may have to be done through parallel tracking of other kinds of information generated independently from the productivity metric.[15] In general, until adjustments can be made to productivity metrics to ac-

---

[15]In practice, we see quality measures deployed to monitor whether learning quality changes with changes in production methodology, as, for example, in course redesign projects such as those conducted by the National Center for Academic Transformation. This requires that institutions take steps to ensure that departments maintain a robust internal quality control system.

count for quality differences, it will be inappropriate to rely exclusively on them when making funding and resource reallocation decisions. A productivity metric is only one piece of information to weigh in most decision-making environments. Uncritical use could result in creating the wrong incentives, such as penalizing institutions that accept economically disadvantaged (less prepared) students. This is also why we emphasize the need to segment and array institutions for purposes of comparison. At the national level, quality adjustment is a concern only if there are changes over time in the preparedness of students and the value of education, or in the percentages attending various kinds of institutions—for example, a big shift into community colleges. The problem of quality is more acute when attempting to compare institutions, departments, and systems.

5.3.1. Variation of Inputs

As emphasized throughout this report, full measurement of inputs and outputs is more complicated than simply counting hours, dollars, or degrees. The hours for a given task are not fixed, and students, instructors, institutions, and degrees are not homogenous. Among the host of factors that change over time or vary across institutions and departments—and which in turn affect measured productivity—is the mix of students. Students may vary along dimensions such as preparedness and socioeconomic background. Prior research shows that standard outcome measures (graduation and persistence rates, for example) are related to variables such as entry test scores and family income (Webber and Ehrenberg, 2010). Heterogeneity of student characteristics surely must be taken into consideration when interpreting measures of institutional productivity.

The heterogeneity issue regularly arises when interpreting performance implications of simple metrics such as graduation rates. For purposes of making comparisons across institutions (or states, or nations), it is essential to take into account incoming student ability and preparation. Highly selective institutions typically have higher completion rates than open-access institutions. This may reflect more on the prior learning, preparation, and motivation of the entrants than on the productivity of the institution they enter. Therefore, in the context of resource allocation, performance assessment, or other high stakes decisions, the marginal success effect attributable to this input quality effect should be taken into consideration. A conventional approach, widely applied in the empirical literature, is to use SAT scores and other indicators of student quality (e.g., high school rank, ethnicity, socioeconomic variables such as educational status and income of parents) as explanatory variables in regression analysis to make the needed adjustments.

Legal constraints may prevent reporting of data on the individual student level, but much could still be learned from a more complete school-wide census of incoming freshmen on demographic and preparedness measures. Beyond the data offered by IPEDS on SAT/ACT scores and enrollment by gender and race for first-time freshmen, more empirical traction could be gained by making available the following data at the school level: distributions of family income by entering freshman cohort (some of which could be gleaned from federal student loan applications); distributions of Advanced Placement test taking and scores by cohort; distribution of parents' education by cohort; distribution of SAT/ACT scores by gender, race, and cohort; distributions of need-based aid (both in-house and government) by income categories and cohort; and other relevant information that schools commonly collect but do not report. It may be possible for schools to report a census of applicants or matriculants that would include variables such as acceptance rates by race, gender, and household income.

In the spirit of monitoring quality (in this case, of the student input) in parallel with the proposed productivity statistic, student distributions could be reported at the quartile or quintile level so as not to make reporting excessively costly, rather than simple averages. Dispersion is likely to be an informative metric in quality-adjusted productivity.[16] Schools commonly track at least some of these data, but this advance would require a mandate by IPEDS to elicit widespread cooperation. This kind of partial quality adjustment is better than nothing and contributes to researchers, practitioners, and policy makers having a more precise and informative picture to learn from.

Segmenting institutions is the alternative (or in some case complementary) approach to controlling for variation in student characteristics and other kinds of educational inputs and outputs. As outlined in Section 4.3, institutions are assigned to different groups and productivity estimates are made for each group. Representatives of the segments themselves would have to make the case that any increments to resource utilization per unit of output, as compared to other segments, are justified in terms of quality, research emphasis, or other factors.

Even within an institutional segment, it is still desirable to account for differences in the mix of degree levels and majors. Institution-level cost data indicate that the resources required to produce an undergraduate degree vary, sometimes significantly, by major. Variation in degree cost is linked to, among other things, systematic differences in the amount of time and technology (e.g., engineering) needed to complete a degree. Some majors take an average of four years while others may take four-and-a-half or five years (engineering tracks, for example, typically entail eight or more additional credits due to course requirements and

---

[16]For a simple example, suppose two schools have an entering class with the same average SAT score, but the first school has a higher variance. If students below a certain preparation threshold are more likely to drop out, then, all else equal, the school with the fattest lower tail would have a larger attrition rate and hence, a lower measured productivity if means alone were considered. Even though their student inputs are comparable as measured by the first moment of the distribution, the second moment (and others) may still contain meaningful information on quality differentials.

accreditation rules).[17] Similarly, there is variation in associate degree program lengths. A nursing A.S., for example, is often more than 60 credit hours; 72 hours is typical. Also, some majors are associated with larger class sizes and others with smaller ones; and some majors are associated with lower graduation rates.[18] If this variation were not taken into account—that is, if only degrees and credits were counted—schools with an expensive field mix would fare poorly on a cost-per-degree metric; and, if such a performance measure were tied to high stakes decisions, institutional policy makers might have an incentive to gravitate toward less costly majors. If an institution's students were increasingly enrolled in high-cost majors, expenditures per student must rise or, if they remain constant, one would expect a decline in graduation and persistence rates or in quality.

Faculty salaries also vary widely across fields of study (Turner, 2001). Institutions that educate a greater share of their students and employ a greater share of their faculty in fields associated with rising relative salaries will see greater cost pressures on their faculty resources, other factors held constant. Institutions may respond by reducing faculty size as salary costs rise or shifting to lower-paid nontenure-track teachers which, as noted earlier in the chapter, may potentially affect student learning and graduation outcomes. This suggests that productivity measures must control for changes in the distribution of faculty type and salaries over time.[19] For these reasons, changes in the mix of majors must be accounted for when estimating the denominator of the productivity measure.

Recommendation (9): The productivity model should include an adjustment for field of study. This adjustment should reflect different course requirements, pass rates, and labor input costs associated with various fields.

Even if the initial baseline model does not adjust for field of study, research to create future versions that do so should be encouraged. In our data recommenda-

---

[17]A gradual increase in credit-hour requirements has occurred since the 1970s, possibly in response to credit-hour funding incentives. Before that, almost all bachelor's programs were 120 credit hours. They are now gradually decreasing again under pressure from states. Productivity metrics will help avoid incentives to inflate requirements and extend students' time.

[18]Blose, Porter, and Kokkelenberg (2006) look at the distribution of majors and the cost of producing a degree for each field of the State University of New York system.

[19]At the national level, using a national average of faculty salaries by field is appropriate. When thinking about changes in productivity at individual institutions, it becomes a more complicated problem. Not only do faculty salaries vary across fields, but the ratio of faculty salaries in different fields (e.g., average salary in economics to average salary in English) also varies widely across institutions. Ehrenberg et al. (2006) suggest that if, say, the economics department at a university gets higher salaries relative to the English department, the relative salary advantage of economists will increase, leading average faculty salaries at the institution to increase. In measuring changes in productivity at that institution, it is unclear whether this institution-specific change in relative faculty salaries should be factored in.

tions (next chapter), we advise that credit-hour data for productivity analyses be collected in a way that follows students in order to estimate the role of various departments associated with a given type of degree.

5.3.2. Quality Variation and Change of Outputs

The major types of information needed to ideally adjust for in an output measure relate to learning outcomes and degree and credit value. If salaries of graduates are used as a quality metric of outputs, which we do not blindly advise, controlling for field in the model is essential. Even with field of study level granularity, acting on the recommendations in this report will produce nothing like a complete quality-adjusted productivity measure. The goal here is to initiate a methodology that provides a real and necessary step toward better measures that can be further developed as data and research advance.

Because of its complexity, the prospect of quality adjustment calculations seems at first blush daunting. However, some information is already available. For example, in thinking about outputs (educated and credentialed graduates), a wide range of degrees already include some kind of external certification that involve quality assessment, at least in terms of student competency outcomes.[20] These include engineering, accounting, nursing, and a range of technical fields.

Recommendation (10): Where they already exist, externally validated assessment tools offer one basis for assessing student learning outcomes. For fields where external professional exams are taken, data should be systematically collected at the department level. This could subsequently become a part of IPEDS reporting requirements.

While this kind of information cannot be included in the productivity metric as specified above, it can be evaluated alongside it to help determine if instructional quality is holding constant as input and output variables change.[21] Similarly, empirical power could be created if something like the College and Beyond (C&B) survey conducted by Bowen and Bok (1998) were done so on a nationally representative sample of schools. A limiting aspect of the C&B survey is that it concentrates only on highly selective schools that are not reflective of the overall college market.

Student learning is inherently complex and therefore difficult to measure, particularly when it comes to the higher-order thought process presumably

---

[20]On the other hand, many of the fields taught within colleges of liberal arts do not have learning assessments based on field competency tests.

[21]Additional information, such as students' college entrance test scores, would make the professional exam data even more useful. On their own, the latter data do not indicate the value added by a school, but rather students' absolute level of achievement relative to a threshold of passing.

needed to pursue a college education. But steps have been taken, and a number of states produce data on learning results. All University of Texas system schools use the Collegiate Learning Assessment (CLA) test as a means of assessing value-added of each general education curriculum. South Dakota uses the Collegiate Assessment of Academic Proficiency (CAAP) to, among other things, "compute student gains between taking the ACT as high school students and the CAAP as rising juniors. Gains are computed by comparing student scores on the two exams and then categorizing students as making lower than expected progress, expected progress, or higher than expected progress."[22] If learning assessments such as these are to be included as an adjustment factor in a productivity measure, the test selected needs to be one that has national norms. Accreditation is moving in this direction. The Accreditation Board for Engineering and Technology accredits over 3,100 programs at more than 600 colleges and universities worldwide.

A complete monitoring of the value added to students by degrees earned would also require an initial baseline to capture an incoming student's level of preparation. One approach to assessing student learning would be to encourage institutions to implement data systems for cataloguing tests and test results of their graduates. To some extent, these test-based assessments presume that development of cognitive skills is the goal. However, returns to noncognitive skills—for example, improved networking, social skills, citizen awareness of civic responsibility—may also be a goal but do not appear in many efforts to assess learning. Much more thought will have to be given to appropriate characteristics of tests and how they should be applied and interpreted. Existing high-stakes exams should obviously be utilized to the extent possible. Pilot tests could be developed to analyze validated credit hours at meaningful levels; some departments have information that would be useful in learning assessments. To accurately reflect learning patterns, these tests must carry high enough stakes to motivate students to take them seriously; such a testing system would be difficult to create.

Given that quality assessment in higher education remains very much a work in progress, the panel is not prepared to recommend a single measure of quality for use in adjusting the productivity model's output metric. Likewise, we are not in a position to recommend specific methods for adjusting the quality of student and teacher inputs to higher education. As discussed in Chapter 4, there are promising approaches to measuring student readiness (e.g., testing) and faculty effectiveness (e.g., course sequence grade analysis). Results from this research could provide context for interpreting more narrowly defined productivity metrics and other performance measures, particularly when policy choices are being weighed.

As put forward in Chapter 4, however, we do propose that effective quality assurance systems be maintained to ensure that output quality does not decline

---

[22]For details, go to http://www.educationsector.org/sites/default/files/publications/Subcategories_49.pdf, page 1 [June 2012].

as a result of quantitative productivity measurements. These could be based on extant accreditation systems, on the methods of academic audit being used effectively in Tennessee and certain overseas venues, and on the other quality-reviewing initiatives now being conducted at the state level (see Massy, Graham, and Short, 2007). All such methods can and should make use of the growing body of quality measures that are developing. Whatever the approach, however, its usefulness for achieving the goals of this report will depend upon full transparency, which is not always maintained in the existing systems.

We believe the groundwork exists for implementing effective quality monitoring, and that a committee (that, beyond accreditors, might include representation from governors and state legislators, Congress, state governing boards, consumer advocacy groups, and college guidebook publishers) could usefully review external quality assessment, with specific reference to the contents of this report, and make recommendations about the way forward.

Recommendation (11): A neutral entity, with representation from but not dominated or controlled by the country's existing higher education quality assurance bodies, should be charged with reviewing the state of education quality assessment in the United States and recommending an approach to assure that quantitative productivity measurement does not result in quality erosion.

This is an important recommendation: the time is right for an overarching impartial review. Failing such a review, the development of badly needed improvement in the quantitative dimension of productivity could lead to unintended negative outcomes.

6

Implementation and Data Recommendations

6.1. GENERAL STRATEGIES

This report contains two types of recommendation for improving productivity measurement: those that are conceptual and those that address issues related to implementation of new measures and data development. The model presented in Chapter 4 requires specific data inputs and, while considerable progress can be made using existing sources such as the Integrated Postsecondary Education Data System (IPEDS) of the National Center for Education Statistics (NCES), an ideal productivity measure will require new or improved capabilities as well.

In moving forward with plans to implement productivity measurement, program administrators will not be able to do everything suggested by this panel (and by others[1]) all at once. It is helpful, initially, to simply take stock of information that is available on input and output trends at various units of analysis, and then consider how far—with that data—one can get in constructing measures. This type of demonstration was a major motivation for working through the model presented in Chapter 4 using real data examples.

More generally, both with and beyond our model, we want to know how well—with current data and approaches—we can address questions of policy interest that arise:

- If measurable outputs have increased while resources have been stable or declining, has quality suffered?

---

[1] See recommendations by the National Postsecondary Education Cooperative (2010).

- If outputs have declined while resources have increased or remained stable, has quality changed correspondingly?
- How do productivity trends in comparable states, institutions, or departments compare?
- Have changes in education delivery mode, student characteristics or important contextual variables (economic, demographic, political, institutional) had a measurable bearing on the trends?
- Are there clear indicators (spikes, dives, or other anomalies) that suggest data problems to be cleaned (as opposed to sudden changes in performance)?
- What evidence or further research could be brought to bear to answer these questions in the next step of the conversation?

The more accustomed administrators, researchers, and policy makers become to conversations that incorporate these kinds of questions, the better the selection of metrics and the potential to understand them are likely to become, and the more evident the need for high-quality data.

A general strategy of implementing improved metrics for monitoring higher education begins with the following assertions:

- Productivity should be a central concern of higher education.
- Policy discussions of higher education performance will lack coherence in the absence of a well-vetted and agreed upon set of metrics.
- Quality of inputs and outputs—and particularly changes in them—should always be a core part of productivity measurement discussions, even when it is not fully or explicitly captured by the metrics. Alternatively put, productivity measurement is not meaningful without at least a parallel assessment of quality trends and, at best, a quality dimension built directly into the metric.
- Some elements relevant to measuring productivity are difficult to quantify. This should not be used as an excuse to ignore these elements or to avoid discussions of productivity. In other words, current methodological defects and data shortcomings should not stunt the discussion.

Additionally, in devising measures to evaluate performance and guide resource allocation decisions, it is important to anticipate and limit opportunities to manipulate systems. The potential for gaming is one reason many common performance metrics should not be relied on, at least not exclusively, in funding and other decision-making processes. *Simply rewarding throughput can create distortions and counterproductive strategies in admissions policies, grading policies, or standards of rigor. Clearly, a single high-stakes measure is a flawed approach; a range of measures will almost always be preferable for weighing overall performance.* We note, however, that monitoring productivity trends would not be introducing incentives to a world without them. Among the major incentives now in place are to enroll students, acquire research grants, improve standing in rankings, raise money, and win athletic competitions. The recommendations in this report are merely adding another incentive (and one more worthy than a number already in play) that will help round out the current set.

6.2. RECOMMENDATIONS FOR IMPROVING THE DATA INFRASTRUCTURE

A major element of the prescription for improving productivity measures for higher education involves developing more accurate and new kinds of information. Thus, identifying data needs is a key part of the panel's charge. Much has been implied in this regard throughout the report and some specific data needs were highlighted in Chapter 4. Here, we reemphasize these in the form of additional recommendations. In thinking about new approaches, the panel had an advantage over practitioners and administrators in being able to think in terms of future goals by recommending changes to IPEDS, coordination of other existing data sources, or development of new data approaches altogether.

6.2.1. Data Demanded by the Conceptual Framework

The categories of data demanded by the modeling framework are, broadly:

- Output/Benefit information. Basic institutional data on credits and degrees can be enhanced through linkages to longitudinal student databases. In addition to their role in sharpening graduation rate statistics, longitudinal student surveys are needed to more accurately estimate degree costs, degree earnings value, and input/output quality.[2]
- Input/Cost information. Sources include institution and state-based expenditure accounting data; basic information about faculty time allocations[3]; and student unit records.

Ideally, for higher education, underlying data for productivity measurement would be as detailed and accurate as it is for the best-measured sectors of the economy. Information requirements—including the need for data at more granular levels,

---

[2]Data Quality Campaign, *10 Essential Elements of a State Longitudinal Data System*, see http://www.dataqualitycampaign.org/survey/elements [January 2012].

[3]IPEDS provides some data on teaching loads; the Delta Cost Project (2009) includes some data on staffing. One could push for time use surveys of faculty time allocations, including hourly accounts of research activity, instruction, and service. This would be difficult though as faculty do not bill by the minute or hour, and much research is done off-campus; furthermore, how would conceptual breakthroughs or mental crafting of language be accounted for when they occur during the course of another activity, such as teaching or hiking?

and input and output quality indicators—extend beyond what is currently available in IPEDS and other sources, though these provide an excellent start.

Another logical source of information to support productivity measurement is the quinquennial economic census surveys, a reliable source of expenditure and other data—including total labor costs and total hours—for most sectors of the economy, including many nonprofits. Statistics for other service industries have improved a great deal in recent years, in part as a result of periodic enhancements to the economic census. However, Bosworth (2005:69) notes that "the higher education community successfully lobbied to be exempted from these reporting requirements; thus the Census Bureau is blocked from gathering data and we lack even the most basic information about the education industry. For example, we do not know with any degree of detail who is employed in higher education, how much capital is being spent, or how many computers are being used."

The higher education sector has not been covered in the economic census since 1977, when it was introduced there (it only appeared once). This decision to omit this sector should be revisited, specifically to evaluate the costs of reintroducing it to the census and the benefits in terms of value added to existing data sources.

Recommendation (12): Every effort should be made to include colleges and universities in the economic census, with due regard for the adequacy of alternative data sources and for the overall value and costs added, as well as difficulties in implementation.

The Department of Education could require that institutions file the census forms in order to maintain eligibility to participate in Title IV programs.

For purposes of constructing the National Income and Product Accounts (NIPAs) and productivity measures, BEA and BLS may also benefit from such a reversal of policy. Census data would provide details on employment by broad categories (it is now difficult to find statistics on employment in higher education industry), along with a range of other operational and performance information. It would facilitate construction of value-added statistics for most of the inputs (including capital goods) that are useful for broad measures of productivity. Additionally, participation in the economic census would harmonize data reporting formats used in other industries. An alternative to this recommendation would be to take advantage of the established IPEDS framework, which includes institution identifiers, and then import economic census style questions into it.

6.2.2. Envisioning the Next Generation IPEDS

IPEDS provides valuable information annually (or biannually) on institutional characteristics, degree completions, 12-month enrollment, human resources (employees by assigned position, fall semester staff, salaries), fall semester enrollment, finance, financial aid, and graduation rates for all private and public, nonprofit and for-profit postsecondary institutions that are open to the general public and that provide academic, vocational, or continuing education for credit.[4] Even so, fully specified productivity measurement of the type envisioned by the panel requires more complete and different kinds of information than what is currently available in IPEDS. For some purposes, greater data disaggregation, such as at departmental levels, and quality dimensions are needed. More comprehensive longitudinal student databases are essential for calculating better tailored and more clearly defined graduation rates and for estimating full degree costs and values.

Box 6.1 summarizes IPEDS data that may be useful in the measurement of higher education productivity, enumerating its significant advantages and remaining challenges for its improvement.

For the model proposed in Chapter 4, institutional data submission requirements are not exceedingly onerous. As noted above, many of the needed variables—credit hours, enrollments, degrees—are already reported to IPEDS. The most significant change required to fully implement output differentiation is to link credit hours to degree or field.

Recommendation (13): Institutions should collect credit-hour data that track both individual students and the departments of record. The necessary information exists in most institutions' student registration files. IPEDS should report these data along with the numbers of degrees awarded.

Chapter 4 provides details about how exactly the credit-hour data should be structured and the statistics extracted.[5]

A side benefit of following students is that it creates new opportunities for calculating more sophisticated graduation rates as well. Cohort-based statistics such as those produced through IPEDS Graduation Rate Survey typically restrict the denominator to first-time, full-time students. For institutions that enroll large numbers of part-time students and beginning transfers, this will not yield a meaningful number.[6] Including these students in the cohort allows for more

---

[4]See http://nces.ed.gov/ipeds/ [July 2012].

[5]In applying this approach to, among other things, discover the course components that go into producing a certain kind of degree, credit hours could be calculated by degree program and institution one time and the results applied in subsequent cohorts for that institution. The calculation may not have to be done every year, though that might not be such an onerous task once systematized. "One-time" benchmarks that are refreshed periodically may be adequate.

[6]NPEC (2010) offers recommendations for (1) counting and defining the composition of an initial cohort of students; (2) counting and defining who is a completer; (3) understanding the length or time of completion; and (4) incorporating students who transfer out of an institution. Available: http://nces.ed.gov/pubs2010/2010832.pdf [July 2012]. The panel agrees with most of these recommendations.

BOX 6.1
Integrated Postsecondary Education Data System (IPEDS)

IPEDS describes itself as "the primary source for data on colleges, universities, and technical and vocational postsecondary institutions in the United States." Elements of IPEDS will be essential to most attempts to measure productivity in a consistent manner across state lines, within states that do not have their own consistent statewide reporting processes for all public institutions, and across both public and private institutions. IPEDS collects detailed descriptive data from all public and private institutions in the United States that wish to be eligible for federal student financial aid, which almost all do.

Productivity-Related Content

Completions

Degrees and certificates awarded are the only elements of the IPEDS system that are broken down by discipline. They are reported for every institution, with field of study and degree level (e.g., associate, bachelor, > one-year certificate, etc.), first/second major, and student demographic characteristics.

Finances

Expenditures are reported by the purpose of the expense (e.g., instruction, research, public service, student services, academic support, etc.) and by the type of expense (i.e., salaries, benefits, plant operations, depreciation, and other). For measurement of instructional productivity using IPEDS data, the direct instructional and student services expenses, plus a prorated share of academic support, institutional support, and plant operations constitute the relevant portion of the total expenditure.

Enrollment

Student credit hours are a core measure for productivity analysis. IPEDS collects only aggregate data on undergraduate and graduate enrollments for each institution. Definitions provided to reporting institutions allow for translation among different calendar systems and for calculation of full-time equivalent enrollments based on numbers of semester/quarter/clock or other units.

Institutional Characteristics

This file contains elements that could be used to group like institutions for productivity analysis. Relevant groups include Carnegie classification, public or private control, Historically Black College and Universities, geographical details, etc.

Human Resources

For degree-granting institutions, the number of employees and their compensation are reported by faculty and tenure status, and equal employment opportunity (EEO) category:

Staff whose primary responsibility is instruction, research, and/or public service:

- Executive/administrative/managerial
- Other professionals (support/service)
- Technical and paraprofessionals
- Clerical and secretarial
- Skilled crafts
- Service/maintenance

Advantages

- IPEDS is the primary national data source for cross-sector and cross-state comparisons.
- Terms are defined independently of state or system-level categories.
- Completions data are reported at a high level of detail.
- IPEDS does not change quickly. Most data fields have been consistently defined over many years, allowing for reliable analysis of trends.

Challenges

- Credit-hour enrollments, staffing patterns, and finance data are available as aggregate numbers only, with no discipline-level detail.
- Incoming student data are limited. Other than a few average data points in the Institutional Characteristics file, IPEDS does not have information about students' level of academic preparation (including remediation or advanced placement), credits transferred in, socioeconomic background, or academic objectives at time of entry.
- IPEDS does not change quickly. Changes typically require strong consensus among institutions, Congressional action, or both, and take many years to implement fully.
- Institutional interpretations of human resources categories, and to a lesser extent finance and degree discipline classifications, vary widely in practice. Required human resources files are designed primarily for equal opportunity reporting and auditing, rather than productivity analysis.
- For cross-institution comparisons of costs and outcomes, researchers need data on discipline mix. Many state systems already identify enrollment by major in their data sources. Classification structures in IPEDS are complicated by varying levels of interdisciplinarity among institutions, different types of academic organization, evolution of categories over time, and external factors such as financial incentives to encourage students to major in STEM fields or to award more degrees in those areas. Weights assigned to disciplines for the purpose of assessing productivity would also risk creating external pressure to adjust discipline classification. Data on distribution of degrees granted across majors has been shown to be an important predictor of six-year graduation rates in many educational production function studies. Given this coverage, it is not clear that collecting data on departmental level progression of students makes sense, especially since there is so much movement of students across fields of study during their period of college enrollment.

completeness; however it can also create new problems because part-time students have differing credit loads and transfer students bring in varying numbers of previously earned credits. This renders fair comparisons difficult because, unlike the first-time full-time population, not all subpopulations are starting from the same baseline.

On the labor input side of the production function, it would be helpful to have data that clarifies more detailed categories for employees. IPEDS does not distribute labor hours into all categories; it does include the proportion of FTE allocated to instructional time. A complete dataset underlying productivity measurement would identify major job categories and how time is allocated on average at a given level of aggregation. In Chapter 5, we recommended that institutions be charged with collecting data on employees by personnel category, making time allocation approximations—focusing on instruction, research, and service—and reporting the results in a revised IPEDS submission that would be subject to the same kind of audit used by other agencies in data collection.

A number of international data efforts are already heading in these new directions, developing microdata and quantitative indicators for higher education institutions, including time in research and other activities. The European Commission, for example, appointed the EUMIDA Consortium to "explore the feasibility of building a consistent and transparent European statistical infrastructure at the level of individual higher education institutions" (Bonaccorsi, Daraio, and Simar, 2006). The goal of the project is to "provide institutions and policy makers with relevant information for the benchmarking and monitoring of trends for modernisation in higher education institutions. . . . [M]ost European countries collect data on their universities, either as part of R&D and higher education statistics or as part of budgeting/auditing systems."[7] U.S. educational institutions and the Department of Education may benefit from assessing these efforts.

6.2.3. Administrative Data Sources

Beyond IPEDS, a number of existing administrative databases can be tapped in constructing useful performance measures. The potential of the kinds of administrative data sources described below depends heavily on the ability of researchers and policy analysts to link records across state boundaries and across elementary, secondary, postsecondary, and workforce boundaries (Prescott and Ewell, 2009). This, in turn, depends upon the presence of secure unique identifiers, such as social security numbers, in all the databases of interest. At present, use of such identifiers is limited (or, more importantly, is perceived to be limited) by the provisions of Family Educational Rights and Privacy Act (FERPA) regulations. Clarification or re-regulation of FERPA might considerably enhance the usefulness of these administrative databases.

---

[7]See http://isi.fraunhofer.de/isi-de/p/projekte/us_eumida.php [July 2012].

Much of the potential of source linking involves data collected and maintained at various levels, ranging from local to federal. For example, administrative data such as that maintained by the IRS's Statistics of Income program and by the Social Security Administration (SSA) can enhance the robustness of studies of the economic benefits associated with postsecondary education (Dale and Krueger, 2002). In principle (and with due attention to legal confidentiality), longitudinal files linking individuals' earning and their educational attainment can be created. BLS data and states' Unemployment Insurance Wage Records could be substitutes for this as well; typically, this kind of research must take place in census data centers.

Institutional and System-Level Data

In many instances, information on higher education inputs and outputs can be obtained inexpensively from institutions' accounting and management systems. In fact, much of the detailed data on human resources and finances needed for ideal analysis of productivity is maintained only by institutions. Many systems and institutions have studies that distinguish expenditures and staffing by discipline and course level in ways that are well suited to the type of analyses recommended in this report.

Micro-level data related to learning outcomes and program quality—for example, exam results and assignments, course evaluations, student surveys, and faculty and staff credentials—are also available in some cases. As has been noted throughout this report, longitudinal student data is especially valuable for tracking the quality of incoming students and the value of higher education attainment. An example of this kind of resource is the longitudinal study recently developed for the University of Virginia that collects data on students following them from kindergarten through college, and then adds the capacity to link to unemployment insurance job records thereafter.[8]

Among the advantages of institution and state-level data are their high levels of detail and accuracy, which are necessary to support evaluation of quality within programs, departments, institutions, and systems. Among the challenges found in institution and state-level data are that methods developed to support day-to-day business operations are often not well configured for research and analysis. Further, data are often not comparable across institutions or across time since they have been built up historically using different practices, and tend to focus more on financial information than on the physical data needed for productivity measurement (see Figure 6.1).

---

[8]The project is being developed by the State Council of Higher Education for Virginia, which makes higher education public policy recommendations, and it will be available to researchers with appropriate safeguards to ensure confidentiality of records.

STATE UNIVERSITY SYSTEM
20092010 EXPENDITURE ANALYSIS
COSTS PER CREDIT HOUR
UCF - REPORT VIII - BY DISCIPLINE

BUDGET ENTITY: E & G
COLL SUBCOMP: Not coded by college

COST ACTIVITIES	FACULTY	GRAD. ASSIST HOUSE STAFF FACULTY ADJ. OTHER OPS	(SUPPORT STAFF) A&P/USPS RESIDUAL	(OPS SUPPORT) STU. ASSIST	SUMMARY
DIS CODE: 14 Engineering					
INSTRUCTION					
Lower	0.7424	1.6945	1.6863	0.0000	4.1232
Upper	23.8723	15.8074	27.4581	0.0000	67.1378
Graduate I	15.8712	7.5400	16.2004	0.0000	39.6116
Graduate II	16.5434	6.6349	16.0393	0.0000	39.2176
Grad III	0.0000	0.0000	0.0000	0.0000	0.0000
Clinical Professional	0.0000	0.0000	0.0000	0.0000	0.0000
*** SUB TOTAL INST ***	57.0293	31.6768	61.3841	0.0000	150.0902
OTHER ACADEMIC AREAS					
Academic Advising	1.4936	0.0000	1.0335	0.0000	2.5271
Academic Administration	10.2040	0.2490	7.2334	0.0000	17.6864
Public Service	4.1460	0.0000	2.8690	0.0000	7.0150
Research	38.6094	7.6083	31.9825	0.0000	78.2002
*** TOTAL I&R PERYEARS ***	111.4823	39.5341	104.5025	0.0000	255.5189

FIGURE 6.1 "Person-years" reported for Engineering at one university, by activity type, 2009-2010.
SOURCE: State University System of Florida Expenditure Reports. Available: http://www. flbog.org/about/budget/expendanalysis.php [October 2012].

State Student Unit-Record Databases

All but five states have constructed databases that cover enrollments and degrees granted in higher education (Garcia and L'Orange, 2010). At minimum, student-level databases contain one record for every student enrolled in a given term or year in all of the state's public institutions. Many have expanded data content that includes detailed academic activities such as specific course enrollments, placement test scores and remedial work, and financial aid sources. Many of these state sources have also begun including data from nonpublic institutions (both proprietary and not-for-profit). Records can, in principle, be linked together to create the kinds of longitudinal databases required to analyze retention, degree completion, and patterns of student flow among institutions within a state. Increasingly, they are being linked with similar databases addressing elementary and secondary schooling and entry into the workforce to enable large-scale human capital studies.

The primary challenges to effective use of these databases are (a) the lack of standardized definitions across them, (b) incomplete institutional and content coverage, and (c) relative inexperience in linking methodologies to create comprehensive longitudinal databases. Federal action to standardize data definitions and to mandate institutional participation in such databases as a condition of receiving Title IV funding would help stimulate productive use.

Recommendation (14): Standardization and coordination of states' student record databases should be a priority. Ideally, NCES should revive its proposal to organize a national unit record database.

Such a data system would be extremely valuable for both policy and research purposes. This is a politically difficult recommendation that may take years to realize. In the meantime, progress can be made through the adoption of standard definitions, based on IPEDS and the Common Data Set, for all data elements in state longitudinal databases, plus linkages among them.[9]

Valuable administrative data are also collected and maintained by state and federal agencies. Wage record and employment data are among the most relevant for estimating productivity and efficiency measures.

Unemployment Insurance Wage Record Data

Under federal guidance, all states maintain databases of employed personnel and wages paid for the purpose of administering unemployment compensation programs. These employment and earnings data can be linked via Social Security Numbers (SSNs) to educational data by researchers interested in estimating such things as return on investment for various kinds of postsecondary training programs and placement rates in related occupations.

The comparative advantage of Unemployment Insurance (UI) data is in its capacity to provide aggregate estimates of outcomes—earnings by industry—for graduates and nongraduates. Additionally, such data are not easily subject to manipulation. The value of UI data for productivity measurement is most obvious for comparatively sophisticated models wherein outputs (i.e., degrees) are weighted in proportion to their contribution to students' short-term or lifetime earnings potential or other career-related outcomes; or studies that make use of employment records to track and compare the earnings of graduates in different disciplines to establish weights. There may also be uses for these data in assessing compensation of higher education personnel and in establishing the quantities or weights of inputs in calculations of productivity.

Though a powerful national resource, the potential of UI data is limited by several factors. First, most UI systems contain data only at the industry level for the reported employee, and not the actual occupation held within that industry. Industry is not always a good proxy for occupation. Universities, for example, employ police officers, landscapers, and social workers. Some employees may thus be misclassified when conducting placement studies—for example, a nurse working in a lumber camp being classified as a forest products worker. A simple

---

[9]This kind of work is being piloted by the Western Interstate Commission for Higher Education, Gates Foundation data sharing project. The panel also applauds work ongoing by the Common Data Standards Project, currently under way at the State Higher Education Executive Officers association.

fix that federal authorities could make would be to mandate inclusion of the Standard Occupational Classification (SOC) code in all state UI wage records. Second, each state maintains its own UI wage record file independently under the auspices of its labor department or workforce agency. And, whether for post-secondary education or employment, it is difficult to coordinate multi-state or national-level individual unit record databases. For this reason, state databases cannot track cohorts of graduates or nongraduates across state lines without some agreement to do so.

> **Recommendation (15): The Bureau of Labor Statistics should continue its efforts to establish a national entity such as a clearinghouse to facilitate multi-state links of UI wage records and education data. This would allow for research on issues such as return on investment from postsecondary training or placement rates in various occupations.**

Such an entity could also begin to address a third major limitation of UI wage records—the fact that they do not contain data on individuals who are self-employed or employed in the public sector. Linkages to public employee and military personnel databases could be established on a national basis and self-employment earnings and occupation data, with the appropriate privacy safeguards, might be obtained from the IRS. Additionally, economic analyses of earnings often require looking many years after graduation to see the economic value of some degrees (some biology majors, for example, may have low reported earnings during medical school and residency programs, but very high wages afterward).

State Longitudinal Databases

Many states have databases that allow for longitudinal studies of students from K-12 education through postsecondary enrollment, degree completion, and beyond. The U.S. government has contributed significant resources in an effort to create or expand these databases over the last several years. For example, late in 2010, the U.S. Department of Labor, through its Workforce Data Quality Initiative, awarded more than $12 million to 13 states to build or expand longitudinal databases of workforce data that could also be linked to education data. As described in Chapter 2, these kinds of data are essential for research into and policy analysis of the link between employment and education, and the long-term success of individuals with varying levels and kinds of education.

Databases vary in age, depth, and breadth, all of which affect how they can be used for productivity measurement. The state-maintained databases all contain student-level enrollment and degree completion information, usually with aggregate numbers of credit hours—all useful for productivity measurement. They vary in the extent to which they include specific course-level detail. Many contain data about K-12 preparation, which affects productivity in higher education in the sense that similar degrees represent different quantities of achievement (levels of preparedness) for different students. Many also include at least some data from private postsecondary institutions. Another asset of these kinds of databases is that they allow for analysis that crosses institutional boundaries. They also present many challenges: (1) the nature of the gaps in data vary by state; (2) access to records can be subject to state political considerations; (3) they are less useful in states with substantial mobility across state lines; and (4) they include no or only limited amounts of financial or human resources data.

National Student Clearinghouse

The National Student Clearinghouse (NSC) is a national postsecondary enrollment and degree warehouse that was established about fifteen years ago to house data on student loan recipients. It has since been expanded to include enrollment records for more than 94 percent of the nation's postsecondary enrollments and almost 90 percent of postsecondary degrees, essentially rendering it a national database.[10] Its primary function is administrative, verifying attendance and financial aid eligibility for the Department of Education, among other things. It also provides limited research services.

Proof of concept studies have demonstrated that the data contained in NSC records are capable of grounding accurate longitudinal tracking studies of college entrance and completion regardless of place of enrollment, thus overcoming one of the major limitations of state SUR databases (Ewell and L'Orange, 2009). Often when a student fails to re-enroll at an institution or within a state system of higher education, there is no record to indicate whether the student transferred or re-enrolled elsewhere, and therefore no way to know whether the credits earned prior to departure are part of an eventual credential. Similarly, when a degree is awarded, there is often imperfect information about the different institutions a student may have attended prior to the degree award from the graduating institution. NSC's matching service can fill in some of these gaps for institutional or state-level cohorts of students. The major advantage is that it can provide information about cross-institution, cross-state, and cross-sector enrollments and degrees awarded that would not otherwise be available.

The major drawback of harnessing these data for such purposes, however, is the fact that reporting to the NSC is voluntary: institutions provide data because they get value in return in the form of the ability to track, and therefore account for, students who have left their institutions with no forwarding information. As a result, some safeguards on the use of NSC data for research purposes would need to be established and enforced. Additionally, only the enrollment and degree award events are recorded. Although 94 percent of college enrollments are represented, states and institutions with a disproportionate share of the nonparticipants

---

[10] Available: http://www.studentclearinghouse.org/ [July 2012].

may not be able to benefit. Some researchers are also reporting problems with the matching algorithms that make the data difficult to use and interpret correctly.[11]

6.2.4. Survey-Based Data Sources

In this section, we describe several survey-based data sources that have value to developers of productivity and other performance metrics. A fuller accounting of data sources is provided in Appendix C.

NCES Postsecondary Sample Surveys

The National Center for Education Statistics conducts a number of relevant surveys: Baccalaureate and Beyond (B&B), Beginning Postsecondary Students (BPS), National Postsecondary Student Aid Survey (NPSAS), National Survey of Postsecondary Faculty (NSOPF), and the Postsecondary Education Transcript Study (PETS).[12] These surveys use large national samples to provide research and policy answers to questions that cannot be addressed from IPEDS. They include information about students' level of academic preparation, transfer patterns, socioeconomic status, financial resources, aid received, academic and non-academic experiences during college, and persistence and degree attainment. NSOPF includes data about faculty activities, but have not been administered since 2003-2004. The samples are structured to provide reliable samples at the level of institutional sector (public four-year, two-year, private four-year, etc.) across the United States. Only limited additional disaggregation is possible without losing statistical significance.

This set of surveys includes content in a number of areas that is relevant to productivity measurement. What an institution contributes to a student's education should ideally be separated from what a student brought with him or her, in terms of credits earned elsewhere, level of preparation in earlier levels of education, and other experiences and aptitudes. NPSAS and its offshoots can help to assign the contribution share for degrees to multiple institutions or sectors when students transfer (as a significant percentage do), and to distinguish what institutions are contributing from what students bring with them at entry.

The BPS survey, conducted on a subset of NPSAS participants, is especially important for understanding sector-level productivity nationally, and has typically been started with a new cohort every eight years.

---

[11]See http://www.spencer.org/resources/content/3/documents/NSC-Dear-colleagues-letter.pdf [July 2012].

[12]Baccalaureate and Beyond: http://nces.ed.gov/surveys/b%26b/; Beginning Postsecondary Students: http://nces.ed.gov/surveys/bps/; National Postsecondary Student Aid Survey: http://nces.ed.gov/surveys/npsas/; National Survey of Postsecondary Faculty: http://nces.ed.gov/surveys/nsopf/; and Postsecondary Education Transcript Study: https://surveys.nces.ed.gov/pets/ [July 2012].

These datasets have several positive attributes. Samples attempt to represent all students in U.S. higher education; longitudinal follow-ups track attainment across institutions, sectors, state lines; and students entering with different levels of preparation can be distinguished. They also present a number of challenges. National surveys are, by design, not useful as state- or institution-level resources; surveys are administered infrequently; and surveys are costly to implement and to scale up.

National Science Foundation

The National Science Foundation (NSF) conducts surveys on sciences and engineering graduate and postgraduate students.[13] Information is collected on type of degree, degree field, and graduation date. Data items collected in NSF surveys are more attuned toward understanding the demographic characteristics, source of financial support and posteducation employment situation of graduates from particular fields of science, health, and engineering. These data are useful in understanding trends in salaries of science, technology, engineering, and mathematics (STEM) graduates.

NSF surveys concentrate on degree holders only. The sampling frame does not include individuals who have not graduated from a higher educational institution. There is no information on credits completed by degree and nondegree holders. Although the sampling frame is limited for purposes of calculating institutional productivity for undergraduate programs, it does collect information on post-bachelor degree holders, postdoctoral appointees, and doctorate-holding nonfaculty researchers. Sampling techniques and data items collected also make the NSF data useful for calculating department level (within STEM fields) output in terms of research and academic opportunities available to graduates.

The NSF survey of academic R&D expenditures is valuable to federal, state, and academic planners for assessing trends in and setting priorities for R&D expenditures across fields of science and engineering, though it is not directly related to instructional productivity.[14] It has potential for indirect use in estimating the volume of research expenditure, by discipline, at different institutions in order to better untangle joint products. In contrast, IPEDS provides only aggregate research expenditure, with no disciplinary detail. This NSF survey may be the only national source for this limited purpose.

---

[13]See http://nsf.gov/statistics/survey.cfm [July 2012].

[14]Survey description: http://www.nsf.gov/statistics/srvyrdexpenditures/ and WebCaspar data access: https://webcaspar.nsf.gov/ [July 2012].

Census and the American Community Survey

The American Community Survey (ACS), which replaced the Census long form, is a national sample survey of 2 million households that became fully implemented in 2005. ACS data are used to produce estimates for one-year, three-year, and five-year periods. Each month, the ACS questionnaire is mailed to 250,000 housing units across the nation that have been sampled from the Census Bureau's Master Address File.[15] As with the long-form of the Census, response to the ACS is currently required by law. The questionnaire has items on sex, age, race, ethnicity, and household relationship. Each observation is weighted to produce estimates. Weighting is done via a ratio estimation procedure that results in the assignment of two sets of weights: a weight to each sample person record, both household and group quarters persons, and a weight to each sample housing unit record. There are three education-related variables in the ACS: college or school enrollment in the three months preceding the survey date, current grade level, and educational attainment, including field of bachelor's degree. ACS collects data from households and group quarters. Group quarters include institutions such as prisons and nursing homes but also college dormitories.

In terms of value for productivity measurement, no information is collected on credit hours and colleges or universities attended or completed by survey respondents enrolled in college. The questionnaire has items on various sources and amounts of income, and details on occupation and work in the year preceding date of survey. ACS data thus provides descriptive statistics of educational status of various population groups (even in small geographic areas like census tracts), but it lacks relevant information to calculate institutional productivity. In the ACS, survey respondents change from year to year. No household or person is followed over time. Therefore it is difficult to understand educational pathways which other education-related data sources address. At best, ACS provides a snapshot of educational status of the U.S. population based on a sample size larger than that of other data sources.

The major attraction of the ACS, for the purposes here, is its comprehensive population coverage. Its limitations are that it is a relatively new survey, with data available from 2006; only three education-related variables are present and the data are not longitudinal.

Bureau of Labor Statistics

The Bureau of Labor Statistics (BLS) conducts two longitudinal surveys, the National Longitudinal Survey of Youth 1979 (NLSY79) and National Longitudinal Survey of Youth 1997 (NLSY97). These gather information on education and employment history of young individuals. The survey begun in 1979 is still ac-

---

[15]See http://www.census.gov/acs/www/ [June 2012].

tive, over three decades later.[16] The schooling survey section collects information on the highest grade attended or completed, earning of GED/high school diploma, ACT and SAT scores, Advanced Placement (AP) test (grades, test taken date, subject of test, highest AP score received), range of colleges applied to, college enrollment status, field of major and type of college degree (bachelor or first professional), number and types (two-year or four-year) of colleges attended, credits received, major choice, college GPA, tuition and fees, sources and amounts of financial aid. Survey respondents were administered Armed Services Vocational Aptitude Battery test and Armed Forces Qualifications Test (only for NLSY79 respondents and Peabody Individual Achievement Test for NLSY97 respondents) and the respective scores are available in the dataset. The employment section has items on types of occupations, education requirements and income in different occupations and pension plans. Along with sections on employment and schooling, both the surveys cover areas such as health, family formation, relationships, crime and substance abuse, program participation, etc.

The National Longitudinal Surveys of Youth are important. They can track a survey respondent over time across more than one educational institution. For each institution attended by the respondent, information on credit hours, degree attained and other associated variables are collected. Information about each institution attended (IPEDS code) is available in restricted files. Using the IPEDS code a researcher can access the institutional information available in IPEDS survey files. The database is also helpful in looking at multiple enrollment patterns, kinds of jobs held, and information on graduates' salaries. The National Longitudinal Surveys of Youth are among the longest-running longitudinal surveys in the country.

Even though the NLSY samples are representative of the U.S. youth population, one cannot calculate institutional productivity for single colleges or universities, unless a sufficient number of observations is available. The survey collects information on institutions attended by survey respondents. Therefore it is not comprehensive because data covering a reasonable period of time are not available for all institutions.

Student and Faculty Engagement Surveys

Student and Faculty Engagement surveys gather information on learning gains and are available in different formats for different types of institutions. For two-year and four-year undergraduate institutions, both students and faculty

---

[16]See http://www.bls.gov/nls/ [June 2012].

are surveyed. For law schools, only students are surveyed. Participation in these surveys is optional.[17]

The National Survey of Student Engagement and the Law School Survey do not gather information on final output such as degrees and credit hours. Rather, their focus is on intermediate outputs, such as learning during enrollment. The community college engagement survey asks students to report the range of credit hours completed rather than the exact number of credit hours. The faculty surveys collect information on full-time/part-time status, number of credit hours taught and rank. There is no survey of nonfaculty staff. No information is collected on faculty or staff salaries. Information gathered in the surveys can be supplemented by individual institutions by linking student responses to other institutional data. Results from the survey can be used to estimate sheepskin effects. As students report a field of major, the results can be used to deduce learning gains in various fields.

The most useful attribute of student and faculty engagement surveys is that they collect data at the individual institution level and can be tailored to specific needs. Among their drawbacks is that participation at institutional, faculty, and student level is optional; and facility to convert survey results to productivity measures has not been developed.

---

[17]Beginning College Survey of Student Engagement: http://bcsse.iub.edu/; Community College Faculty Survey of Student Engagement: http://www.ccsse.org/CCFSSE/CCFSSE.cfm/; Community College Survey of Student Engagement: http://www.ccsse.org/aboutsurvey/aboutsurvey.cfm/; Faculty Survey of Student Engagement: http://fsse.iub.edu/; Law School Survey of Student Engagement: http://lssse.iub.edu/about.cfm/; and National Survey of Student Engagement: http://nsse.iub.edu/html/about.cfm/ [July 2012]. The Community College Leadership Program at the University of Texas, Austin, conducts the community college survey. Other surveys are conducted by the Indiana University Center for Survey Research in cooperation with its Center for Survey Research.

References and Bibliography

Adelman, C.
  1999.   *Answers in the Tool Box: Academic Intensity, Attendance Patterns, and Bachelor's Degree Attainment.* Washington, DC: U.S. Department of Education.
Archibald, R.B., and Feldman, D.H.
  2011.   *Why Does College Cost So Much?* Oxford, England: Oxford University Press.
Arum, R., and Roksa, J.
  2010.   *Academically Adrift: Limited Learning on College Campuses.* Chicago: University of Chicago Press.
Astin, A.W.
  1993.   *What Matters in College: Four Critical Years Revisited.* San Francisco, CA: Jossey-Bass.
Atkinson, R.C., and Geiser, S.
  2009.   Addressing the graduation gap. [Review of *Crossing the Finish Line: Completing College at America's Public Universities*]. *Science* (325):1343-1344.
Atkinson Commission
  2005.   *Atkinson Review: Final Report, Measurement of Government Output and Productivity for the National Accounts.* United Kingdom Department for Education and Skills. Hampshire, England: Palgrave Macmillan.
  2005.   *Measuring Government Education Output in the National Accounts: An Overview of Several Methods Developed as Part of The Atkinson Review.* United Kingdom: Department for Education and Skills. Available: https://www.education.gov.uk/publications/eOrderingDownload/RW45.pdf [June 2012].
Avery, C., Fairbanks, A., and Zeckhauser, R.
  2003.   *The Early Admissions Game: Joining the Elite.* Cambridge, MA: Harvard University Press.
Babcock, P.S., and Marks, M.
  2011.   The falling time cost of college: Evidence from half a century of time use data. *Review of Economic Statistics 93*(May 2011):468-478.

Bailey, T., and Kienzl, G.S.
1999.   *What Can We Learn About Postsecondary Vocational Education from Existing Data?* Paper presented at the Independent Advisory Panel Meeting, National Assessment of Vocational Education, Washington, DC. Available: http://www2.ed.gov/rschstat/eval/sectech/nave/bailey.html [June 2012].

Bailey, T., Kienzl, G., and Marcott, D.E.
2004.   *The Return to a Sub-Baccalaureate Education: The Effects of Schooling, Credentials and Program of Study on Economic Outcomes.* Washington, DC: U.S. Department of Education.

Ballou, D., and Springer, M.G.
2008.   *Achievement Trade-offs and No Child Left Behind.* Peabody College of Vanderbilt University. Available: http://www.vanderbilt.edu/schoolchoice/documents/achievement_tradeoffs.pdf [July 2012].

Barro, R.J., and Lee, J.W.
2010a.   *A New Data Set of Educational Attainment in the World.* NBER Working Paper No. 15902. Cambridge, MA: National Bureau of Economic Research.
2010b.   *Educational Attainment Dataset.* Available: http://www.barrolee.com/ [June 2012].

Barrow, C.
1990.   *Universities and the Capitalist State: Corporate Liberalism and the Reconstruction of the American Higher Education, 1894-1928.* Madison: University of Wisconsin Press.

Baumol, W.J., and Bowen, W.G.
1966.   *Performing Arts: The Economic Dilemma.* Cambridge, MA: MIT Press.

Bettinger, E., and Long, B.T.
2006.   The increasing use of adjunct instructors at public institutions: Are we hurting students? In R.G. Ehrenberg (Ed.), *What's Happening to Public Higher Education?: The Shifting Financial Burden.* Westport, CT: Praeger.

Blose, G.L., Porter, J.D., and Kokkelenberg, E.C.
2006.   The effects of institutional funding cuts on baccalaureate graduation rates in public higher education. In R.G. Ehrenberg (Ed.), *What's Happening to Public Higher Education?: The Shifting Financial Burden.* Westport, CT: Praeger.

Bonaccorsi, A., Daraio, C., and Simar, L.
2006.   Advanced indicators of productivity of universities: An application of robust nonparametric methods to Italian data. *Scientometrics* 66(2):389-410.

Booher-Jennings, J.
2005.   Below the bubble: "Educational triangle" and the Texas accountability system. *American Educational Research Journal* 42(2):231-268.

Bosworth, B.
2005.   *A Jobless Recovery?: Offshoring of Jobs Versus Productivity Growth at Home.* The Forum for the Future of Higher Education, EDUCAUSE. Available: http://net.educause.edu/ir/library/pdf/FFP0503S.pdf [June 2012].

Bound, J., Groen, J., Kezdi, G.G., and Turner, S.
2004.   Trade in university training: Cross-state variation in the production and stock of college-educated labor. *Journal of Econometrics* 121(1-2):143-173.

Bound, J., Lovenheim, M.F., and Turner, S.
2010.   Why have college completion rates declined? An analysis of changing student preparation and collegiate resources. *American Economic Journal: Applied Economics* 2(3):129-157.

Bowen, W., and Bok, D.
1998.   *The Shape of the River: Long-Term Consequences of Considering Race in College and University Admissions.* Princeton, NJ: Princeton University Press.

Bowen, W.G., Chingos, M.M., and McPherson, M.S.
  2009.   *Crossing the Finish Line: Completing College at America's Public Universities.* Princeton, NJ: Princeton University Press.
Brady, H., Hout, M., Stiles, J., Gleeson, S., and Hui, I.
  2005.   *Return on Investment: Educational Choices and Demographic Change in California's Future.* Berkeley: Survey Research Center, University of California.
Brand, J., and Xie, Y.
  2010.   Who benefits most from college?: Evidence for negative selection in heterogeneous economic returns to higher education. *American Sociological Review 75*:273-302.
Breneman, D.W.
  2001.   *The Outputs of Higher Education.* Ford Policy Forum, University of Virginia. Available: http://net.educause.edu/ir/library/pdf/ffpfp0101.pdf [July 2012].
Brinkman, P.T.
  1990.   Higher education cost functions. Pp. 107-128 in S.A. Hoenack and E.L Collins (Eds.), *The Economics of American Universities.* Albany: State University of New York Press.
Brownell, J.E., and Swaner, L.E.
  2009.   Outcomes of high-impact educational practices: A literature review. *Diversity and Democracy 12*(2):4-6.
Bureau of Economic Analysis
  2012.   *GDP and Personal Income Interactive Table.* Available: http://www.bea.gov/iTable/index_nipa.cfm [June 2012].
Bureau of Labor Statistics
  2007.   *Technical Information about the BLS Multifactor Productivity Measures.* Available: http://www.bls.gov/mfp/mprtech.pdf [June 2012].
Card, D.
  1999.   The causal effect of education on earnings. *Handbook of Labor Economics 3*(1):1801-1863.
Carey, K.
  2011.   "Trust us" won't cut it anymore. *The Chronicle of Higher Education,* January 18, Online Edition. Opinion and Ideas: Commentary Section. Available: http://chronicle.com/article/Trust-Us-Wont-Cut-It/125978/ [June 2012].
Carneiro, P., Heckman, J.J., and Vytlacil, E.J.
  2010.   *Estimating Marginal Returns to Education.* NBER Working Paper No. 16474. Cambridge, MA: National Bureau of Economic Research.
Carnevale, A.P., Smith, N., and Strohl, J.
  2010.   *Help Wanted: Projections of Jobs and Education Requirements Through 2018.* Georgetown University Center on Education and the Workforce. Available: http://www9.georgetown.edu/grad/gppi/hpi/cew/pdfs/HelpWanted.FullReport.pdf [July 2012].
Carpenter, A.N., and Bach, C.N.
  2010.   Learning assessment: Hyperbolic doubts versus deflated critiques. *Analytic Teaching and Philosophical Praxis 30*(1):1-11.
Carrell, S.E., and West, J.E.
  2010.   Does professor quality matter?: Evidence from random assignment of students to professors. *Journal of Political Economy 118*(3):409-432.
Caves, D.W., Christensen, L.R., and Diewert, W.E.
  1982.   The economic theory of index numbers and the measurement of input, output, and productivity. *Econometrica 50*(6):1393-1414.
Chakrabarti, R.
  2007.   *Vouchers, Public School Response, and the Role of Incentives: Evidence from Florida.* Federal Reserve Bank of New York Staff Reports No. 306. Available: http://www.newyorkfed.org/research/staff_reports/sr306.pdf [June 2012].

Chiang, H.
 2009.   How accountability pressure on failing schools affects student achievement. *Journal of Public Economics* 93(9):1045-1057.
Christensen, L., Jorgensen, D.W., and Lau, L.J.
 1973.   Transcendental logarithmic production frontiers. *Review of Economics and Statistics* 55(1):28-45.
Christian, M.
 2006.   *Measuring the Education Function of Government in the United S*tates. Paper prepared for the joint OECD/ONS/Government of Norway Workshop on Measurement of Nonmarket Output in Education and Health. London, Brunei Gallery, October 3-5. Available: http://www.oecd.org/dataoecd/24/48/37053888.pdf [June 2012].
Clark, B.R.
 1995.   *Places of Inquiry.* Berkeley: University of California Press.
Cole, J.R.
 2009.   *The Great American University: Its Rise to Preeminence, Its Indispensable National Role, Why It Must Be Protected.* New York: Public Affairs.
The Conference Board
     Total Economy Database. Available: http://www.conference-board.org/data/economydatabase/ [June 2012].
Cooke, M.L.
 1910.   *Academic and Industrial Efficiency: A Report to the Carnegie Foundation for the Advancement of Teaching.* New York: Carnegie Foundation for the Advancement of Teaching.
Dale, S.B., and Krueger, A.B.
 2002.   Estimating the payoff to attending a more selective college: An application of selection on observables and unobservables. *The Quarterly Journal of Economics* 117(4):1491-1527.
Daraio, C., Bonaccorsi, A., Geuna, A., Lepori, B., Bach, L., Bogetoft, P., Cardoso, M.F., Castro-Martinez, E., Crespi, G., Fernandez de Lucio, I., Fried, H., Garcia-Aracil, A., Inzelt, A., Jongbloed, B., Kempkes, G., Llerena, P., Matt, M., Olivares, M., Pohl, C., Raty, T., Rosas, M.J., Sarrico, C.S., Simar, L., Slipersaeter, S., Teixeira, P.N., and Vanden Eeckaut, P.
 2011.   The European university landscape: A micro characterization based on evidence from the Aquameth project. *Research Policy* 40(1):148-164.
Dasgupta, P., and David, P.A.
 1994.   Toward a new economics of science. *Research Policy* 23(5):487-521.
Data Quality Campaign
     Undated. *10 Essential Elements of a State Longitudinal System.* Available: http://www.dataqualitycampaign.org/build/elements/ [June 2012].
Davies, S., and Guppy, N.
 1997.   Fields of study, college selectivity, and student inequalities in higher education. *Social Forces* 74(4):1417-1438.
DeGroot, H., McMahon, W.W., and Volkwein, J.F.
 1991.   The cost structure of American research universities. *The Review of Economics and Statistics* 73(3):424-431.
Delta Cost Project.
 2009.   *Metrics for Improving Cost Accountability.* Issue Brief # 2. Available: http://www.deltacostproject.org/resources/pdf/issuebrief_02.pdf [June 2012].
DesJardins, S.L., Kim, D.-O., and Rzonca, C.S.
 2003.   A nested analysis of factors affecting bachelor's degree completion. *Journal of College Student Retention: Research, Theory and Practice* 4(4):407-435.
Diewert, W.E.
 1971.   An application of the Shepherd duality theorem: A generalized Leontief production function. *Journal of Political Economy* 79:481-507.

Ehrenberg, R., and Monks, J.
  1999.   *The Impact of* U.S. News & World Report *College Rankings on Admissions Outcomes and Pricing Policies at Selective Private Institutions.* NBER Working Paper No. 7227. Cambridge, MA: National Bureau of Economic Research.
Ehrenberg, R.G.
  2012.   American higher education in transition. *Journal of Economic Perspectives 26*(1):193-216.
Ehrenberg, R.G., and Zhang, L.
  2005.   Do tenured and tenure-track faculty matter? *Journal of Human Resources 40*(3):647-659.
Ehrenberg, R.G., McGraw, M., and Mrdjenovic, J.
  2006.   Why do field differentials in average faculty salaries vary across universities? *Economics of Education Review 25*:241-248.
Eurostat
  2001.   *Handbook on Price and Volume Measures in National Accounts.* Luxembourg: Office for Official Publications of the European Communities.
Ewell, P.T.
  2009.   *Assessment, Accountability, and Improvement: Revisiting the Tension.* National Institute of Learning Outcomes Assessment. Occasional Paper Series 1. Available: http://www.learningoutcomeassessment.org/documents/PeterEwell_005.pdf [June 2012].
Ewell, P.T., and L'Orange, H.P.
  2009.   *The Ideal State Postsecondary Data System:15 Essential Characteristics and Required Functionality.* National Center for Higher Education Management Systems and State Higher Education Executive Officers, Boulder, CO. Available: http://www.sheeo.org/pcn/Uploads/ideal_data_system.pdf [June 2012].
Feller, I.
  2009.   Performance measurement and the governance of the American academics. *Minerva 47*(3):323-344.
Figlio, D., and Rouse, C.
  2006.   Do accountability and voucher threats improve low-performing schools? *Journal of Public Economics 90*(1-2):239-255.
Figlio, D., and Winicki, J.
  2005.   Food for thought? The effects of school accountability plans on school nutrition. *Journal of Public Economics 89*(1-2):381-394.
Flores-Lagunes, A., and Light, A.
  2007.   *Identifying Sheepskin Effects in the Return to Education.* Working Paper 22, Education Research Section, Princeton University.
Garcia, T.I., and L'Orange, H.P.
  2010.   *Strong Foundations: The State of State Postsecondary Data Systems.* State Higher Education Executive Officers, Boulder, CO. Available: http://www.sheeo.org/sspds/StrongFoundations_Full.pdf [June 2012].
Gates, S.M., Augustine, C.H., Benjamin, R., Bikson, T.K., Kaganoff, T., Levy, D.G., Moini, J.S., and Zimmer, R.W.
  2002.   *Ensuring Quality and Productivity in Higher Education: An Analysis of Assessment Practices—ASHE-ERIC Higher Education Report, Volume 29, Number 1.* San Francisco, CA: Jossey-Bass.
Grewal, R., Dearden, J.A., and Lilien, G.L.
  2008.   *Merit Aid and Competition in the University Marketplace.* Working paper, Department of Economics, College of Business and Economics, Pennsylvania State University. Available: http://www.lehigh.edu/~incntr/publications/documents/DeardenMeritAid04-08.pdf [June 2012].
Griliches, Z.
  1977.   Estimating the returns to schooling: some econometric problems. *Econometrica 45*(1):1-22.

Griliches, Z., and Mason, W.M.
    1972.   Education, income and ability. *Journal of Political Economy 80*(3):S74-S103.
Habley, W.R., and McClanahan, R.
    2004.   *What Works in Student Retention?: Four-Year Public Colleges.* Iowa City, IA: American College Testing. Available: http://www.act.org/research/policymakers/pdf/droptables/FourYearPrivate.pdf [June 2012].
Hamilton, L.S., Stecher, B.M., Julie, A., Marsh, J.A., McCombs, J.S., Robyn, A., Russell, J.L., Naftel, S., and Barney, H.
    2007.   *Standards-Based Accountability under No Child Left Behind: Experiences of Teachers and Administrators in Three States.* Santa Monica, CA: RAND.
Haney, W.
    2000.   The Myth of the Texas Miracle in Education. *Education Policy Analysis Archives 8*(41). Available: http://epaa.asu.edu/ojs/article/view/432 [June 2012].
Hansson, B.
    2008.   *OECD Measures on Human Capital and Potential Use in Educational Accounts.* Presentation at the Workshop on the Measurement of Human Capital, November 4, Turin, Italy.
Hanushek, E., and Kimko, D.
    2000.   Schooling, labor force quality, and the growth of nations. *American Economic Review 90*(5):1184-1208.
Hanushek, E., and Raymond, M.
    2004.   Does school accountability lead to improved school performance? *Journal of Policy Analysis and Management 24*(2):297-327.
Hare, P., and Wyatt, G.
    1988.   Modeling the determination of research output in British Universities. *Research Policy 17*(6):315-328.
Harris, D., and Goldrick-Rab, S.
    2011.   *Higher Education in Wisconsin: A 21st Century Status Report.* Madison: Wisconsin Covenant Foundation.
Hodge, A.W., Corea, R.J., Green, J.M., and Retus, B.A.
    2011.   Returns for domestic nonfinancial business. Pp. 24-28 in Bureau of Economic Analysis, *Survey of Current Business.* Washington, DC: U.S. Department of Commerce.
Horn, L.J., and Kojaku, L.K.
    2001.   High school academic curriculum and the persistence path through college: Persistence and transfer behavior of undergraduates 3 years after entering 4-year institutions. *Education Statistics Quarterly 3*(3):65-72.
Hout, M.
    2012.   Social and economic returns to college education in the United States. *Annual Review of Sociology 38*(August):379-400.
Hoxby, C.M.
    1997.   *How the Changing Market Structure of U.S. Higher Education Explains College Tuition.* NBER Working Paper No. 6323. Cambridge, MA: National Bureau of Economic Research.
    2000.   The return to attending a more selective college: 1960 to the present. Pp. 13-42 in M. Devlin and J. Meyerson (Eds.), *Forum Futures: Exploring the future of Higher Education, 2000.* Forum Strategy Series, Volume 3. San Francisco, CA: Jossey-Bass. Available: http://net.educause.edu/ir/library/pdf/ffp0002.pdf [June 2012.]
    2009.   The changing selectivity of American colleges. *Journal of Economic Perspectives 23*(4): 95-118.
Immerwahr, J., Johnson, J., and Gasbarra, P.
    2008.   *The Iron Triangle: College Presidents Talk About Costs, Access, and Quality.* San Jose, CA: The National Center for Public Policy and Higher Education and Public Agenda.

Jacob, B., and Levitt, S.
2003. Rotten apples: An investigation of the prevalence and predictors of teacher cheating. *Quarterly Journal of Economics 118*(3):843-877.
Jaeger, D.A., and Page, M.E.
1996. Degrees matter: New evidence on sheepskin effects in the returns to education. *The Review of Economics and Statistics 78*(4):733-740.
Johnson, N.
2009. *What Does a College Degree Cost?: Comparing Approaches to Measuring "Cost Per Degree."* Delta Cost Project White Paper Series. Available: http://www.deltacostproject.org/resources/pdf/johnson3-09_WP.pdf [June 2012].
Jorgenson, D.W., and Fraumeni, B.M.
1992. The output of the education sector. In *Output Measurement in the Service Sectors*. Cambridge, MA: National Bureau of Economic Research.
Jorgenson, D.W., and Vu, K.
2009. Growth accounting within the International Comparison Program. *ICP Bulletin 6*(1):3-19.
Kleiner, M., and Krueger, A.
2008. *The Prevalence and Effects of Occupational Licensing in the United States.* NBER Working Paper No. 14308. Cambridge, MA: National Bureau of Economic Research.
Klor de Alva, J., Schneider, M.S., and Klagge, J.
2010. *Proof of Concept Study on Proposed Changes Needed to Improve IPEDS Data.* Tempe, AZ: Nexus Research and Policy Center. Available: http://nexusresearch.org/2/ipeds_4-year.pdf [June 2012].
Kokkelenberg, E.C., Sinha, E., Porter, J.D., and Blose, G.L.
2008. *The Efficiency of Private Universities as Measured by Graduation Rates.* Working Paper No. 113. Ithaca, NY: Cornell Higher Education Research Institute.
Krieg, J.
2008. Are students left behind?: The distributional effects of the No Child Left Behind Act. *Education Finance and Policy 3*(2):250-281.
Kuh, G.D.
2002. *The College Student Report 4th Edition.* National Survey of Student Engagement, Center for Postsecondary Research and Planning, Indiana University, Bloomington.
2003. What we're learning about student engagement from NSSE. *Change 35*(2):24-32.
2008. Advising for student success. In V.N. Gordon, W.R. Habley, T.J. Grites, and Associates (Eds.), *Academic Advising: A Comprehensive Handbook* (2nd ed.). San Francisco, CA: Jossey-Bass and NACADA.
Kuh, G.D., and Pascarella, E.T.
2004. What does institutional selectivity tell us about educational quality? *Change 36*(5):52-58.
Kuh, G.D., Cruce, T., Shoup, R., Kinzie, J., and Gonyea, R.
2008. Unmasking the effects of student engagement on first-year college grades and persistence. *Journal of Higher Education 79*(5):540-563.
Ladd, H.F., and Lauen, D.L.
2010. Status versus growth: The distributional effects of school accountability policies. *Journal of Policy Analysis and Management 29*:426-450.
Lester, R.K.
2005. *Universities, Innovation, and the Competitiveness of Local Economies.* Summary report from the local innovation project—Phase I. Industrial Performance Center Working Paper, Massachusetts Institute of Technology.
López Turley, R.N.
2003. When do neighborhoods matter?: The role of race and neighborhood peers. *Social Science Research 32*(1):61-79.

López Turley, R.N., Santos, M., and Ceja, C.
  2007.   Social origin and college opportunity expectations across cohorts. *Social Science Research* *36*(3):1200-1218.
Martinez, M., and Klopott, S.
  2003.   *Improving College Access for Minority, Low-Income, and First-Generation Students.* Boston, MA: Pathways to College Network.
Massy, W.F.
  2003.   *Honoring the Trust: Quality and Cost Containment in Higher Education.* San Francisco, CA: Jossey-Bass.
  2010.   *A Departmental Activity Model for Productivity Improvement.* Unpublished paper. [Research paper in preparation.]
  2012.   *Productivity Indices for Nonprofit Enterprises.* Unpublished paper, Florence, MA.
Massy, W.F., Graham, S.W., and Short, P.M.
  2007.   *Academic Quality Work: A Handbook for Improvement.* San Francisco, CA: Jossey-Bass.
McCormick, A.C., and McClenney, K.
  2012.   Will these trees *ever bear* fruit?: A response to the Special Issue on Student Engagement. *The Review of Higher Education 35*(2):307-333.
McPherson, P., and Shulenburger, D.
  2010.   Understanding the cost of public higher education. *Planning for Higher Education 38*(3): 15-24.
National Association of Colleges and Universities Business Officers
  2002.   *Explaining College Costs: NACUBO Methodology for Identifying the Costs of Delivering Undergraduate Education.* Available: http://www.nacubo.org/documents/research/cofc finalreport.pdf [June 2012].
National Association of State Budget Officers
  2011.   *State Expenditure Report Examining Fiscal 2009-2011 State Spending.* Available: http://www.nasbo.org/sites/default/files/2010%20State%20Expenditure%20Report.pdf [June 2012].
National Postsecondary Education Cooperative
  2010.   *Suggestions for Improving the IPEDS Graduation Rate Survey Data Collection and Reporting.* (NPEC 2010-832). Prepared by Brenda Albright for Coffey Consulting, Washington, DC.
National Research Council
  2002.   *At What Price?: Conceptualizing and Measuring Cost-of-Living and Price Indexes.* Panel on Conceptual Measurement and Other Statistical Issues in Developing Cost-of-Living Indexes, C. Schultze and C. Mackie (Eds.). Committee on National Statistics, Division of Behavioral and Social Sciences and Education. Washington, DC: National Academy Press.
  2005.   *Beyond the Market: Designing Nonmarket Accounts for the United States.* Panel to Study the Design of Nonmarket Accounts, K.G. Abraham and C. Mackie (Eds.). Committee on National Statistics, Division of Behavioral and Social Sciences and Education. Washington, DC: The National Academies Press.
  2010a.   *Accounting for Health and Health Care: Approaches to Measuring the Sources and Costs of their Improvement.* Panel to Advance a Research Program on the Design of National Health Accounts. J.P. Newhouse and C. Mackie (Eds.). Committee on National Statistics. Division of Behavioral and Social Sciences and Education. Washington, DC: The National Academies Press.
  2010b.   *A Data-Based Assessment of Research-Doctorate Programs in the United States.* J.P. Ostriker, C.V. Kuh, and J.A. Voytuk (Eds.). Committee to Assess Research-Doctorate Programs. National Research Council. Washington, DC: The National Academies Press.

2011. *Incentives and Test-Based Accountability in Education.* Committee on Incentives and Test-Based Accountability in Public Education, M. Hout and S.W. Elliot, (Eds.). Board on Testing and Assessment, Division of Behavioral and Social Sciences and Education. Washington, DC: The National Academies Press.

National Science Board

2010. *Science and Engineering Indicators 2010.* Arlington, VA: U.S. National Science Foundation.

Neal, D., and Schanzenbach, D.W.

2010. Left behind by design: Proficiency counts and test-based accountability. *Review of Economics and Statistics 92*(2):263-283.

Nerlove, M.

1972. On tuition and the costs of higher education: Prolegomena to a conceptual framework. *Journal of Political Economy 80*(3):S178-S218.

Organisation for Economic Co-operation and Development

2001. *Measuring Productivity, Measurement of Aggregate and Industry-Level Productivity Growth.* Paris: Organisation for Economic Co-operation and Development.

2009. *Review on Quality Teaching in Higher Education.* Paris: Organisation for Economic Co-operation and Development.

Ozek, U.

2010. *One Day Too Late?: Mobile Students in an Era of Accountability.* UI Working Paper. Washington, DC: Urban Institute.

Park, J.H.

1999. Estimation of sheepskin effects using the old and the new measures of educational attainment in the Current Population Survey. *Economics Letters 62*(2):237-240.

Pascarella, E.T.

2001. Cognitive growth in college: Surprising and reassuring findings from the national study of student learning *Change 33*(6):20-27.

Pascarella, E.T., and Terenzini, P.T.

1991. *How College Affects Students: Findings and Insights from Twenty Years of Research.* San Francisco, CA: Jossey-Bass.

2005. *How College Affects Students: A Third Decade of Research.* San Francisco, CA: Jossey-Bass.

Paulos, J.

2010. Metric mania. *New York Times,* May 16, Sunday Magazine. Available: http://www.nytimes.com/2010/05/16/magazine/16FOB-WWLN-t.html [June 2012].

Porter, S.R.

2003- Understanding retention outcomes: Using multiple data sources to distinguish between
2004. dropouts, stopouts, and transfer-outs. *Journal of College Student Retention: Research, Theory & Practice 5*(May):53-70.

Powers, W., Jr.

2011. How to measure the learning experience at the University of Texas. *Austin American Statesman,* June 7. Available: http://www.statesman.com/opinion/powers-how-to-measure-the-learning-experience-at-1525080.html [June 2012].

Prescott, B.T., and Ewell, P.

2009. *A Framework for a Multi-State Human Capital Development Data System.* Western Interstate Commission for Higher Education. Available: http://www.wiche.edu/pub/13129 [June 2012].

Reback, R., Rockoff, J., and Schwartz, H.

2011. *Under Pressure: Job Security, Resource Allocation, and Productivity in Schools Under NCLB.* NBER Working Paper No. 16745. Cambridge, MA: National Bureau of Economic Research.

Rockoff, J., and Turner, L.
2010.   Short run impacts of accountability on school quality. *American Economic Journal: Economic Policy* 2(4):119-147.

Rothschild, M., and White, L.J.
1995.   The analytics of the pricing of higher education and other services in which the customers are inputs. *Journal of Political Economy* 103(3):573-586.

Rouse, C., Hannaway, J., Goldhaber, D., and Figlio, D.
2007.   *Feeling the Florida Heat?: How Low-Performing Schools Respond to Voucher and Accountability Pressure.* NBER Working Paper No. 13681. Cambridge, MA: National Bureau of Economic Research.

Sampson, S.E.
2010.   The unified service theory: A paradigm for service science. Pp. 107-131 in P.P. Maglio, C. Kieliszewski, and J.C. Spohrer (Eds.), *Handbook of Service Science.* New York: Springer.

Schreyer, P.
2001.   The OECD productivity manual: A guide to the measurement of industry-level and aggregate productivity. *International Productivity Monitor* (2)(Spring):37-51.

Shavelson, R.J.
2010.   *Measuring College Learning Responsibly: Accountability in a New Era.* Stanford, CA: Stanford University Press.

Shedd, J.
2003.   The history of the student credit hour. *New Directions for Higher Education 122*:5-19.

Shulman, L.
2007.   Counting and recounting: Assessment and the quest for accountability. *Change 39*(1): 20-25.

Simon, S., and Banchero, S.
2010.   Putting a price on professors. *Wall Street Journal,* October 22, Online Edition. Life and Culture Section. Available: http://online.wsj.com/article/SB10001424052748703735804575536322093520994.html [June 2012].

Soete, L., Guy, K., and Praest Knudsen, M.
2009.   *The Role of Community Research Policy in the Knowledge-Based Economy.* Expert Group Report to DG Research, European Commission. Luxembourg: Publications Office of the European Union. Available: http://ec.europa.eu/research/era/pdf/community_research_policy_role.pdf [June 2012].

Spence, M.
1973.   Job market signaling. *Quarterly Journal of Economics* 87(3):355-374.

State University.com
        College and its Effect on Students: Early Work on the Impact of College, Nine Generalizations, Later Studies, Pascarella and Terenzini. Available: http://education.stateuniversity.com/pages/1844/College-its-Effect-on-Students.html#ixzz1kgrG689w [June 2012].

Swaner, L.E., and Brownell, J.E.
2009.   *Outcomes of High Impact Practices for Underserved Students: A Review of the Literature.* Washington, DC: Association of American Colleges and Universities.

Torche, F.
2011.   Is a college degree still the great equalizer? Intergenerational mobility across levels of schooling in the U.S. *American Journal of Sociology 117*(3):763-807.

Trent, J.W., and Medsker, L.L.
1968.   *Beyond High School.* San Francisco, CA: Jossey-Bass.

Triplett, J.E.
2009. *Output and Productivity Measures for Medical Care and Education.* Paper prepared for the University of Rome Workshop on Medical Care and Education Productivity, Rome, April. Available: http://www.brookings.edu/~/media/research/files/papers/2009/4/medical%20 measures%20triplett/04_medical_measures_triplett.pdf [June 2012].

Triplett, J.E., and Bosworth, B.P.
2002. *Baumol's Disease Has Been Cured: IT and Multifactor Productivity Growth in the U.S. Services Industries.* Paper presented at the Brookings Workshop on Economic Measurement: Service Industry Productivity (May). Available: ftp://ftp.zew.de/pub/zew-docs/div/ IKT03/Triplett.pdf [June 2012].

Turner, S.
2001. The evolving production functions of schools of education. Pp. 103-124 in W. Tierney (Ed.), *Faculty Work in Schools of Education: Rethinking Roles and Rewards for the Twenty-first Century.* Albany, NY: SUNY Press.

2004. Going to college and finishing college: Explaining different educational outcomes. Pp. 13-56 in C.M. Hoxby (Ed.), *College Choices: The Economics of Where to Go, When to Go, and How to Pay for It.* Chicago, IL: University of Chicago Press.

Twigg, C.
2005. *Improving Quality and Reducing Costs: The Case for Redesign.* NCAT monograph. National Center for Academic Transformation. Available: http://www.thencat.org/monographs.html [June 2012].

U.S. News & World Report
Rankings. Available: http://colleges.usnews.rankingsandreviews.com/best-colleges.

Webber, D.A., and Ehrenberg, R.G.
2010. Do expenditures other than instructional expenditures affect graduation and persistence rates in American higher education? *Economics of Education Review 29*(6):947-958.

Webster, T.
2001. A principal component analysis of the *U.S. News & World Report* tier rankings of colleges and universities. *Economics of Education Review 20*(3):235-244.

Weisbrod, B.A., and Karpoff, P.
1968. Monetary returns to college education, student ability and college quality. *Review of Economics and Statistics 50*(4):491-497.

Wellman, J.V.
2010. *Connecting the Dots Between Learning and Resources.* National Institute of Learning Outcomes Assessment. Occasional Paper Series 3. Available: http://learningoutcomes assessment.org/documents/wellman.pdf [June 2012].

White, K., and Rosenbaum, J.
2008. Inside the black box of accountability: How high-stakes accountability alters school culture and the classification and treatment of students and teachers. In A.R. Sadovnik, J.A. O'Day, G.W. Bohrnstedt, and K.M. Borman (Eds.), *No Child Left Behind and the Reduction of the Achievement Gap: Sociological Perspectives on Federal Education Policy.* New York: Routledge.

Wong, M., Cook, T.D., and Steiner, P.M.
2010. *No Child Left Behind: An Interim Evaluation of Its Effects on Learning Using Two Interrupted Time Series Each With Its Own Nonequivalent Comparison Series.* IPR Working Paper 09-11. Evanston, IL: Institute for Policy Research, Northwestern University. Available: http://www.ipr.northwestern.edu/publications/workingpapers/2009/wp0911.pdf [June 2012].

Wood, T.
   2009.   *The Sheepskin Effect.* New York: National Association of Scholars. Available: http://www.
          nas.org/articles/The_Sheepskin_Effect [June 2012].
Zhang, L.
   2005.   Do measures of college quality matter? The effect of college quality on graduates' earn-
          ings. *Review of Higher Education* 28(4):571-596.
Zimmerman, D.J.
   2003.   Peer effects in academic outcomes: Evidence from a natural experiment. *The Review of
          Economics and Statistics* 85(1):9-23.

Appendix A

Commonly Used Performance Metrics for Higher Education

This appendix elaborates on some of the proxy measures for productivity and efficiency that were described briefly in Chapter 2. As discussed, the proxies vary in their efficacy and, therefore, in their usefulness for accountability. They relate to the concept of productivity as discussed in this report, but they should not be confused with it.

GRADUATION RATES

Since being fixed in law by the Student Right-to-Know and Campus Security Act and established as a statistical reporting requirement in the Graduation Rate Survey (GRS) of the National Center for Education Statistics, graduation rates have become a staple of accountability reporting in higher education. As defined by the GRS, the standard graduation rate for four-year institutions is computed as the percentage of a starting fall term cohort of first time in college full-time attending students who have completed a bachelor's degree within six years (150 percent) of college entry. The parallel rate for two-year institutions allows a three-year window for completion of an associate's degree. All other graduation rate statistics are modeled on the GRS, but allow varying time frames, different degree designations, and different inclusion standards in the denominators that describe the cohort. Principal variations allow adjustments for part-time student starters and incoming transfer students in the cohort. Dropout rates are more colloquial and are not defined as consistently as graduation rates. Typically, they are calculated on the basis of the same tracking cohort and are defined as the percentage of the cohort that remains enrolled for at least one credit one year later (i.e., the following fall term) or one term later (i.e., the following spring term).

Although widely used, cohort-based graduation and dropout rates are subject to many limitations. For example, the GRS restricts the denominator to first-time, full-time students, which may represent only a small fraction of beginning students at institutions that enroll large numbers of part-time students and beginning transfers. Including these students in the cohort allows for more completeness, but causes further problems because part-time students have differing credit loads and transfer students bring in wide ranging numbers of previously-earned credits. This renders fair comparisons difficult because, unlike the first-time full-time population, not all subpopulations are starting from the same baseline.

Graduation data, such as that produced by IPEDS, thus penalize certain types of institutions since they do not account for differences in entering students' characteristics or resources available to the college. Graduation rates also reflect admission standards, the academic strength of the enrolled students, and the resources institutions devote to instruction, to remediation, and to retention. Because of this heterogeneity in student types and institutional missions, any increase in the production of graduates (either through increased graduation rates or expanded enrollment) will likely happen at lower ranking institutions; highly selective schools are not going to change and are already operating at capacity.

These are legitimate issues, but if those were the only ones, a case could still be made for the public policy value of graduation rates, with appropriate caveats attached. The primary reason to de-emphasize IPEDS graduation rates in public policy is that, when used in the aggregate for a whole state or a group of institutions, the information that many believe is being conveyed simply is not. To illustrate, Table A.1 contrasts the average IPEDS graduation rate for community colleges nationally with the more comprehensive picture of student persistence and attainment from the Beginning Postsecondary Student (BPS) Survey. The data are for the same cohort of students; IPEDS includes all students who entered as full-time students at community colleges in fall 2003. The BPS results are from a comprehensive survey of a sample of the same students. As expected, the same-institution graduation rate is within the survey's margin of error, at a little over 20 percent, but there is also much more information about what happened to the other 80 percent.

A number of institutions have taken steps to produce additional statistics that give greater context to graduation rate information. The Minnesota's state college system maintains an "accountability dashboard"[1] for each of its campuses. Beyond the number of students completing degrees), its variables indicate, for example, the condition of facilities and pass rates of graduates taking professional licensing exams. The California State University system attempts to approximate the value of degrees, posting online the median starting and mid-career salaries for graduates of each campus, as well as their average student loan debt.[2]

---

[1] See http://www.mnscu.edu/board/accountability/index.html [July 2012].
[2] See http://www.calstate.edu/value/systemwide/ [July 2012].

TABLE A.1 Comparison of IPEDS Graduation Rate and BPS Persistence and Attainment for Fall 2003 First-Time, Full-Time, Degree-Seeking Students

IPEDS GRS 2003-2006 (%)		BPS 2003-2004/2009 (%)	
Graduated within 150% of normal time	21.5	Graduated in less than 3 years (by spring 2006) at the same institution	22.5
Unknown outcomes	78.5	Graduated in less than 3 years, but at another institution	1.9
		Graduated in 3-6 years, at different institution	14.0
		Graduated in 3-6 years, at same institution	6.0
		No degree after 6 years, but still enrolled at four-year institution	7.4
		No degree after 6 years, but still enrolled at less-than-four-year institution	10.5
		No degree, never returned	37.3

The IPEDS graduation rate correctly shows the proportion of full-time, first-time, degree-seeking students who started in a two-year public college and completed a certificate or degree within 150 percent of normal time at the same institution.[3] Members of the higher education community generally recognize these subtleties but, in practice, the figures above are often condensed in public statements to "21.5 percent of community college students graduate," which many leaders have come to believe is the entire story.

There is much more to it, however, as the results of the BPS survey show. Based on the BPS sample, about 44 percent of the same cohort of students had graduated by 2009. Many had transferred to four-year institutions and finished their bachelor's degrees, or were still working on a bachelor's degree in 2009. They skipped the associate credential entirely. Others took longer than three years to get an associate degree or certificate. If half of those still enrolled at two- or four-year institutions eventually complete a credential, the true graduation rate for the population probably approaches 50 percent. This is not a number to brag about, and the extended time many students require to complete is a significant policy issue in itself, but it has little to do with the IPEDS rate. The same would be true at most four-year colleges, although the gap between the IPEDS rate and the actual graduation rate would be smaller.

---

[3]IPEDS/Digest of Education Statistics: see http://nces.ed.gov/programs/digest/d09/tables/dt09_331. asp [July 2012].

COMPLETION AND ENROLLMENT RATIOS

An alternative to cohort-based graduation rates is a ratio measure that divides credentials awarded by the total student population to create a rough measure of enrollment efficiency. This approach has the virtue of including all enrollments, in contrast to cohort-based measures that address a subset of students who begin their enrollment at the same time. There are no standard definitions of this measure, but a typical calculation counts undergraduate degrees (associate's and bachelor's) for a given academic year and divides by an unduplicated undergraduate headcount for the same period (Klor de Alva, Schneider, and Klagge, 2010). A common variation is to use undergraduate full-time equivalent (FTE) enrollment as the denominator, which shifts the perspective of the measure toward output per unit of instructional activity.

Although more inclusive than cohort-based statistics, ratio measures such as these are also subject to serious limitations. First, they are not truly valid because the degrees that are counted are not awarded to the particular students that constitute the population count. If the students constituting the numerator and the denominator have differing characteristics—e.g., levels of academic ability or demographic profiles—that affect their chances of graduating, the statistic will be misleading. More important, the measure is sensitive to changing population size. If enrollment is growing rapidly, for example, the ratio will understate student success because the degrees conferred in a given period are awarded to students from an earlier period characterized by smaller entering classes. Some approaches try to correct this defect by counting enrollments four to six years earlier, but the lag amount is arbitrary, so this correction is never entirely satisfactory.

TIME TO DEGREE

Another commonly used performance measure is average lengths of time required to earn a degree. This can be calculated for specific degrees at specific institutions or at more aggregated levels. This statistic can be forward-looking, applied to an entering cohort to estimate a graduation rate (like the GRS) by averaging the elapsed time from beginning of enrollment to the award of the degree. More commonly, it is backward-looking, selecting all those students who were awarded a particular degree in a given term and identifying each student's first term of enrollment. A significant decision must be made between counting pure elapsed time (for example, the number of elapsed terms between entry and degree award) or the number of terms in which the student was actively enrolled. The first approach may more closely corresponds to most people's understanding of the underlying concept, but it implicitly holds institutions responsible for outcomes over which they have no control, such as a student's decision to take a year off, or other exogenous factors that slow otherwise normal progress toward degree completion.

The major drawback to using time-to-degree measures is that they are difficult to interpret. Extended duration to degree may reflect shortcomings of the institution, such as unusually complex curricula or insufficient course offerings and scheduling complication resulting in lack of available courses and students ultimately taking far more credits than the minimum needed for graduation.[4] Whether or not students can get into classes they need for prerequisites is a very important determination of time to degree.

Many other factors affect time to completion that are unrelated to an institution's administrative and operational effectiveness. Among the most prominent are students electing to take smaller course loads, interrupt schooling, or pursue specialized accreditation requirements (for example, in engineering) that add to time to degree. Many institutions also serve predominantly part-time students and working adults, or underprepared student populations. Uninformed comparisons will result in these institutions appearing less efficient in terms of degree production (i.e., exhibiting longer time values), yet they may be functioning reasonably well, given their mission and student characteristics. The ways students finance their educations, and particularly whether they are employed while enrolled, also affects time to graduation.

Time to degree relates to and raises a number of policy issues and may provide insight into the broader value to individuals of college other than the degree. For example, only a very small percentage of students attempt to earn a B.S. or B.A. degree in three years, while many continue to complete coursework beyond the conventional four-year period. In valuing the college experience, it may be worth considering the benefits of social interactions and engagement to students, including their contribution to the learning process. And, for many, college undeniably includes a consumption component that has value (part of the multi-product essence of the sector): it can be an enjoyable experience. On the other hand, when students are pushed to a five-year plan, or if choice of major or other options are affected because of insufficient course offerings, this is closer to a productivity problem.

Time use studies indicate that students engage in patterns of homework and other time use behaviors at different levels of intensity depending, for example, on their majors or enrollment status. The American Time Use Survey provides some information on student input hours (Babcock and Marks, 2011). Enrollment status is important in other ways as well. Commuting students and residential

---

[4]Bowen et al. (2009) rightly argue that time to degree is a serious policy concern, and demonstrate that students who take additional time to graduate often accumulate remarkable numbers of credit hours. This may be because they change majors or experience "start-and-stop" problems, but it may also be compounded by the schedule of course offerings by the institution.

students may have very different experiences and this may correlate with probability of success.

In summary, time to degree is not a measure that can be used to rank or compare all institutions along a meaningful quality or cost continuum. Adjustment factors that reflect mix of student populations need to be added to time-to-degree statistics in order for them to be used in cross-institution or cross-system (and, in some instances, departmental) comparisons. Failure to take enrollment status into account leads to problems when time-to-degree statistics are used as a performance metric.

COSTS PER CREDIT OR DEGREE

Some measures attempt to capture the cost of producing an academic credit or degree by documenting all the inputs involved in generating the credit and calculating their costs. Cost per credit or degree is generally produced for a particular setting, such as an academic program or department. All the credits generated by a program within a particular time period (for example, an academic year or term) are added to create the denominator. The numerator is produced by calculating the total cost of offering the program for the same time period. The two figures are then cast as a ratio. For example, among potential performance metrics being considered by the National Governors Association and some state higher education systems is "credentials and degrees awarded per $100,000 state, local, tuition, and fee revenues—weighted by STEM and health (for example, public research universities in Virginia produce 1.98 degrees per $100,000 in state, local, tuition, and fee revenues)."[5]

Despite their obvious use value, degree or credit cost measures present several problems. First, aggregating total costs and credits rather than summing from the lowest unit of activity (for example, individual classes) may obscure important differences across micro-environments and may lead to false conclusions because of the disproportionate impact of a few outliers.[6] Second, costs do not necessarily reflect underlying relationship between inputs and outputs because similar inputs may be priced differently. For example, if one department or institution is staffed largely by tenured faculty with relatively high salaries and another staffed by low-cost adjunct faculty, differences in cost per credit between them may be considerable even though the same numbers of teaching hours are involved. Similar differences encumber cost comparisons across disciplines because of typically high salaries in some (e.g., business) and low salaries in others

---

[5]National Center for Higher Education Management Systems presentation to the Virginia Higher Education Advisory committee, July 21, 2011.

[6]There are also smaller technical issues. For example, in the NGA measure, what is the proper time frame to assign the $100,000 expenditure? It is reasonable to assert that "this year's degrees" should be attributed in some fashion to expenditures weighted across periods t, t – 1, . . . going back at least to t – 4.

(e.g., English). If these factors are ignored, the policy implication will always be to substitute low cost inputs for higher cost ones. Finally, the cost calculation itself is subject to the joint-use problem because the same faculty member may be doing more than one thing with his or her time (see Section 3.1).

Cost-per-degree and per-credit statistics are less controversial and perhaps more appropriate for tracking trends at the national level. At this level, the effects of student and institutional heterogeneity are diluted and the problem of transfers is eliminated. Still, sampling issues remain.

STUDENT-FACULTY RATIOS

Student-faculty ratios are similar to cost per credit in that they relate presumed teaching output (students taught) to presumed teaching input (faculty assignment). Like cost per credit, moreover, these ratios are constructed on an aggregate basis rather than being built up from individual classes. Because this measure is constructed using physical entities, it is not subject to many of the distortions associated with cost per credit, but it still suffers from the aggregation and joint-use issues noted above. Perhaps more important, student-faculty ratios can lead to serious misunderstandings about quality, as a high value is usually interpreted as a signal of efficient instruction while a low value is usually interpreted as a mark of quality. These contradictory conclusions are possible because the student-faculty ratio does not capture the actual output of the relationship, student learning. Yet both common sense and empirical evidence suggests that high student-faculty ratios are not invariably linked to poor academic outcomes. Larger classes can be made qualitatively different from smaller ones through the use of technology and altered pedagogy where students can learn from one another. Meanwhile, there is growing empirical evidence from the large course redesign projects undertaken by the Center for Academic Transformation that it is possible to increase enrollment in a course while simultaneously improving learning outcomes.

Appendix B

Methods for Measuring Comparative Quality and Cost Developed by the National Center for Academic Transformation

The National Center for Academic Transformation (NCAT) is an independent nonprofit organization that describes itself as "dedicated to the effective use of information technology to improve student learning outcomes and reduce the cost of higher education."[1] NCAT works with institutions to analyze their instructional models and identify ways to efficiently leverage technology, faculty, graduate students, peer interactions, and other learning resources to improve quality and efficiency. In the NCAT model, students are transformed from "passive note takers" in a standard lecture format to active participants in their own learning, leveraging a set of tools and resources. Based on a review of the participating institutions, NCAT has identified six redesign models that vary in format, student experience, and use of technology.

Course redesigns focus primarily, but not exclusively, on large-enrollment, introductory courses in multiple disciplines, including 16 in the humanities (developmental reading and writing, English composition, fine arts, history, music, Spanish, literature, and women's studies), 60 in quantitative subjects (developmental and college-level mathematics, statistics, and computing), 23 in the social sciences (political science, economics, psychology, and sociology), 15 in the natural sciences (anatomy and physiology, astronomy, biology, chemistry, and geology) and 6 in professional studies (accounting, business, education, engineering, and nursing).

---

[1] This appendix draws heavily from the NCAT Web site: http://www.thencat.org/ [November 2011].

QUALITY

NCAT requires each participating institution to conduct a rigorous evaluation of the impact of the redesign on learning outcomes as measured by student performance and achievement. National experts have provided consultation and oversight regarding the assessment of learning outcomes to ensure that the results are as reliable and valid as possible. To date, results show improved student learning in 72 percent of the redesigns, with the remaining 28 percent showing learning outcomes equivalent to traditional formats. Other qualitative outcomes achieved in the course redesigns include increased course-completion rates, improved retention, better student attitudes toward the subject matter, increased student performance in downstream courses and increased student satisfaction with the mode of instruction.

All NCAT redesign projects compare student learning outcomes in the traditional format with those achieved in the redesigned format. This is done by either running parallel sections of the course in the two formats or comparing baseline data from an offering of the traditional course to a later offering of the redesigned course, looking at differences in outcomes from before and after. The four measurement methods used to assess student learning are Comparisons of Common Final Exams, Comparisons of Common Content Items Selected from Exams, Comparisons of Pre- and Post-tests, and Comparisons of Student Work Using Common Rubrics.

COST

NCAT requires each participating institution to establish a team of faculty and staff to conduct the redesign. Each team develops a detailed cost analysis of both the traditional and the redesigned course formats. All 120 course redesigns have reduced costs—by 37 percent, on average, with a range of 9 percent to 77 percent. The 120 redesigned courses have affected more than 160,000 students nationwide and produced a savings of about $9.5 million each year.

Each team analyzes and documents "before and after" course costs using activity-based costing. NCAT developed a spreadsheet-based course planning tool (CPT) that allows institutions to (1) determine all personnel costs; (2) identify the tasks associated with preparing and offering the course in the traditional format and determine how much time each type of personnel spends on each of the tasks; and (3) identify the tasks associated with preparing and offering the course in the redesigned format, and determine how much time each type of personnel spends on each of the tasks. The CPT then automatically converts the data to a comparable cost-per-student measure. At the beginning of each project, baseline cost data for the traditional course and projected redesigned course costs are collected; actual redesigned course costs are collected at the end.

Completing the CPT allows faculty members to consider changes in specific instructional tasks, make decisions about how to use technology (or not) for specific tasks, visualize duplicative or unnecessary effort and complete a cost/benefit analysis regarding the right type of personnel for each instructional task. The CPT consists of four worksheets: Instructional Costs per Hour, used to determine all personnel costs involved in the course and to express each kind of cost as an hourly rate; Traditional Course Activities and Cost, used to determine the activities involved in and the costs of preparing and delivering the course in its traditional format; Redesigned Course Activities and Cost, used to determine the activities involved in preparing and delivering the course in its redesigned format when it is fully operational; and Annual Cost Comparison, used to compare the annual costs of the traditional course and the redesigned course.

Among the assumptions of the NCAT Model are the following:

Developmental costs are not included. NCAT's model compares the before costs (current/historical/ traditional) and the after costs (what the course will cost when it is fully operational)—i.e., it asks the team to plan what the redesigned course will look like at the end of the developmental process. It does not include the up-front developmental costs of either the traditional or the redesigned course.

Institution-wide support services, administrative overhead, infrastructure and equipment costs are not included. The assumption is that these costs are constant—are part of the campus environment—for both the traditional and redesigned courses. Campus networking, site licenses for course management systems and desktop PCs for faculty, for example, are part of the campus-wide IT environment. Costs that are particular to the course are included in "other costs."

EXAMPLES (CASE STUDIES)

Research University: Louisiana State University

Louisiana State University (LSU) redesigned College Algebra, a three-credit course enrolling 4,900 students annually. The university moved all structured learning activity to a computer lab where students work with an instructional software package—which includes interactive tutorials, computational exercises, videos, practice exercises, and online quizzes—and receive just-in-time assistance from instructors and undergraduate assistants. Instructors also meet students in a once-a-week focus group which builds community among students and instructors.

The redesign reduced costs by serving the same number of students with half of the personnel used in the traditional model. Section size stayed at 40-44 students, but the number of class meetings each week was reduced from three to one. The redesigned format allows one instructor to teach twice as many students as in the traditional format without increasing class size and without increasing workload. In the traditional format, each instructor taught one three-day-a-week section with 44 students. In the redesigned format, that same instructor teaches two sections of 44 students and spends four hours tutoring in the lab. This can be accomplished because the class only meets once a week and because no hand-grading is required. While the cost of adding tutors in the computer lab as well as increased time for coordination and systems administration reduced the net savings, the redesign reduced the cost-per-student from $121 to $78.

Learning outcomes were measured by comparing medians on a common final exam. Final exam medians for traditional fall sections ranged from 70 percent to 76 percent. After redesign, the final exam median in fall 2006 was 78 percent, the highest ever achieved. In the traditional format, final exams were graded by individual instructors and partial credit was allowed. In the redesigned format, final exams were group-graded, which means that grading was more consistent from one section to the next, and partial credit was not allowed, yet exam medians were higher. The success rate (grades of C or better) for College Algebra in the five years prior to the redesign averaged 64 percent. In fall 2006, after full implementation of the redesign, students had a success rate of 75 percent.

Comprehensive Four-Year Institution: The University of Southern Mississippi

The University of Southern Mississippi (USM) redesigned World Literature, a course enrolling more than 1,000 students each term, in order to eliminate course drift and inconsistent student learning experiences. The traditional course was offered in 16 sections of about 65 students each: 8 sections taught by full-time faculty and 8 by adjuncts. The redesign placed all students in a coherent single online section and replaced the passive lecture environment with media-enriched presentations that required active student engagement. A course coordinator directed the team teaching of four faculty members, each of whom taught his or her area of expertise of four weeks, and four graduate teaching assistant (GTA) graders. The faculty team offered course content through a combination of live lectures with optional attendance and required Web-delivered, media- and resource-enhanced presentations.

USM reduced the number of sections from 30 to 2 and increased the number of students in each section from 65 to 1,000. These changes enabled the university to reduce the number of faculty teaching the course from 16 to the equivalent of 2 full-time faculty and 4 GTAs. USM eliminated adjuncts completely. The course is now taught 100 percent by full-time faculty supported by GTAs for writing assignment grading. By making these changes, six full-time faculty were freed to teach other courses, and the funds previously used to hire adjuncts were made available for a variety of academic enhancements in the department. The cost-per-student was reduced from $70 to $31.

Student performance improved on multiple dimensions in the redesign. Grades on weekly quizzes with common content showed an increase in grades of C or better from 68 percent in the traditional course to 88 percent in the re-designed course. Writing scores of C or better increased from 61 percent to 77 percent. Essay scores increased in from 7.11 in the traditional mode to 8.10 in the redesigned format. In the traditional version of the course, faculty-taught sections typically retained about 75 percent of their students, while adjunct- and GTA-taught sections retained 85 percent. In the fall 2003 semester of full implementation of the redesign, retention was 87 percent, with all students being taught solely by full-time faculty. At the same time, the rate of D and F grades dropped from 37 percent to 27 percent in the redesigned course.

Private, Liberal Arts Institution: Fairfield University

Fairfield University, a comprehensive Jesuit university with 3,100 full-time undergraduates, redesigned its general biology course to improve the quality of student learning and to reduce its cost. The traditional biology course was taught in a multiple-section model, with 35-40 students per section, and met three times per week with a three-hour lab. Four faculty members provided lectures; additional faculty and professionals were needed to staff the labs. The cost of offering the traditional course to 260 students annually was $131,560, which translates to a per-student cost of $506.

Significant cost savings were realized from reducing faculty time in three major areas: (1) materials development for lectures; (2) out-of-class course meetings; and (3) in-class lectures and labs. The number of faculty needed to teach the course declined from seven to four. Faculty time was reconfigured to support a division of teaching responsibilities so that the four faculty members now teach from their areas of expertise. Faculty time devoted to this course decreased from 1,550 hours to 1,063 hours. Consolidation of the seven lecture sections into two in the redesigned course and the introduction of computer-based modules in the lecture and laboratory resulted in a cost-per-student reduction from $506 to $350.

Students in the redesigned course performed significantly better on benchmark exam questions. The questions on the new exams were designed to test higher order thinking and allow students to synthesize material from the basic concepts.

In addition, specific exam questions incorporated in the second year genetics course (required of all biology majors) were used to measure the retention of key concepts and compare the performance of traditional students and redesign students. Students from the redesigned course performed significantly better on this set of questions than did students from the traditional course (88 percent correct vs. 79 percent correct, respectively). The DFW rate dropped: only 3 percent of the students in the redesign dropped the course compared to an average of 8 percent in previous years. The number of students who decided to enroll in the second semester of the course approached 85 percent compared to less than 75 percent in previous years.

Community College: Tallahassee Community College

Tallahassee Community College (TCC) redesigned College Composition, a required course serving approximately 3,000 students annually. The traditional format, which combined lecture and writing activities in sections of 30 students each, made it difficult to address individual needs. The redesign used technology to provide diagnostic assessments resulting in individualized learning plans; interactive tutorials in grammar, mechanics, reading comprehension, and basic research skills; online tutorials for feedback on written assignments; follow-up assessments; and discussion boards to facilitate the development of learning communities. The classroom was restructured to include a wide range of learner-centered writing activities that fostered collaboration, proficiency, and higher levels of thinking. By shifting many of the basic instructional activities to technology, faculty could focus the classroom portion of the course on the writing process.

TCC reduced the number of full-time faculty involved in teaching the course from 32 to 8 and substituted less expensive adjunct faculty without sacrificing quality and consistency. In the traditional course, full-time faculty taught 70 percent of the course, and adjuncts taught 30 percent. In the redesigned course, full-time faculty teach 33 percent of the course, and adjuncts teach 67 percent. Overall, the cost-per-student was reduced from $252 to $145, a savings of 43 percent. Full-time faculty were freed to teach second-level courses where finding adjuncts was much more difficult.

Five final out-of-class essays were selected randomly from the traditional and redesigned sections and were graded by an independent group of faculty using an established holistic scoring rubric. Students in the redesigned composition course scored significantly higher ($p = 0.03$) and had an average score of 8.35 compared to 7.32 for the students in the traditional course. Students in redesigned sections had a 62 percent success rate (grades of C or better) compared with 56 percent in traditional sections, representing a 13.6 percent decrease in the DFW rate. Success rates of students in the second-level English course increased (79.3 percent success for redesigned compared to 76.1 percent for traditional).

Appendix C

Overview of Data Sources

The purpose of this appendix is to provide an overview of data sources on education statistics. Data sources can be categorized by their unit of analysis or their collecting agencies. Unit of analysis may be an institution, faculty, student, or household. Collection agencies include federal agencies, state agencies, or private data-collection agencies. A tabular summary of the available education data sources is presented in the following pages (Table C.1). More detailed explanation of each data source follows the table.

Much of the text of the appendix is reproduced from the government websites referenced herein, especially sites maintained by the National Center for Education Statistics and the National Science Foundation. Direct links to Web pages are provided as footnotes where appropriate.

TABLE C.1 Summary of Education Data Sources

Name of Survey	Collection Agency	Objective of the Survey	Unit of Analysis	Time Period	Survey Components[a]
Integrated Postsecondary Education Data System (IPEDS)	National Center for Educations Statistics (NCES)	Collect data on postsecondary education in the United States.	Educational Institutions	Collected annually from 1989	Institutional Characteristics, Institutional Prices, Enrollment, Student Financial Aid, Degrees and Certificates Conferred, Student Persistence and Success, and Institutional Human and Fiscal Resources.
Higher Education General Information Survey (HEGIS)	NCES	Predecessor to IPEDS. Currently not active. The Higher Education General Information Survey (HEGIS) system was conducted by the NCES between 1966 and 1985. These surveys collected institution-level data on such topics as institutional characteristics, enrollment, degrees conferred, salaries, employees, financial statistics, libraries, and others. Surveys were sent to approximately 3,400 accredited institutions of higher education.			
National Study of Postsecondary Faculty (NSOPF)	NCES	Provide data about faculty to postsecondary education researchers, planners, and policy makers.	Faculty	Four Cycles: 1987-1988; 1992-1993; 1998-1999; and 2003-2004	Institution Survey; Department Chairperson Survey and Faculty Survey
National Postsecondary Student Aid Study (NPSAS)	NCES	Examine how students and their families pay for postsecondary education. NPSAS data provide the base-year sample BPS and B&B.	Student. Nationally representative sample of all students (graduate, first-professional, and undergraduate) enrolled in postsecondary education institutions.	Six Cycles: 1986-1987; 1989-1990; 1992-1993; 1995-1996; 1999-2000; and 2003-2004	Major Field of Study; Tuition and Fees; Date First Enrolled, and Other Information from Institution Records

Baccalaureate and Beyond (B&B)	NCES	Follow students who complete their baccalaureate degrees. Initially, students in the NPSAS surveys are identified as being in their last year of undergraduate studies.	Student. Drawn from NPSAS sample. Students who completed bachelor's degrees in academic year of the NPSAS survey.	Three Cycles: 1993-1994, 1997, 2003; 2000-2001; and 2008	Time to Bachelor's Degree; Undergraduate Education; Employment; Postbaccalaureate Enrollment and Student Characteristics
Recent College Graduates (RCG)	NCES	Analyze the occupational outcomes and educational experiences of bachelor's and master's degree recipients who graduated from colleges and universities in the continental United States.	Student	Periodically: 1976-1991. B&B replaced RCG	Degree Programs; College Experiences; Employment Opportunities; Student Work Experiences and Teaching Credentials

continued

TABLE C.1 Continued

Name of Survey	Collection Agency	Objective of the Survey	Unit of Analysis	Time Period	Survey Components[a]
Beginning Postsecondary Students Longitudinal Study (BPS)	NCES	Collect information on all students who entered postsecondary education for the first time. Includes all types of postsecondary educational institutions: public institutions; private, not-for-profit institutions; and private, for-profit institutions.	Student. Drawn from NPSAS sample. Students identified as first-time beginning students.	Three academic years: 1989-1990, 1990-1991, and 1991-1992	Student Characteristics; Institutional Characteristics and Degree Programs; Student Educational Experiences; Financing Postsecondary Education; Student Work Experiences; Marriage and Family Information; Civic Participation and Noncredit Education Activities
National Household Education Survey (NHES)	NCES	Collect information from households on a variety of educational issues.	Household	Nine Cycles: 1991, 1993, 1995, 1996, 1999, 2001, 2003, 2005, and 2007	Adult Education; Before- and After-School Programs and Activities; Early Childhood Program Participation; Parent and Family Involvement in Education; Civic Involvement; Household Library Use; School Readiness; School Safety and Discipline

| Wisconsin Longitudinal Study of 1957 | National Institute on Aging (NIA) | Provide study of life course from late adolescence to early/mid-60s. | Student. Random sample of 10,317 men and women who graduated from Wisconsin high schools in 1957 and of their randomly selected brothers and sisters. Survey data were collected from the original respondents or their parents in 1957, 1964, 1975, and 1993, and from a selected sibling in 1977 and 1994. | Five Cycles: 1957, 1964, 1975-1977, 1992-1994, 2002-2005 (47 years) | Data from the original respondents or their parents from 1957 to 1975 cover social background, youthful and adult aspirations, schooling, military service, family formation, labor market experience, and social participation. The 1992-1993 surveys cover occupational histories; income, assets, and economic transfers; social and economic characteristics of parents, siblings, and children; and mental and physical health and well-being. Parallel interviews have been carried out with siblings in 1977 and 1993-1994. The current round of survey data collection from graduates, siblings, and their spouses or widows began late in 2003. These new data repeat many previous measures, but add more extensive data on health, health behaviors, health insurance, psychological and cognitive functioning, family relations, social and civic participation, religiosity, and preparation for retirement and for the end of life. |

continued

TABLE C.1 Continued

Name of Survey	Collection Agency	Objective of the Survey	Unit of Analysis	Time Period	Survey Components[a]
National Longitudinal Survey of Class of 1972 (NLS 72)	NCES	Provide ongoing and updated database of sample of high school seniors and their experiences.	Student. Participants in the study were selected when they were seniors in high school in the spring of 1972, and in a supplementary sample drawn in 1973.	Follow-up surveys in 1973, 1974, 1976, 1979, and 1986 (14 years)	General Information; Education and Training; Work Experience; Family Status; Military Service; Activities and Opinions and Background Information
High School and Beyond (HSB)	NCES	Follow the educational, vocational, and personal development of young people.	Student. Consists of two cohorts: 1980 senior class, and the 1980 sophomore class.	Both cohorts were surveyed every 2 years through 1986, and the 1980 sophomore class was also surveyed again in 1992. (6 years)	Background Information; Work Experience; Periods of Unemployment; Education; Other Training; Family Information; Income; Experiences and Opinions
National Education Longitudinal Study of 1988 (NELS 88)	NCES	Same as above.	Student. Cohort of students who were in the eighth grade in 1988.	First follow-up in 1990. Second one in 1992 and third one in 1994. Final follow-up in 2000. (12 years)	Demographic Characteristics and Eighth-Grade Status; Education; Current Activities; Employment and Income; Marriage and Parental Status; Volunteer and Leisure Time Variables

Study	Agency	Purpose	Sample	Timeline	Content
Educational Longitudinal Study of 2002 (ELS 2002)	NCES	Monitor the progress of sample of tenth graders from high school to postsecondary education to work.	Student. Nationally representative sample of high school sophomores in 2002 spring term.	First follow-up in 2004 and second follow-up in 2006. Third follow-up planned in 2012. (10 years)	Student: School Experience and Activities; Plans for the Future; Language; Money and Work; Family and Beliefs and Opinions About Self. Teacher: Teacher Background and Activities. Library and Media Center: Policies, Facilities, Staffing, Technology; School Administrator: Student and Teacher Characteristics; Structure and Policies.
High School Longitudinal Study of 2009 (HSLS 2009)	NCES	Understand the trajectory of sample of ninth graders from high school to postsecondary education to work. Concentration on factors determining choices toward STEM fields.	Student. Cohort of ninth graders in 2009.	First follow-up is planned for 2012. Final follow-up in 2021. (13 years)	Student: Student Background, Previous School Experience, Math Experiences, Science Experiences, Home and School, Postsecondary Education Plans, Life After High School. Parent: Family Structure, Origin and Language, Parental Education and Occupation, Student's Educational Experience, Parental Involvement, Student's Future. Teacher: Background, Math and Science Department and Instruction, Beliefs about Teaching and Current School. School Counselor: Staffing and Practice, Program and Policies, Math and Science Placement, Opinions and Background. School Administrator: School Characteristics, Student Population, School's Teachers, Courses Offered, Goals and Background.

continued

TABLE C.1 Continued

Name of Survey	Collection Agency	Objective of the Survey	Unit of Analysis	Time Period	Survey Components[a]
National Longitudinal Survey of Youth 1979 (NLSY 79)	Bureau of Labor Statistics (BLS)	Study changes over time and examines cause-effect relationships.	Student. Nationally representative sample of 12,686 young men and women who were 14-22 years old when they were first surveyed in 1979.	These individuals were interviewed annually through 1994 and are currently interviewed on a biennial basis. (32 years in 2010)	Attitudes, Expectations, and Noncognitive Tests; Crime and Substance Use; Education, Training, and Cognitive Tests; Employment; Health; Income, Assets, and Program Participation; Fertility, Children, and Childcare; Parents, Family Processes, and Childhood; Household, Geographic, and Contextual Variables; Relationships, Dating, and Sexual Activity
National Longitudinal Survey of Youth 1997 (NLSY 97)	BLS	Study changes over time and examines cause-effect relationships.	Student. NLSY 97 consists of a nationally representative sample of 8,984 youths who were 12 to 16 years old as of December 31, 1996.	These individuals were interviewed annually. 13 rounds have taken place so far. (13 years in 2009)	Aptitude and Achievement Scores; Education; Employment; Expectations, Attitudes, Behaviors, and Time Use; Family Background and Demographic Characteristics; Health; Income, Program Participation, and Assets; Marital History, Childcare and Fertility; Training

Survey of Graduate Students and Postdoctorates in Science and Engineering	National Science Foundation-National Institutes of Health (NSF-NIH)	Provide data on the number and characteristics of graduate students, postdoctoral appointees, and doctorate-holding nonfaculty researchers in science and engineering (S&E) and selected health fields.	Student and Academic Unit. All academic institutions in the United States and its territories that grant research-based master's degrees or doctorates, appoint postdocs, or employ doctorate-holding nonfaculty researchers in S&E and selected health fields are eligible.	Collected periodically.	Enrollment Status, Gender, Race/Ethnicity, Citizenship, Primary Source and Mechanism of Support, Highest Degree Attained
Survey of Earned Doctorates (SED)	NSF	Provide data on number and characteristics of individuals receiving research doctoral degrees.	Student. All individuals receiving research doctorates from accredited U.S. institutions are asked to complete the survey.	Collected periodically from 1957-1958.	Enrollment Status, Gender, Race/Ethnicity, Citizenship, Primary Source and Mechanism of Support, Highest Degree Attained

continued

TABLE C.1 Continued

Name of Survey	Collection Agency	Objective of the Survey	Unit of Analysis	Time Period	Survey Components[a]
Survey of Doctorate Recipients (SDR)	NSF	Gather information from individuals who have obtained a doctoral degree in a science, engineering, or health field.	Student. Recipients of doctoral degree in a science, engineering, or health field living in the U.S. during the survey reference week, who are noninstitutionalized and under age 76. Longitudinal survey follows recipients of research doctorates from U.S. institutions until age 76.	Collected biennially. Before 1993 data collected by National Research Council. For NSF. Under NSF there had been seven cycles till now– 1993, 1995, 1997, 1999, 2001, 2003, and 2006.	Enrollment Status, Gender, Race/ Ethnicity, Disability Status, Citizenship, Primary Source and Mechanism of Support, Highest Degree Attained, Marital Status and Number of Children, Salary, Satisfaction and Importance of Various Aspects of Job, Occupation, Postdoctorate Status
National Survey of College Graduates (NSCG)	NSF	Provide data on the number and characteristics of experienced individuals with education and/ or employment in science and engineering (S&E, or S&E-related fields).	Student. Respondents are individuals who recently received bachelor's or master's degrees in an S&E field from a U.S. institution, were living in the U.S. during the survey reference week, and are under age 76.	Two decade long biennial longitudinal surveys. One started in 1993 and the second one in 2003.	Demographic Characteristics, Immigrant Module (Year of Entry, Type of Visa, etc.), Number of Children; Educational History, School Enrollment Status; Employment Status, Salary, Satisfaction and Importance of Various Aspects of Job, Sector of Employment, Academic Employment and Work-Related Training; Publications and Patent Activities

National Survey of Recent College Graduates (NSRCG)	NSF	Gather information about individuals who recently obtained bachelor's or master's degrees in a science, engineering, or health (SEH) field.	Student. Respondents are individuals who recently received bachelor's or master's degrees in an SEH field from a U.S. institution, were living in the U.S. during the survey reference week, and are under age 76.	Collected biennially from 1993.	Enrollment Status, Gender, Race/Ethnicity, Disability Status, Citizenship, Primary Source and Mechanism of Support, Highest Degree Attained, Marital Status and Number of Children, Salary, Satisfaction and Importance of Various Aspects of Job, Occupation, Parental Education
State Student Unit-Record (SUR) Databases	Varies across states. Mostly State Higher Education Executive Officers Agency	Link statewide student record databases.	Student. Information on student's background and academics.	The inception varies from state to state. California in 1970, Texas and Wisconsin in 1973. Latest to join is Kansas in 2002.	Demographics, Academic Background, Enrollment Status, Academic Activity, and Academic Attainment
National Survey of Student Engagement (NSSE)	Center for Survey Research supported by Pew Charitable Trust	Time use of undergraduate students and gains in learning from college/university education.	Student in a participating institution.	Annual survey starting from year 2000. Participation of institutions is by choice.	College Activities, Educational and Personal Growth, Opinions About Your School, Background Information

continued

TABLE C.1 Continued

Name of Survey	Collection Agency	Objective of the Survey	Unit of Analysis	Time Period	Survey Components[a]
Beginning College Survey of Student Engagement (BCSSE)	Center for Survey Research and Center for Postsecondary Research	Measure gains in learning from high school education and college experiences of first-year entering students.	Student in a participating institution.	Annual survey starting from year 2007. Institutions participating in NSSE are eligible.	High School Experiences, College Experiences, Additional Information
Faculty Survey of Student Engagement (FSSE)	Center for Survey Research and Center for Postsecondary Research	Measure faculty expectations of student engagement.	Faculty in a participating institution.	Annual survey starting from year 2003. Institutions participating in NSSE are eligible.	Student Engagement, Faculty-Student Interaction, Opinions About Learning and Development, Time Use
Community College Survey of Student Engagement (CCSSE)	Community College Leadership Program at UT Austin	Measure gains in learning from community college education. Provide data on time use by community college students.	Student in a participating institution.	Annual survey starting from year 2001.	College Activities, Educational and Personal Growth, Opinions About Your School, Background Information Starting in 2006 supplemental questions added with a different focus each year
Community College Faculty Survey of Student Engagement (CCFSSE)	Center for Survey Research and Center for Postsecondary Research	Measure faculty expectations of student engagement in community colleges.	Faculty in a participating institution.	Annual survey starting from year 2005.	Student Engagement, Faculty-Student Interaction, Opinions About Learning and Development, Opinions About Services Provided, Time Use, Background Information

Survey	Organization	Purpose	Population	Timing	Survey Components
Law School Survey of Student Engagement (LSSSE)	Center for Postsecondary Research. Co-sponsored by Association of American Law Schools and the Carnegie Foundation for the Advancement of Teaching.	Provide data on time use by law students and gains in learning from law school.	Student in a participating institution.	Annual survey starting from year 2004.	College Activities, Educational and Personal Growth, Opinions About Your School, Background Information
International Student Enrollment Survey	Institute for International Education	Gather information on international students enrolled in United States.	International Student. An individual who is studying at an institution of higher education in the United States on a temporary visa that allows for academic coursework.	Data collected since 1919.	Enrollment, Primary Source of Funding, Field of Study, Places of Origin, Academic Level, Institutions Enrolled in
Study Abroad Survey	Institute for International Education	Gather information on U.S. students taking courses in foreign institutions.	U.S. Student receiving credit from an institution of higher education in the United States after study abroad experience.	Data collected since 1985.	Destination Country, Field of Study, Duration of Stay, Foreign Institution, Academic Level, Gender, Ethnicity, Visa Status
National Student Clearinghouse (NSC)	National Student Clearinghouse	Verify student degrees, certifications, student enrollment statuses.	Student. Gather data on student loan recipients.	Started in 1995. Data collected annually.	Name, Birth Date, School Name, Dates of Attendance, Degree Earned

[a]The survey designs and instruments of most of the surveys listed have changed over time. The survey components column reflects the items in the most recent cycle of the survey.

INTEGRATED POSTSECONDARY EDUCATION DATA SYSTEM

The Integrated Postsecondary Education Data System (IPEDS)[1] consists of seven interrelated surveys conducted annually by the U.S. Department of Education's National Center for Education Statistics (NCES). IPEDS gathers information from every college, university, and technical and vocational institution that participates in the federal student financial aid programs. More than 6,700 institutions complete IPEDS surveys each year. These include research universities, state colleges and universities, private religious and liberal arts colleges, for-profit institutions, community and technical colleges, nondegree-granting institutions such as beauty colleges, and others. IPEDS collects data on postsecondary education in the United States in seven areas: institutional characteristics, institutional prices, enrollment, student financial aid, degrees and certificates conferred, student persistence and success, and institutional human and fiscal resources. The seven survey components covering the seven areas are

- Institutional Characteristics Survey (IC)
- Fall Enrollment Survey (EF)
- Completions Survey (C)
- Graduation Rate Survey (GRS)
- Student Financial Aid Survey (SFA)
- Finance Survey (F)
- Fall Staff Survey (S)
- Employees by Assigned Position (EAP)
- Reporting Salaries Survey (SA)

The data collection cycle of IPEDS is summarized in Table C.2.

Reporting by institutions to IPEDS is mandatory under Title IV of the Higher Education Act of 1965, as amended (20 U.S.C. 1094, Section 487(a)(17) and 34 CFR 668.14(b)(19)). Starting in 1991, IPEDS data is available on institutional characteristics, enrollment, completions, and finance. Data on enrollment by age, fall staff and residence of first-time freshman are available in alternate years. Other surveys have been added: the Graduation Rate Survey (GRS) in 1997, Student Financial Aid (SFA) in 1999, and Employees by Assigned Position (EAP) in 2001.

The Institutional Characteristics (IC) survey collects basic institutional information including mission, system affiliations, student services, and athletic association. The IC survey also collects institutional pricing data from institutions for first-time, full-time, degree- or certificate-seeking undergraduate students. This includes tuition and fee data as well as information on the estimated budgets

---

[1] See http://nces.ed.gov/ipeds/about/ [October 2010].

TABLE C.2 Data Collection Cycle of IPEDS

Fall (Sept.-Nov.)	Institutional Characteristics, Completions
Winter (Dec.-Feb.)	Human Resources, Enrollment, Finance
Spring (March-May)	Enrollment, Finance, Student Financial Aid, Graduation Rates

for students based on living situations (on-campus or off-campus). Enrollment data is collected in various forms: fall enrollment, residence of first-time full-time students, age distribution of enrolled students, unduplicated head count of students enrolled over a 12-month period, total credit and/or contact hours delivered by institutions during a 12-month period, the number of incoming students (both freshman and transfer) due to various institutional missions and points of access. The percentage of full-time, first-degree, or certificate-seeking students who receive different types of grants and loans and the average dollar amount of aid received is available from SFA.

IPEDS collects data on the number of students who complete a postsecondary education program by type of program and level of award (certificate or degree). In 2003, IPEDS also started collecting information on persistence rates. EAP has information on all employees by full- or part-time status, faculty status, and occupational activity. SA and S surveys contain information on number of full-time instructional faculty by rank, gender, and length of contract/teaching period; total salary outlay and fringe benefits; and demographic and occupational characteristics. Finance data includes institutional revenues by source, expenditures by category, and assets and liabilities. IPEDS data forms the institutional sampling frame for other NCES postsecondary surveys, such as the National Postsecondary Student Aid Study and the National Survey of Postsecondary Faculty.

National Study of Postsecondary Faculty

The National Study of Postsecondary Faculty (NSOPF)[2] was a nationally representative sample of full- and part-time faculty and instructional staff at public and private not-for-profit two- and four-year institutions in the United States. It provided data about faculty and instructional staff to postsecondary education researchers and policy makers. The study was initially conducted during the 1987-1988 school year and was repeated in 1992-1993, 1998-1999, and 2003-2004.

The 1987-1988 wave consisted of three major components: an institutional survey, a faculty survey, and a department chair survey. The institutional survey used a stratified random sample of 480 institution-level respondents and had a

---

[2]See http://nces.ed.gov/surveys/nsopf/ [November 2010].

response rate of 88 percent. The faculty survey used a stratified random sample of 11,013 eligible faculty members within the participating institutions and had a response rate of 76 percent. The department chair survey used a stratified random sample of 3,029 eligible department chairpersons (or their equivalent) within the participating two-year and four-year institutions and had a response rate of 80 percent. The 1988 NSOPF gathered information on backgrounds, responsibilities, workloads, salaries, benefits, and attitudes of full-time and part-time instructional faculty in higher educational institutions. Information was collected on faculty composition, turnover and recruitment, retention and tenure policies from institutional and department-level respondents.

The second cycle of NSOPF was conducted by NCES with support from the National Science Foundation and National Endowment for Humanities. NSOPF:93 was limited to surveys of institutions and faculty, but with a substantially expanded sample of 974 colleges and universities, and 31,354 faculty and instructional staff. NSPOF:99 included 960 degree-granting postsecondary institutions and approximately 18,000 faculty and instructional staff. The fourth cycle of NSOPF was conducted in 2003-2004 and included 1,080 degree-granting postsecondary institutions and approximately 26,000 faculty and instructional staff. There are no plans to repeat the study. Rather, NCES plans to provide technical assistance to state postsecondary data systems and to encourage the development of robust connections between faculty and student data systems so that key questions concerning faculty, instruction, and student outcomes can be addressed.

National Postsecondary Student Aid Study

The purpose of National Postsecondary Student Aid Study (NPSAS)[3] is to compile a comprehensive research dataset on financial aid provided by the federal government, the states, postsecondary institutions, employers, and private agencies. The dataset is based on student-level records and includes student demographic and enrollment data. NPSAS uses a nationally representative sample of all students (graduate, first-professional, and undergraduate) enrolled in postsecondary educational institutions. Students attending all types and levels of institutions are represented in the samples, including public and private for-profit and not-for-profit institutions and from less-than-two-year institutions to four-year colleges and universities.

NPSAS data come from multiple sources, including institutional records, government databases, and student interviews. Detailed data on participation in student financial aid programs are extracted from institutional records. Data about family circumstances, demographics, education and work experiences, and student expectations are collected from students through a Web-based multi-mode interview (self-administered and computer-assisted telephone interview, CATI).

---

[3]See http://nces.ed.gov/surveys/npsas/about.asp [November 2010].

The first study (NPSAS:87) was conducted during the 1986-1987 school year; subsequently, NPSAS has been conducted triennially.

Each study is designed to cover students enrolled in a postsecondary institution from July 1 through June 30 financial aid award year. In the first study, data was gathered from 1,130 institutions, 55,000 students, and 16,000 parents. In the 1989-1990 survey, the number of students increased to 70,000. These data provided information on the costs of postsecondary education, distribution of financial aid and characteristics of unaided and aided students and their families.

Content areas in NPSAS include student demographics (birth date, gender, ethnicity/race), household composition, high school degree details, languages spoken, expectations, marital status, number of dependents; enrollment and education-admission tests taken, year taken, scores in admission tests, level of degree in the survey year, type of degree program, cumulative GPA, field of study, transfer credits if any, requirements for degree, tuition and charges for all terms enrolled during the survey year, factors in college choice; financial aid-receipt of aid, amount of aid received under various federal, state programs, institutional grants and scholarships and other award; student aid report-number of members in the student family, their educational status, if any of the members are currently enrolled in college, income tax details of student, parents and spouse, social security and investment details of parents, reasons for pursuing college degree, expectation of highest degree; employment and living expenses.

NPSAS data provide the base-year sample for the Beginning Postsecondary Students (BPS) longitudinal study and the Baccalaureate and Beyond (B&B) longitudinal study. For BPS, the longitudinal cohort consisted of students beginning their postsecondary education during the NPSAS year (NPSAS:90, NPSAS:96, and NPSAS:04); BPS surveys followed these students over time to examine such issues as persistence and the effects of financial aid on subsequent enrollment. For B&B, NPSAS provided the base-year sample of students obtaining a baccalaureate degree during the NPSAS year (NPSAS:93 and NPSAS:2000); the B&B surveys followed these students over time to examine issues such as the transition from college to work and access to graduate school.

Baccalaureate and Beyond Longitudinal Study

Baccalaureate and Beyond Longitudinal Study (B&B)[4] examines students' education and work experiences after they complete a bachelor's degree, with a special emphasis on the experiences of new elementary and secondary teachers. Following several cohorts of students over time, B&B looks at bachelor's degree recipients' workforce participation, income and debt repayment, and entry into and persistence through graduate school programs, among other indicators. It addresses several issues specifically related to teaching, including teacher prepara-

---

[4]See http://nces.ed.gov/surveys/b&b/about.asp [November 2010].

tion, entry into and persistence in the profession, and teacher career paths. B&B also gathers extensive information on bachelor's degree recipients' undergraduate experience, demographic backgrounds, and expectations regarding graduate study and work, and participation in community service.

The first B&B cohort (about 11,000 students) was drawn from the 1993 NPSAS and followed up by surveys in 1994, 1997, and 2003. It sampled students who completed bachelor's degrees in academic year 1992-1993. The base-year interview collected information from students, institutions and parents on background characteristics, enrollment, employment, and education financing including financial aid. Students who received a degree during the survey period were asked additional questions about plans for the future, plans to pursue a graduate degree, and plans to pursue a teaching career in K-12. The first follow-up, conducted in 1994, provides information on the activities of these bachelor's degree recipients in the year after graduation. Topics covered in the first follow-up were cumulative GPA, courses taken, grades earned, first and second majors' field of study, job search, job training and transition to employment, family formation, civic participation and finances (student loans, debt and income). Transcript data was also collected from postsecondary institutions attended by respondents.

A second follow-up of the 1993 cohort, conducted in 1997, gathered information on postbaccalaureate enrollment, including degrees sought, enrollment intensity and duration, finances, and degree attainment. Employment information and experiences, such as the number of jobs held since the last interview, occupations, salaries, benefits, and job satisfaction, were also collected. Those already in or newly identified for teaching careers were asked questions about their preparation to teach, work experience at the K-12 level, and satisfaction with teaching as a career. The follow-up also updated information on family formation and civic participation.

The final follow-up interview of the B&B:93 cohort in 2003 (B&B:93/03) was conducted 10 years following degree completion. The 2003 interview covered topics related to continuing education, degree attainment, employment, career choice, family formation, and finances. Respondents were asked to reflect on the value of their undergraduate education and any other education obtained since receiving the bachelor's degree to their lives now. There was a separate questionnaire for new teachers and those who left or continued in the teaching profession.

The second B&B cohort (about 10,000 students) was chosen from the 2000 NPSAS and followed up in 2001. The dataset contains information on enrollment, attendance, and student demographic characteristics. The second follow-up of second cohort covered topics such as high school education, undergraduate enrollment history, academic history, and debt burden. There were separate set of questions on first-year's and first college's enrollment status, marital status, academic performance, residence, employment, and financial aid. Information on civic and volunteer participation, postbaccalaureate enrollment, employment, job training, and current demographics was also collected. Just as in the third follow-up of first cohort, there were supplemental sections for respondents in the teaching profession. The third cohort was drawn from the 2008 NPSAS sample. This group of approximately 19,000 sample members was followed up in 2009 and will be surveyed again in 2012.

Beginning Postsecondary Students Longitudinal Study

Beginning Postsecondary Students Longitudinal Study[5] 90/92 followed students identified as first-time beginning students in the academic year 1989-1990 from the National Postsecondary Student Aid Study 1990 sample. The population of interest in BPS is all students who entered postsecondary education for the first time in academic year 1989-1990. The sample was designed to include students enrolled in all types of postsecondary education—public institutions; private, not-for-profit institutions; and private, for-profit institutions. The sample also included students enrolled in occupationally specific programs that lasted for less than two years. Institutions offering only correspondence courses, institutions enrolling only their own employees, and U.S. service academies were not eligible for NPSAS or BPS. Students eligible for BPS were identified in two stages.

Of the NPSAS 1990 sample, those who were identified as first-time enrollees were eligible for BPS and were retained in the 1992 interview. BPS data are nationally representative by institution level and control, but like NPSAS are not representative at the state level. A database of 11,700 NPSAS:90 participants that was believed to contain all possible full-time beginning students in the NPSAS:90 sample was used as the basis for selecting the BPS:90/92 sample. The initial set of 11,700 potential full-time beginning students contained 10,566 students who had been identified as probable undergraduate students, and 1,134 students who had been identified as probable graduate or first-professional students. A computer-assisted telephone interview (CATI) was conducted two years after the NPSAS:90 survey. It obtained information concerning student characteristics, institutional characteristics and degree programs, student educational experiences, financing postsecondary education, student work experiences, marriage and family information, civic participation, and noncredit education activities.

The BPS:90/94 study was the second follow-up survey of the first cohort. The questionnaire had eight sections covering topics such as education experiences, employment experiences, other education or training, family and demographics, education financing, financial information, graduate school plans, and public service. The second cohort of BPS was constituted of individuals who started their postsecondary education in the 1995-1996 academic year. Data elements in the first follow-up of the second cohort (which took place in 1998) are first-time beginner status, basic demographic information, enrollment status in survey year, enrollment history, enrollment characteristics, financial aid and debt,

---

[5]See http://nces.ed.gov/surveys/bps/about.asp [November 2010].

employment status, learning experience and outcomes, expectations, goals, and plans. A separate section addressed nontraditional students—those not pursuing college education immediately after high school. The second follow up of BPS:96 took place in 2001. It put more emphasis on employment, earnings, financial circumstances, postbaccalaureate enrollment, civic participation, and future goals. The third cohort of BPS constituted individuals who started their postsecondary education in the 2003-2004 academic year. They were followed up in 2006 and 2008. Data elements from BPS:04 were very similar to the second follow-up of BPS:96.

National Household Education Survey

The chief goal of the National Household Education Surveys (NHES)[6] is to describe Americans' educational experiences, thereby offering policy makers, researchers, and educators a variety of statistics on the condition of education in the United States. The NHES has been conducted in the springs of 1991, 1993, 1995, 1996, 1999, 2001, 2003, 2005, and 2007. Surveys include the following:

NHES Surveys	Data Collection Years
Adult Education	1991, 1995, 1999, 2001, 2003, 2005
Before- and After-School Programs and Activities	1999, 2001, 2005
Early Childhood Program Participation	1991, 1995, 1999, 2001, 2005
Parent and Family Involvement in Education	1996, 1999, 2003, 2007
Civic Involvement	1996, 1999
Household Library Use	1996
School Readiness	1993, 1999, 2007
School Safety and Discipline	1993

NHES is designed as a telephone survey of the noninstitutionalized civilian population. U.S. households in the survey are selected randomly using random digit dialing methods. Data is collected using CATI procedures. About 60,000 households were screened for NHES:91. In the Early Childhood Education component, about 14,000 parents/guardians of 3- to 8-year-olds provided information about their children's early educational experiences: participation in nonparental care/education, care arrangements and school, and family, household, and child characteristics. The Adult Education component of the survey questionnaire was administered to 9,800 persons 16 years of age and older. They were identified as having participated in an adult education activity in the previous 12 months. Data were collected on programs of up to four courses, including the subject matter, duration, sponsorship, purpose, and cost. Information on the household and the adult's background and current employment also were collected.

---

[6]Digest of Education Statistics 1995-2009 [November 2010].

In NHES:93, the sample size increased to 64,000 households. About 11,000 parents of 3- to 7-year-olds were interviewed for the School Readiness component. This included topics such as developmental characteristics of preschoolers, school adjustment and teacher feedback to parents of kindergartners and primary students, center-based program participation, early school experiences, home activities with family members, and health status. In the School Safety and Discipline component, about 12,700 parents of children in grades 3 through 12, and about 6,500 youth in grades 6 through 12, were interviewed about their school experiences. Topics included school learning environment, discipline policy, safety at school, victimization, the availability and use of alcohol/drugs, alcohol/drug education and peer norms for behavior in school and substance use. Extensive family and household background information and characteristics of the school attended by the child was also collected.

In NHES:95 survey, the Early Childhood Program Participation component and the Adult Education component were similar to those in 1991. In the Early Childhood component, about 14,000 parents of children from birth to third grade were interviewed. For the Adult Education component, 23,969 adults were sampled; 80 percent (19,722) completed the interview. In the spring of 1996, Parent and Family Involvement in Education and Civic Involvement were covered. For the Parent and Family Involvement component, nearly 21,000 parents of children in grades 3 to 12 were interviewed. For the Civic Involvement component, about 8,000 youth in grades 6 to 12, about 9,000 parents, and about 2,000 adults were interviewed. The 1996 survey also addressed public library use. Adults in almost 55,000 households were interviewed to support state-level estimates of household public library use.

NHES:99 collected end-of-decade estimates of key indicators from the surveys conducted throughout the 1990s. Approximately 60,000 households were screened. Key indicators are expected to include participation of children in non-parental care and early childhood programs, school experiences, parent/family involvement in education at home and at school, youth community service activities, plans for future education, and adult participation in educational activities and community service.

NHES:2001 included two surveys that were largely repeats of similar surveys included in earlier NHES collections. The Early Childhood Program Participation Survey and Adult Education and Lifelong Learning Survey were similar in content to NHES:1995. The Before- and After-School Programs and Activities Survey had a number of new items that collected information about what children were doing during the time spent in child care or in other activities, what parents were looking for in care arrangements and activities, and parent evaluations of care arrangements and activities. Nearly 10,900 adults completed Adult Education and Lifelong Learning Survey interviews. Parents of approximately 6,700 preschool children were interviewed. Parents of 9,600 children in K-8 completed Before- and After-School Programs and Activities Survey interviews.

NHES:2003 included two surveys, Adult Education for Work-Related Reasons and Parent and Family Involvement in Education. The adult education survey provides in-depth information on participation in training and education that prepares adults for work or careers and maintains or improves their skills.

NHES:2005 included surveys that covered Adult Education, Early Childhood Program Participation, and After-School Programs and Activities. Data were collected from about 8,900 adults, parents of about 7,200 preschool children and parents of nearly 11,700 children in K-8 for the After-School Programs and Activities survey. These surveys were very similar to NHES:2001, except for the Adult Education Survey (which included as a new topic informal learning activities for personal interest) and the Early Childhood Program Participation Survey and After-School Programs and Activities Survey (which did not collect information about before-school care for school-age children).

NHES:2007 fielded the Parent and Family Involvement in Education Survey and the School Readiness Survey. These surveys were similar in design and content to NHES:2003 and NHES:1993, respectively. The Parent and Family Involvement Survey included new questions about supplemental education services provided by schools and school districts (including use of and satisfaction with such services). There were questions to identify the school attended by the sampled students. School Readiness Survey included questions that collected details about television programs watched by the sampled children. For the Parent and Family Involvement Survey, interviews were completed with parents of 10,370 students enrolled in public or private schools and a sample of 311 home-schooled children in K-12. For the School Readiness Survey, interviews were completed with parents of 2,633 sampled children ages 3 to 6 years and not yet in kindergarten. Parents who were interviewed about children in K-2 were also asked some questions about these children's school readiness.

Wisconsin Longitudinal Study of 1957

The Wisconsin Longitudinal Study (WLS)[7] follows a cohort of men and women born in 1939. The study is a rich data source to study trends as the cohort ages. WLS is also the first of the large, longitudinal studies of American adolescents, and it thus provides the first large-scale opportunity to study the life course from late adolescence through the later decades in the context of a complete record of ability, aspiration, and achievement. The WLS is a long-term study of a random sample of 10,317 men and women who graduated from Wisconsin high schools in 1957. Survey data were collected from the original respondents or their parents in 1957, 1964, 1975, and 1993, and from a selected sibling in 1977

---

[7]See http://www.ssc.wisc.edu/wlsresearch/ [December 2010].

and 1994. The data provide a full record of social background, youthful aspirations, schooling, military service, family formation, labor market experiences, and social participation of the original respondents. The survey data from earlier years have been supplemented by mental ability tests (of primary respondents and 2,000 of their siblings), measures of school performance, and characteristics of communities of residence, schools and colleges, employers, and industries.

The WLS records for primary respondents are also linked to those of three same-sex high school friends within the study population. In 1977 the study design was expanded with the collection of parallel interview data for a highly stratified sub-sample of 2,000 siblings of the primary respondents. In the 1992-1993 round of the WLS, the sample was expanded to include a randomly selected sibling of every respondent with at least one brother or sister, and the content was extended to obtain detailed occupational histories and job characteristics; incomes, assets, and inter-household transfers; social and economic characteristics of parents, siblings, and children and descriptions of the respondents' relationships with them; and extensive information about mental and physical health and well-being. Approximately 2,800 additional siblings were interviewed in the 1993-1994 round of the study. The WLS sample is mainly of German, English, Irish, Scandinavian, Polish, or Czech ancestry. Minorities (African American, Hispanic, or Asian persons) are not well-represented in the sample. Currently a project is under way to find all African Americans who graduated from Wisconsin high schools in 1957. About 19 percent of the WLS sample is of farm origin. In all, 8,493 of the 9,741 surviving members of the original sample have been re-interviewed. The retention rate was 86.48 percent in 1964, and dropped to 29.67 percent in 2005.

Data topics in WLS are Alcohol Use, Aspirations, Assets, Care Giving, Children, Cognition, Conflicts Tactics Scale, Education, Employment History Details, Financial Intertransfers, Future Plans and Retirement, Health Insurance, Health Symptoms and Condition, High School Friend, Household, Income (Personal and Family), Job Characteristics, Marital and Fertility History, Menopause, Parents and Parents-in-law, Pensions, Personality, Psychological Distress, Psychological Well-Being, Religion, Selected Siblings, Social Background, Social Participation, Wealth, Work-Family Spillover.

National Education Longitudinal Studies

The National Education Longitudinal Studies (NELS) program was established to study the educational, vocational, and personal development of young people beginning with their elementary or secondary education. Thus far, the NELS program consists of five major studies:

- National Longitudinal Study of the High School Class of 1972 (NLS72),[8]
- High School and Beyond (HS&B),[9]
- National Education Longitudinal Study of 1988 (NELS:88),[10]
- Education Longitudinal Study of 2002 (ELS:2002),[11]
- High School Longitudinal Study of 2009 (HSLS:09).[12]

NLS72 followed the 1972 cohort of high school seniors through 1986, or fourteen years after most of this cohort completed high school. The HS&B survey included two cohorts: the 1980 senior class, and the 1980 sophomore class. Both cohorts were surveyed every two years through 1986, and the 1980 sophomore class was also surveyed again in 1992. NELS:88 started with the cohort of students who were in the eighth grade in 1988, and these students have been surveyed through 2000. ELS:2002 began with a cohort of high school sophomores in 2002. This cohort will be followed through 2012. HSLS:09 began with a cohort of ninth graders in 2009. The first follow-up is planned for 2012 when most of the students will be high school sophomores. Taken together, all the five studies will describe the educational experience of students from five decades—1970s, 1980s, 1990s, 2000s, and 2010s.

National Longitudinal Study of the High School Class of 1972

The National Longitudinal Study of the High School Class of 1972 (NLS72) is one of the longitudinal studies on a single generation of Americans. Participants in the study were selected when they were seniors in high school in the spring of 1972, and in a supplementary sample drawn in 1973. The records include the base year survey; follow-up surveys in 1973, 1974, 1976, 1979, and 1986; high school records; and postsecondary transcripts (collected in 1984). In 1968, NCES conducted a survey to determine the specific data needs of educational policy makers and researchers. The results of the survey pointed out the need for data that would allow inter-temporal comparisons of student outcomes. This finding gave rise to one of the first national longitudinal studies. The base year survey of NLS72 was conducted in spring of 1972 and comprised 19,001 students from 1,061 high schools. Each participating student was expected to complete a student questionnaire and take a 69-minute test battery. The sections in the first follow-up survey were general information, education and training, civilian work experience, military service, information about past and background information. The general information section had questions on occupational status of respondents,

---

[8]See http://nces.ed.gov/surveys/nls72/ [November 2010].
[9]See http://nces.ed.gov/surveys/hsb/ [November 2010].
[10]See http://nces.ed.gov/surveys/nels88/ [November 2010].
[11]See http://nces.ed.gov/surveys/els2002/ [November 2010].
[12]See http://nces.ed.gov/surveys/hsls09/ [November 2010].

receipt of high school degree, marital status and history, income of self and spouse, opinions about pursuing postsecondary education, financial choices and decisions, and attitudes toward life and work. The education and training section gathered information on participation in various training programs and their requisite details, field of study pursued by the respondents, details about high school attendance, reasons for leaving high school (if any), education and training progress after high school, sources and kinds of financial support provided to attend education and training programs after school. The section on civilian work experience asked NLS72 respondents about number of jobs held till survey date, satisfaction with various aspects of current jobs, kind of job (government, private, self-employed, working in family business/farm without pay), work hours per week, weekly earnings, and job search methods. The section on military service asked questions on periods of service, branch in which the respondent served, the field of training, and pay grades. Peer effect, education status, occupation of parents, college choice, and financial aid offered by various colleges was covered in the section on past information. The background information section collected basic information such as residence address, sex, and birth date.

The second follow-up survey was conducted from October 1974 to April 1975. It included a special retrospective survey to obtain key information about prior time points from those who had not provided this information previously. A third follow-up was conducted from October 1976 to May 1977. In the fourth follow-up survey, 5,548 respondents were asked to complete a supplemental questionnaire similar to the retrospective survey in the second follow-up. Additionally a test battery was conducted for 2,648 individuals. New sections on family formation and political participation were included. The retention rate until the fourth follow-up was 78 percent. In 1984, a Postsecondary Education Transcript Study was conducted. It collected transcripts from academic and vocational postsecondary educational institutions that respondents had reported attending.

The final follow-up survey was conducted in the spring of 1986 and included sections on general information, work experience, periods of unemployment, education, family information, child care, background information, income, expectations, and opinions. The general information section contained questions on occupation status, residence address, and birth date. The background information section contained items on race/ethnicity, current location of parents, and interaction with parents. The work experience section contained items on number and kinds of jobs held till survey date, details about each job, satisfaction with various aspects of current jobs, time spent in doing various activities involved in a job, relationship with supervisor, factors influencing job choices, and training programs on and off the job. The education section gathered information on enrollment status in college, details of each college attended, satisfaction with education and training, sources of financial aid, and plans for graduate studies. The income section gathered information on sources of income of respondents. The family formation section had items on spouses, partners and children, their education status, kind of activities the respondent engaged in with them, sharing of financial resources in the household, and work hours of spouse. Questions on divorce, divorce settlements, financial, and custody issues from divorce were also included in this section. Political, community, and religious participation of respondents were addressed in the section on expectations and opinions. There were supplementary questions for individuals who considered a career in teaching.

High School and Beyond (HS&B)

High School and Beyond was designed to inform federal and state policy makers about student outcomes in the 1980s. It began in the spring of 1980 with a sample of 58,000 high school students—30,000 sophomores and 28,000 seniors. Follow-up surveys were conducted every two years; the final follow-up survey occurred in 1986. The 1980 sophomore class was surveyed again in 1992.

HS&B was designed to build on NLS72 in three ways. First, the base year survey of HS&B included a 1980 cohort of high school seniors that was directly comparable with the 1972 cohort. Replication of selected NLS72 student questionnaire items and test items made it possible to analyze changes that occurred subsequent to 1972 and their relationship to recent federal policies and programs in education. Second, the introduction of a sophomore cohort provided data on the many critical educational and vocational choices made between the sophomore and senior years in high school, permitting a fuller understanding of the secondary school experience and its impact on students. Finally, HS&B expanded the NLS72 focus by collecting data on a range of lifecycle factors, such as family-formation behavior, intellectual development, and social participation.

Survey instruments in the base year included student questionnaires, test battery, school questionnaire and parent questionnaire. The student questionnaires focused on individual and family background, high school experiences, work experiences, and plans for the future. The student identification pages included information that would be useful in locating the students for future follow-up surveys, as well as a series of items on the student's use of, proficiency in, and educational experiences with languages other than English. The cognitive tests measured verbal and quantitative abilities in both cohorts. Of the 194 test items administered to the senior cohort, 86 percent were identical to the items administered to NLS72 respondents. School questionnaires, which were filled out by an official in each participating school, provided information about enrollment, staff, educational programs, facilities and services, dropout rates, and special programs for handicapped and disadvantaged students. The teacher comment checklist provided teacher observations on students participating in the survey. The parent questionnaire elicited information about how family attitudes and financial planning affected postsecondary educational goals.

Contents in the 1980 senior cohort first follow-up questionnaire included education (amount and type of postsecondary schooling completed, data on schools attended, school financing, educational expectations and aspirations, and nonschool-based postsecondary training), work (labor force participation, detailed job histories, aspirations, military service), financial status (dependency, income), marital status (spouse's occupation, education, dependents), and demographics (household composition, race, sex, ethnicity, and so forth). Questions on employment and schooling were constructed and arranged in an "event history" format in order to provide information suitable for analyses using advanced techniques for determining parameters of transition models.

The purpose of the sophomore cohort first follow-up questionnaire was to document secondary school experiences. Content areas included education (high school program, courses taken, grades, standardized tests taken, attendance and disciplinary behavior, parental involvement, extracurricular and leisure activities, assessment of quality of school and teachers), postsecondary education (goals, expectations, plans and financing), work/labor force participation (occupational goals, attitudes toward military service), demographics (parents' education, father's occupation, family composition, school age siblings, family income, marital status, race, ethnicity, sex, birth date, physical handicaps) and values (attitudes toward life goals, feelings about self and so forth). There was a separate questionnaire for persons who had dropped out of high school, members of the sophomore cohort who had transferred from their base year sample high school to another high school, and members of the sophomore cohort who graduated from high school ahead of schedule. Dropout supplement content areas included circumstances of leaving school, participation in training programs and other postsecondary education work, financial status, marital status, demographics, and other personal characteristics. Transfer supplement content areas were reasons for transferring and for selecting a particular school, identification of school, location, grade respondent was in at time of transfer, entrance requirements, length of interruption in schooling (if any) and reason, type of school, size of student body and grades. An early graduate supplement addressed reasons for graduating early, when decision was made, persons involved in the decision, course adjustments required, school requirements and postsecondary education and work experience.

The second follow-up survey was conducted in 1984. The senior cohort was asked to update background information and to provide information about postsecondary education, work experience, military service, family information, income and life goals. Event history formats were used for obtaining responses about jobs held, schools attended and periods of unemployment. New items included a limited series on computer literacy, financial assistance received from parents for pursuing postsecondary education, and education and training obtained outside of regular school, college or military programs. As the sophomore cohort was out of school by 1984, the follow-up survey had items taking this change into consideration. The questionnaire asked for detailed information (kind of school attended, hours per week spent in class, kind of degree sought, requirements completed) on schools attended after high school, for up to three schools.

Financial information included questions on tuition and fees and scholarship and on financial aid from parents to respondents and to any siblings. There were items on work history, salary income, work hours per week, unemployment periods, job training and satisfaction. Family information covered the spouse's occupation and education, date of marriage, number of children, and income and benefits received by respondent and spouse.

The third follow-up survey was conducted in 1986. Both the cohorts received the same questionnaire. To maintain comparability, many items were repeated. Respondents provided updated information on items asked in previous surveys. Event history formats were used for obtaining responses about jobs held, schools attended, periods of unemployment, and marriage patterns. New items included interest in graduate degree programs and alcohol consumption habits.

National Education Longitudinal Study of 1988 (NELS:88)

The National Education Longitudinal Study of 1988 (NELS:88) was initiated in 1988 with a cohort of eighth graders. The survey sought to study the transition from elementary education to secondary education and was the first to do so. The cohort was resurveyed through four follow-ups in 1990, 1992, 1994, and 2000. In the 1990 follow-up survey, the sample was augmented with new participants who were tenth graders in 1990. This was done to create a comparison group with HS&B. In the 1992 follow-up survey, the sample was augmented with twelfth graders to focus on transition issues from high school to postsecondary education. Another purpose was to create a dataset so as to make trend analyses with 1972 and 1982 senior classes from NLS72 and HS&B surveys. The freshening of the sample not only provided comparability to earlier cohorts from BLS72 and HS&B, but also enabled researchers to conduct both grade-representative cross-sectional and subsequent longitudinal analyses with the data. Students identified as dropouts in the first follow-up were resurveyed in 1992. In late 1992 and early 1993, high school transcripts were collected and in the fall of 2000 and early 2001, postsecondary transcripts were collected. On the questionnaires, students reported on a range of topics, including school, work, and home experiences; educational resources and support; the role in education of their parents and peers; neighborhood characteristics; educational and occupational aspirations; and other student perceptions.

For the three in-school waves of data collection (when most were eighth-graders, sophomores, or seniors), achievement tests in reading, social studies, mathematics and science were also administered. To further enrich the data, students' parents (1988 and 1992), teachers and school administrators (1988, 1990, 1992) were also surveyed. Coursework and grades from students' high school and postsecondary transcripts were also collected. In the base-year survey conducted from 1987 to 1988, data was collected on educational processes and outcomes of student learning, indicators of dropping out and school effects on students' access to learning programs. Almost 25,000 students across the United States participated in the base-year study. Student questionnaires covered school experiences, activities, attitudes, educational, and occupational plans and aspirations, selected background characteristics and language proficiency. Students also completed a series of curriculum-sensitive cognitive tests to measure educational achievement and cognitive growth between eighth and twelfth grades in four subject areas: reading, mathematics, science, and social studies. School principals completed a questionnaire about the school. The administrator questionnaire gathered descriptive information about the school's teaching staff, the school climate, characteristics of the student body, and school policies and offerings. Two teachers (in two of the four subject areas) of each student were asked to answer questions about the student, themselves (characteristics and classroom teaching practices), course content, and their school. One parent of each student was surveyed regarding family characteristics and student activities. Parent questionnaire included items on parental aspirations for children, family willingness to commit resources to children's education, the home educational support system, and other family characteristics relevant to achievement.

The first follow-up was conducted in 1990 and did not include a parent questionnaire. The study frame included 19,264 students and dropouts, 1,291 principals, and 10,000 teachers. There were two more survey components: base-year ineligible study and high school effectiveness study. Respondents took a tenth grade level cognitive test in the four subject areas. The student questionnaire had items on school and home environments, participation in classes and extracurricular activities, current jobs, their goals and aspirations, and opinions about themselves. The dropout questionnaire collected information on reasons for leaving school, school experiences, absenteeism, family formation, plans for the future, employment, attitudes and self-concept, and home environment. The base-year ineligible study was conducted to ascertain 1990 school enrollment status and 1990 NELS:88 eligibility status of students who were excluded from base-year survey because of a language barrier or a physical or mental disability which precluded them from completing the questionnaire and cognitive test. After the study, 341 students became eligible and completed a supplemental questionnaire. The high school effectiveness study (HSES) was designed to allow augmentation of the within-school student sample to produce a subsample of urban and suburban schools. It allowed researchers to better study school effects on education.

The second follow-up took place in 1992 when most of the respondents are in the second semester of their senior year. Dropouts were also resurveyed. For selected subsamples, data was collected from parents, teachers, school administrators, and transcripts. Respondents took a twelfth grade level cognitive test in four subject areas. Student questionnaire items addressed academic achievement, perceptions and feeling about school and its curriculum, family structure and environment, social relations and aspirations, attitudes and values, and family decision-making structure during transition from school to college or work.

There was a supplement for early graduates. Only one teacher (either math or science) for each student was asked to complete the teacher questionnaire. There was no change in the school administrator questionnaire survey design. The dropout questionnaire had no new items from the previous follow-up. Two new components—high school transcript and course offerings—were initiated in the second follow-up. The high school transcript component collected transcript records from the high school respondents attended. The course offering component was for HSES. It provided a probability sample of schools with tenth graders who had a sizable representation in the within-school sample of students.

The third follow-up in 1994 addressed employment and postsecondary access issues. It was designed to allow continuing trend comparisons with other NCES longitudinal studies. Specific content areas included academic achievement, perceptions and feelings about school and job, detailed work experiences, work-related training and family structure and environment.

The fourth and final follow-up in 2000 included interviews with 12,144 members of the three NELS:88 sample cohorts 12 years after the base-year data collection. Most of the respondents had been out of high school, had already enrolled in postsecondary school or intended to do so, and many had families of their own. Interview topics included experiences with postsecondary education, labor market outcomes, job-related training, community integration and marriage and family formation. This follow-up also collected postsecondary transcripts from institutions that the respondents reported attending.

Education Longitudinal Study of 2002 (ELS:2002)

The Education Longitudinal Study of 2002 (ELS:2002) is designed to monitor the transition of a national sample of young people as they progress from tenth grade through high school and on to postsecondary education and/or employment. ELS:2002 is a multi-level study, in that information is collected from multiple respondent populations representing students and their parents, teachers, librarians, and schools. Student-level data comes from student questionnaires and assessment data and reports from students' teachers and parents. The data collected from their teachers provides direct information about the student as well as the credentials and educational background information of the teacher. School-level data is gathered from a school administrator questionnaire, a library media center questionnaire and a facilities check list. This multi-level focus supplies researchers with a comprehensive picture of the home, school, and community environments and their influences on the student.

The base-year sample was comprised of two primary target populations: schools with a tenth grade and sophomore in those schools in the spring term of the 2001-2002 school year. The sample selection process had two stages. First, schools were selected. These schools were then asked to provide sophomore enrollment lists, from which students were selected. The sample design for

ELS:2002 is very similar to the design of NLS72, HS&B, and NELS:88. Non-public schools (specifically, Catholic and other private schools) were sampled at a higher rate, to ensure a sample large enough to support comparisons with public schools. Similarly, Asian students were sampled at a higher rate than Caucasian, African-American, and Hispanic students, to ensure a sample large enough to support comparisons with those groups. The base-year survey instruments were comprised of two assessments: reading and mathematics, and a student questionnaire asking about attitudes and experiences. Also included in the base-year sample were one parent of the sample student and English and mathematics teachers of the sample students. The parent questionnaire was designed to gauge parental aspiration for their child, child's educational history prior to tenth grade, parental interactions with and opinions about the child's school. The teacher questionnaire collected the teacher's evaluation of the student and information on teaching practices, background and other activities of the teachers. The head librarian or media center director of each school completed the library media center questionnaire which provided information on staffing, available technical resources, collections and expenditures, and scheduling and transactions of library media center. The facilities checklist form collected information on condition of school building and facilities.

The ELS:2002 base-year sample students were surveyed and tested again two years later in 2004 to measure their achievement gains in mathematics, as well as changes in their status, such as transfer to another high school, early completion of high school, or leaving high school before graduation. The sample was also augmented by a sample of students who were in twelfth grade in 2004. Separate questionnaires were given to homeschooled students, early graduates, and dropouts. The student questionnaire was comprised of eight content modules as in the base survey. Part I requested contact information. Part II covered the student's school experiences and activities. Part III, the time use module, inquired about time usage on homework, television viewing, video and computer games, computers, nonschool reading, library utilization, and other activities. Part IV concentrated on plans and expectations for the future. Part V addressed education after high school, including postsecondary planning steps and choice criteria. Part VI dealt with plans for work after high school. Part VII inquired about working for pay, including hours worked per week. Part VIII consisted of items on community, family, and friends. In the dropout questionnaire the respondents supplied their specific reasons for leaving school prior to graduation. Most of the modules in the dropout questionnaire matched those with the student questionnaire. Early graduates completed only a subset of the student questionnaire, complemented by items such as whom they consulted when deciding to graduate early, the basis for that decision and the means by which they did so. Sophomore cohort members who changed their base-year school received the transfer student questionnaire which asked them when they transferred and their reasons for doing so. Homeschooled students were asked about their schooling activities and status such as grades, coursework completed in science and math, steps taken toward college, and the other above-mentioned items from the student questionnaire. Also in autumn of 2004, high school transcripts were requested for all sample members who participated in at least one of the first two student interviews. Thus, dropouts, freshened sample members, transfer students, homeschooled students and early graduated were all included if they responded either in 2002 or 2004. The respondents also took a cognitive test in mathematics. High school transcripts were collected for all students from their base-year school and, if they had changed schools, also their transfer schools. These transcripts provide school archival records on courses completed, grades, attendance, SAT/ACT scores, and so on from grades nine through twelve. The school administrator questionnaire was administered in 2004, but not the teacher questionnaire.

In the third round of data collection in 2006, information was collected about colleges applied to and aid offers received, enrollment in postsecondary education, employment and earnings, and living situation, including family formation. In addition, high school completion status was updated for those who had not completed as of the third round of data collection. Only the student questionnaire was administered that time. There were four modules: high school education, postsecondary education, employment, and community. Section A contained questions on receipt of high school/GED/certificate, date of receipt, reasons for finishing degree, and, for dropouts, reasons for leaving school. Section B consisted of items on college choice, including details on colleges applied to, offers of financial aid from each college, reasons for selecting a college, name of academic field aiming to pursue. It also addressed college experiences, including interaction with faculty, first and second majors' field of study, undergraduate debt, expectation of highest level of degree, and enrollment status. Section C covered employment issues, including paid employment or self-employment, work done for family business or armed forces, occupational category, work hours per week, weekly earnings, job search methods, unemployment periods, details of employment during school or college, current finances, and future employment plans. Section D looked at political and community participation, marital status, biological children, and volunteer service. Cohort members will be interviewed again in 2012 so that later outcomes, such as their persistence and attainment in higher education, or their transition into the labor market, can be understood in terms of their earlier aspirations, achievement, and high school experiences.

High School Longitudinal Study of 2009 (HSLS:09)

The High School Longitudinal Study of 2009 (HSLS:09) is a nationally representative, longitudinal study of more than 21,000 ninth graders in 944 schools who will be followed through their secondary and postsecondary years. The study focuses on understanding students' trajectories from the beginning of high school into postsecondary education, the workforce, and beyond. What students decide to pursue and when, why, and how are crucial questions for HSLS:09, especially but not solely in regards to science, technology, engineering, and math (STEM) courses, majors, and careers. This study features a new student assessment in algebraic skills, reasoning, and problem-solving. It includes, like past studies, surveys of students, their parents, math and science teachers, and school administrators, and also adds a new survey of school counselors. The first wave of data collection for HSLS:09 began in the fall of 2009 and will produce not only a nationally representative dataset but also state representative datasets for each of ten states. The next data collection will occur in the spring of 2012.

National Longitudinal Study of Youth 1979

The National Longitudinal Study of Youth 1979 (NLSY79)[13] is a nationally representative sample of 12,686 young men and women who were 14 to 22 years of age when first surveyed in 1979. During the years since that first interview, these young people typically have finished their schooling, moved out of their parents' homes, made decisions on continuing education and training, entered the labor market, served in the military, married, and started families of their own. The cohort was interviewed annually through 1994. Since 1994, the survey has been administered biennially. Since 1986, detailed information on the development of children born to women in the NLSY79 cohort has supplemented the data on mothers and children collected during the main NLSY79.

NLSY79 is made up of three subsamples. The first is a cross-sectional sample of 6,111 noninstitutionalized youths. The second, supplemental sample of 5,295 youths is designed to oversample Hispanics, Blacks, and economically disadvantaged non-Hispanic and non-Black individuals. The third is a military sample of 1,280 youths enlisted in one of the four branches of the armed forces. The retention rate for the survey remained around 90 percent till 1994, after which it started dropping. In 2002 it was 77.5 percent. The 13 data elements in NLSY79 are

- Labor market experiences
- Training investments
- Schooling, school records, and aptitude information
- Military experience
- Income and assets
- Health conditions, injuries, and insurance coverage
- Alcohol and substance use, criminal behavior
- Attitudes and aspirations
- Geographic residence information
- Family background and demographic characteristics

---

[13] See http://www.bls.gov/nls/handbook/2005/nlshc3.pdf [November 2010].

- Household composition
- Marital and fertility histories
- Child care

Questions in each of the above survey components have undergone several changes. Information about current labor force status, number of jobs held, time periods for each job held, unemployment phases, pay rates, fringe benefits, and wage setting by collective bargaining is provided by the labor market experiences section. In the 1994-2002 labor market experiences' section, questions on job search methods, participation in employer-provided pension plan, receipt of severance pay, and type of position held (temporary, permanent, independent contractor) were included. In 2002, the employer supplement section was expanded to gather information on self-employed respondents and those with nontraditional employment. Training investments surveys have regularly collected detailed information about the types of nongovernment-sponsored vocational or technical training programs in which a respondent had enrolled since the last interview. Prior to 1986, surveys had extensive questions on participation in government-sponsored training programs. In the 1993 and 1994 surveys there were questions on informal methods to learn skills on the current job, potential transferability of skills acquired during various training programs, and whether skills learned in training programs added to skills learned in high school.

The schooling section contain information about respondents' current school enrollment status, the highest grade attended or completed, earning of GED or high school diploma, college enrollment status, field of major and type of college degree. There was also a school survey of the last secondary school attended by respondents. It included both respondent-specific and school-specific information. Transcript data was collected during the 1980-1983 survey, which contained grades scored, credits earned, class rank, attendance records, and aptitude and achievement test scores.

Scores from Armed Services Vocational Aptitude Battery test and Armed Forces Qualifications Test are also available. Military experience section provides information regarding respondent's enlistment intentions, attitudes toward military, dates and branch of service, military occupation, pay grade, income, education/training received and reasons for leaving the military or reenlisting. The income and assets section requests information about the sources and amounts of income received in the past calendar year by the respondent and his or her spouse. Income from TANF, Food Stamps, other public assistance and social security income is also recorded.

Questions on health conditions, injuries, and insurance coverage provide data regarding the respondent's height and weight, as well as the presence and duration of health conditions that prevent or limit labor market activity. Most surveys since 1989 have collected information on participation of respondents, their spouses and their children in private or government health care/hospitalization plan and source of coverage. A new set of health questions was asked for the first time in the 1998 survey to create a baseline health data for respondents aged 40 and older. The questions cover general health status and the influence of health on daily activities and emotional well-being. Questions on alcohol conumption were asked in selected survey years and addressed its frequency, quantity, and impact on schoolwork or job performance. Similar information is gathered on smoking of cigarettes and substance use (marijuana, amphetamines, barbiturates, cocaine, and heroin). Female respondents were also asked to report if they consumed alcohol, cigarettes, or other substances during pregnancy. Data on criminal behavior is gathered from a 1980 supplement which had items on truancy, alcohol or marijuana use, vandalism, shoplifting, drug dealing and robbery, arrest records, and police contacts.

Survey questions dealing with attitudes and aspiratins changed as the respondents moved from adolescence to adult life. In the initial survey, respondents reported on the attitude of the most influential person in their lives on their occupational, residence, and childbearing decisions. In some years the survey included questions on attitudes toward women and work; future expectations about marriage, education, and employment; and occupational aspirations and work commitment. Geographic residence information is available for all respondents. 1992-2000 residence surveys included questions on neighborhood characteristics (safety, apathy, and joblessness) addressed to female respondents. A separate dataset entitled Women's Support Network contains measures of the geographic proximity of residences of relatives, friends, and acquaintances to female respondents interviewed in 1983-1985 surveys. Family background, demographic characteristics, and household composition cover basic information on each respondent's age, racial/ethnic identity, date of birth, country of birth, state of birth, religious affiliations, number of members in the household, and their relationship to the respondent, household members' schooling, and work experience. The 1993 survey gathered information on age, education, and fertility of as many as 13 biological siblings. Marital and fertility histories covered topics such as marital status, cohabitation (since the 2002 surveys), menarche, menopause, abortions, and pregnancies (for female respondents), first sexual intercourse, usage of contraceptive methods, and interaction with children. Childcare items request information about the types of childcare used by female respondents, the associated childcare payments, and hours spent by children in childcare.

National Longitudinal Study of Youth 1997

The National Longitudinal Survey of Youth 1997 (NLSY97)[14] consists of a nationally representative sample of 8,984 youths who were 12 to 16 years old as of December 31, 1996. The sample is designed to be a representative sample

---

[14] See http://www.bls.gov/nls/handbook/2005/nlshc2.pdf [November 2010].

of youth in the United States. Two subsamples within the NLSY97 are a cross-sectional sample of 6,748 respondents and a supplemental sample of 2,236 respondents designed to oversample Hispanics, Latinos, and African Americans. Most of the survey respondents in round one of the survey were in high school. Only in round one, parents were also surveyed. Round one asked questions that addressed the transitioning of students from school to college to work and their choices concerning marriage and children. Retention rate was around 90 percent until 2000. The twelfth round of the survey in 2008 had a retention rate of 83.3 percent.

NLSY97 has 11 data elements:

1. Employment
2. Schooling
3. Training
4. Income, assets, and program participation
5. Family formation
6. Family background
7. Expectations
8. Attitudes, behaviors, and time use
9. Health
10. Environmental variables
11. Event history variables

The employment section has three categories: employee jobs, freelance or self-employment jobs, and gaps between jobs. The data file includes a week-by-week longitudinal work record for each respondent from his or her fourteenth birthday. For the first two employment categories, respondents were asked about the start and end date of employment, number of hours worked, earnings. Respondents reporting employment gaps were asked about the reasons for and period of gap.

The schooling section contains questions on educational attainment, experiences, and coursework. The parent questionnaire was administered in round one to reveal more about the respondent's past and current school experience. Round one also included administration of ASVAB (Armed Services Vocational Aptitude Battery), a military enlistment test, and PIAT (Peabody Individual Achievement Test). ACT and SAT scores were also collected. In the first round, detailed information about Advanced Placement (AP) tests (grade, test date, subject of test, highest AP score received) taken by respondents were also collected. Rounds two to seven recorded only the subject of AP tests taken. NLSY97 also included 1996 and 2000 school surveys, which collected information from all high schools with a twelfth grade in the 147 NLSY97 primary sampling units. The schooling section has items on college and college choice. College choice questions ask about the range of colleges the respondent applied to. Data on the types of scholarships and financial aid offered to the respondent by each institution is also requested. Institutional information is collected so that the IPEDS code can be assigned; it is available in restricted files. College questions ask youths their enrollment patterns, number and types of colleges attended (two-year or four-year), type of degree sought, credits received, major choice, college GPA, tuition, and fees. Sources and amounts of financial aid are also reported.

The training section requests information about participation in training programs-reasons for participation, type of certification, program's length, contents, completion status, and source of funding. If the training is undertaken for a specific employer, respondents are asked about the occupation which he or she aims to pursue and the reason for enrolling in the program.

The section on income, assets, and program participation is similar to the income and assets section in NLSY79. The parent questionnaire included in round one gathered data from parents on the youth's earnings and income in the previous year and the amount of support provided to financially independent youths. Under assets, respondents were asked about their bank accounts. Round seven included a section which asked respondents about their knowledge of welfare programs.

Questions on marriage, fertility, and child care were asked in the family formation section. In round one and rounds four to seven, questions on quality of relationships was included. In the fertility section, female respondents report about the details of failed pregnancies, while male respondents answered questions on fathering a child. The child care section had more detailed questions on persons providing transportation to childcare center, traveling time, etc. The family background section addresses demographic characteristics and household composition. Along with income questions, parents were asked about their history of participation in welfare programs.

In round one, the expectation section asked respondents about the probability of an event occurring in their life by next year, by age 20 and by age 30. These events were getting an academic degree, serving time in prison and working. In round four, similar questions were asked about probability of event occurrence within the next five years. The attitudes section collects information on youths' opinions about their parents, about parent's knowledge of the respondent's activities, whom they turn to for advice, perception of the criminal justice system, peer behavior, attitudes toward teachers, and perception of school environment. The section on domains of influence was introduced in round seven. It collects information about the identity of the persons who offer the respondent advice on financial issues, employment, education, training, and personal relationships. Questions on religious preference and beliefs, and frequency of attendance at religious services are included in the youth and parent questionnaire.

The behavior sections are similar to the alcohol and substance use and behavior section in NLSY79. A series of questions on time use were asked from round one to three. General health statuses of respondents are collected in the health sections. Rounds one to six asked about health-related behaviors and practices such as seatbelt use, nutrition, and exercise.

Environmental variables are created using information provided by respondents. Questions address whether respondent's residence is in a rural or urban area and whether it is located in a metropolitan statistical area (MSA). Other questions address the local unemployment rate. Event history variables are specially created to summarize the timing of a variety of major life events for each respondent. The event history section is divided into four major sections: employment status, marital status, program participation, and schooling experiences. This group of variables denotes the requisite status of the respondent in the four major sections in each month following the fourteenth birthday of the respondent.

National Survey of College Graduates

The National Survey of College Graduates (NSCG)[15] is a longitudinal survey designed to provide data on the number and characteristics of experienced individuals with education and/or employment in science and engineering (S&E), or S&E-related fields in the United States. The two NSCG baseline surveys were conducted in 1993 and 2003. The 1993 survey is a decade-long longitudinal and biannual survey. The 1993 NSCG was a special baseline survey that included all those who had earned a bachelor's degree or higher prior to 4/1/90, regardless of field. The sample for this survey was drawn from 1990 Census Long Form respondents. The target population for this survey was thus more comprehensive than for the usual NSCG. The 1995 NSCG target population covered only the S&E population portion. The sample was selected from 1993 NSCG respondents and 1993 National Survey of Recent College Graduates (NSRCG) respondents. The 1995, 1997, and 1999 surveys had sampling frames similar to 1993, i.e., drawing from previous NSCG and NSRCG respondents. NSCG was not conducted in 2001. NSCG 1993 followed its respondents for six years.

The 2003 NSCG is a baseline survey which draws its sample from the 2000 Census Long Form respondents. 2003 survey respondents were noninstitutionalized individuals living in the U.S. during the reference week of October 1, 2003, holding a bachelor's or higher degree in any field (received prior to April 1, 2000), and under age 76. Those holding a Ph.D. earned in the United States in an S&E field will not be followed in the future NSCG survey cycles as these individuals are covered in Survey of Doctorate Recipients.

The 2003 NSCG is supposed to generate decade-long survey cycles as the 1993 NSCG did. Items in the 2003 survey cycle include demographic variables—age, sex, race/ethnicity, citizenship status, country of birth, country of citizenship, immigrant module (year of entry, type of visa, etc.), disability status, marital status, number of children; educational variables—educational history (field,

---

[15]See http://nsf.gov/statistics/survey.cfm [November 2010].

level, date received for each degree held), school enrollment status; occupation/work related variables—employment status (unemployed, employed part time, or employed full-time), geographic place of employment, occupation (current or previous job), primary work activity (e.g., teaching, basic research, etc.), salary, satisfaction and importance of various aspects of job, sector of employment (e.g., academia, industry, government, etc.), academic employment (positions, rank, and tenure) and work-related training; publications and patent activities.

National Survey of Recent College Graduates

The National Survey of Recent College Graduates (NSRCG)[16] provides information about individuals who recently obtained bachelor's or master's degrees in a science, engineering, or health (SEH) field two years prior to survey date. This group is of special interest to many decision makers, because it represents individuals who have recently made the transition from school to the workplace. The survey also provides information about individuals attending graduate school. Respondents are individuals who recently received bachelor's or master's degrees in an SEH field from a U.S. institution, were living in the United States during the survey reference week, and under age 76. The NSRCG sample is a two-stage sample. First a sample of institutions is selected. This sampling frame is derived from IPEDS. The selected institutions provide a list of graduates from which a sample of individuals is chosen. The first NSF-sponsored NSRCG (then known as New Entrants) was conducted in 1974. Subsequent surveys were conducted biannually. In the initial survey, data were collected only on bachelor's degree recipients, but all ensuing surveys included both bachelor's and master's degree recipients. NSRCG surveys conducted in 1980s contained individuals who received bachelor's degrees in engineering technology. As of 1993, they are no longer part of the sample. Individuals living outside the United States during the survey reference week were also not considered eligible for the survey.

The survey underwent extensive changes in the 1993 cycle. New topics included in the survey questionnaire were educational experience before and after receiving degree, graduate employment characteristics, relationship between education and employment, graduate background, and demographic characteristics. There were changes in the questions on major field and salary. The major field list was made more comparable with the Department of Education's Classification of Instructional Programs (CIP) and the occupation list was made more comparable with the Standard Occupational Classification (SOC) codes. Thus, the 1993 data on the number and percent working in science and engineering occupations are not comparable with previous years' results.

Items in the current survey cycle include demographic variables—age, sex, race/ethnicity, citizenship status, place of birth, country of birth, coun-

---

[16]See http://nsf.gov/statistics/survey.cfm [November 2010].

try of citizenship, disability status, marital status, number of children; educational variables—educational history (for each degree held: field, level, when received), employment status (unemployed, employed part-time, or employed full-time), educational attainment of parents, school enrollment status; financial variables—financial support and debt amount for undergraduate and graduate degree; occupation/work related variables—geographic place of employment, occupation (current or previous job), work activity (e.g., teaching, basic research, etc.), salary, overall satisfaction with principal job, sector of employment (e.g., academia, industry, government, etc.) and work-related training.

Differences Between National Survey of College Graduates and National Survey of Recent College Graduates

The NSCG is conducted by the Census Bureau for the NSF, while the NSRCG is conducted by the NSF itself. The population of interest is very similar in the NSCG and the NSRCG, but their sampling frame and data collection methods are different. The NSCG starts with a baseline survey based on the recent census data, while the NSRCG starts with a survey of institutions based on IPEDS data. In subsequent survey cycles, NSCG's sample is updated by a selected sample of respondents from the NSRCG. Thus, data from the NSRCG feeds into the NSCG. For the NSRCG, data collection starts at the institutional level and then goes down to student level. A two-stage process identifies a sample of selected graduates from selected institutions. In content, the NSCG stresses employment in academic sector, publications and patents and does not delve into financial obligations of the respondents. The NSRCG collects information on debt burden and sources of financial support. NSCG has a separate item on immigration information which is not covered by NSRCG. Under educational variables, NSRCG has an item on educational attainment of parents.

Survey of Graduate Students and Postdoctorates in Science and Engineering

The National Science Foundation-National Institutes of Health Survey of Graduate Students and Postdoctorates in Science and Engineering (also known as GSS)[17] is an annual survey of academic institutions in the United States. It collects data on the number and characteristics of graduate students, postdoctoral appointees, and doctorate-holding nonfaculty researchers in (S&E) and selected health fields. The NSF analyzes the survey data and produces results on graduate enrollment, postdoctoral appointments, and financial support.

The first survey was conducted in 1966. Since then, there have been substantial changes in terms of data collection efforts, sample sizes, and kinds of

---

[17]See http://nsf.gov/statistics/survey.cfm [December 2010].

institutions on whom data are collected. From 1966 through 1971, the NSF collected data from a limited number of doctorate-granting institutions through the NSF Graduate Traineeship Program. It requested data only on those S&E fields supported by NSF. Beginning with the 1972 survey, the NSF assigned this data collection effort to the Universities and Nonprofit Institutions Studies Group. From 1972 to 1975, the effort was gradually expanded to include additional S&E fields and all institutions known to have programs leading to a doctoral or master's degree. Due to this expansion, data for 1974 and earlier years are not strictly comparable with 1975 and later data.

In 1984, the survey design was changed to a stratified random sample with a certainty stratum that included all doctorate-granting institutions; all master's-granting, historically black colleges and universities; and all land-grant institutions. The remaining master's-granting institutions were divided into two sample strata, based on enrollment size. Enrollment data for 1984-1987 have been adjusted to reflect universe totals.

In 1988, surveying the entire eligible survey population was resumed for the first time since 1983. Since 1988 the survey has attempted to cover all institutions with doctoral or master's-granting programs in S&E or selected health fields and has excluded institutions without any such graduate programs. Also in 1988 the NSF reviewed and tightened the criteria for including departments in the GSS. The NSF considered those departments that were not primarily granting research degrees as not meeting the definition of S&E. This review process continued through the 1989-2006 survey cycles.

In 2007, a comprehensive review of the survey-eligible fields led to several changes. Many programs were eligible or were explicitly listed in the taxonomy for the first time, some were determined ineligible and other programs were reclassified from one field to another. The GSS-eligible programs were updated from the NCES 1990 Classification of Instructional Programs (CIP) taxonomy to the NCES 2000 CIP taxonomy. Due to the changes introduced in 2007, data for 2007 and 2008 are not directly comparable with data from previous years. It is important to note that not all data items were collected from all institutions in all survey years.

The GSS survey is a multi-level census on graduate students, postdoctoral appointees, doctorate-holding nonfaculty researchers, and academic institutions. The data collection is done in two stages. First an updated list of units (departments, programs, research centers, and health facilities) is created (to reflect GSS eligibility) by the school coordinator. Then data is collected on graduate students, postdoctoral appointees, and doctorate-holding nonfaculty researchers for each eligible unit. Because the GSS is a multi-level survey, different sets of variables are collected for different categories of survey respondents. Information on graduate students is collected under the following items: sex, race/ethnicity, citizenship, primary source, and mechanism of support and enrollment status. For postdoctoral appointees information is collected on sex, citizenship, primary mechanism of support and whether the individual holds a professional doctorate in a medical or related field. In the case of doctorate-holding nonfaculty researcher, variables collected are sex and whether the individual holds a professional doctorate in a medical or related field. At the institution level, information is available on highest degree granted, institution type, Carnegie classification, state of location and whether it is a historically black college or university.

Survey of Earned Doctorates

The Survey of Earned Doctorates (SED)[18] began in 1957-1958 to collect data continuously on the number and characteristics of individuals receiving research doctoral degrees from all accredited U.S. institutions. The results of this annual survey are used to assess characteristics and trends in doctorate education and degrees. This information is vital for educational and labor force planners within the federal government and in academia. The SED is sponsored by the following six federal agencies: National Science Foundation, National Institutes of Health, U.S. Department of Education, U.S. Department of Agriculture, National Endowment for the Humanities, and National Aeronautics and Space Administration. The Science Resources Statistics Division (SRS) of the NSF monitors the contract to conduct the SED.

All individuals receiving research doctorates from accredited U.S. institutions are asked to complete the survey. Each U.S. graduate school is responsible for providing the survey to their graduates and then submitting completed forms to the survey contractor. The SED is a census of all individuals receiving a research doctorate from a U.S. institution in the academic year (July 1 through June 30 of the next year). M.D., D.D.S., J.D., D.Pharm., and Psy.D degree holders are not included in the survey. The SED collects a complete college education history and therefore coding of institutions is very important. IPEDS provides the coding frame for the U.S. institutions where doctorate recipients earned their baccalaureate and/or master's degrees. As one-third of doctorate recipients from U.S. universities are citizens of foreign countries, a coding manual for foreign institutions of higher education was developed by the U.S. Department of Education, entitled "Mapping the World of Education: The Comparative Database System." This coding frame is used to code the baccalaureate and/or master's degree origins of U.S. doctorate recipients who earned earlier degrees in foreign countries.

From 1957 to 1997, SED data collection was done by the National Research Council (NRC) for the NSF. The National Opinion Research Center has been conducting the survey since then. Starting from 1998, there were changes in the response categories of marital status (new categories introduced) and source of funding (new coding frame by reducing categories). Items collected in the survey include demographic variables—age, sex, race/ethnicity, birth year, county

---

[18]See http://nsf.gov/statistics/survey.cfm [December 2010].

of birth, country of citizenship at graduation, disability status, marital status, number/age of dependents; educational variables—educational history in college, field of degree, baccalaureate-origin institution (U.S. or foreign), academic institution of doctorate, type of academic institution (e.g., historically black institutions, Carnegie codes, control) awarding the doctorate, educational attainment of parents; postgraduation plans—work/postdoc/training, primary and secondary work activities, type and location of employer; financial variables—graduate and undergraduate educational debt, sources of financial support during graduate school.

Survey of Doctorate Recipients

The Survey of Doctorate Recipients (SDR)[19] gathers information from individuals who have obtained a doctoral degree in an SEH field. The SDR is a biannual and longitudinal survey that follows recipients of research doctorates from U.S. institutions until age 76. This group is of special interest to many decision makers, because it represents some of the most highly educated individuals in the U.S. workforce. The SDR results are used by employers in the education, industry, and government sectors to understand and to predict trends in employment opportunities and salaries in SEH fields for graduates with doctoral degrees. The results are also used to evaluate the effectiveness of equal opportunity efforts. The NSF also finds the results important for internal planning, as most NSF grants go to individuals with doctoral degrees. Respondents were individuals with a research doctorate in a SEH field from a U.S. institution, were living in the United States during the survey reference week, noninstitutionalized and under age 76.

Before 1997 data collection for SDR was done by the NRC for the NSF. There were major changes in the 1993 cycle in survey instrument design and content. The format and layout of the questionnaires were changed to make them more accessible for respondents. This included using a larger font size for improved readability, using graphical aids to indicate skip patterns, and using reverse printing to indicate answer spaces. The survey instrument was expanded from eight pages to twenty pages. New questions were added to gather information on such topics as degrees earned since receipt of the first doctorate, relationship of degree to current job, and reasons for making job changes. Sections on employment and demographic characteristics were also modified to facilitate analysis of the relationship between educational attainment and occupational outcomes. Thus, pre-1993 SDR data and post-1993 SDR data are not strictly comparable.

Items in the 2006 survey cycle include demographic variables—age, sex, race/ethnicity, citizenship status, place of birth, country of birth, country of citizenship, disability status, marital status, number of children; educational

---

[19] See http://nsf.gov/statistics/survey.cfm [December 2010].

variables—educational history (for each degree held: field, level, institution, when received), educational attainment of parents, school enrollment status; financial variables—financial support and debt amount for undergraduate and graduate degree; postdoctorate status (current and/or three most recent postdoctoral appointments); occupation/work related variables—employment status (part-time, full-time, unemployed), geographic place of employment, occupation (current or previous job), work activity (e.g., teaching, basic research, etc.), salary, overall satisfaction and importance of various aspects of job, sector of employment (e.g., academia, industry, government, etc.), and work-related training.

The data from the SDR are combined with that from two other NSF surveys of scientists and engineers, the NSCG and the NSRCG. The three surveys are closely coordinated and share the same reference date and nearly identical instruments. The database developed from the three surveys, the Scientists and Engineers Statistical Data System (SESTAT), provides a comprehensive picture of the number and characteristics of individuals with training and/or employment in science, engineering, or related fields in the United States.

Differences Between Survey of Earned Doctorates and Survey of Doctorate Recipients

The SED is a *census* of all individuals who received a research doctoral degree *irrespective of the field of degree*. The graduate schools collect questionnaires from degree recipients at the time of completion of degree. Data from SED does not require sampling, weighting, or adjustments for nonresponse. Survey of Doctorate Recipients (SDR) is a longitudinal *survey* of individuals who have received a research doctoral degree in a *science, engineering, or health field* (SEH). SED respondents are not followed. In each biannual cycle of SDR, its sample frame is augmented by new cohorts of science and engineering doctorate recipients identified by the SED. Thus, SDR draws its sampling frame from SED. The two surveys also differ in key variables collected. The SED concentrates on the type and field of degree received, debt burden, and postgraduation plans, while SDR concentrates more on work experiences after attaining degree. The SED also asks about previously received foreign degrees and educational attainment of parents.

Statewide Longitudinal Data System (SLDS)

The Statewide Longitudinal Data Systems (SLDS)[20] Grant Program, as authorized by the Educational Technical Assistance Act of 2002, Title II of the statute that created the Institute of Education Sciences (IES), is designed to aid state education agencies in developing and implementing longitudinal data sys-

---

[20]See http://nces.ed.gov/programs/slds/ [December 2010].

tems. These systems are intended to enhance the ability of states to efficiently and accurately manage, analyze, and use education data, including individual student records. The data systems developed with funds from these grants should help states, districts, schools, and teachers make data-driven decisions to improve student learning, as well as facilitate research to increase student achievement and close achievement gaps. These competitive, cooperative agreement grants extend for three to five years and provide up to $20 million per grantee. Grantees are obligated to submit annual reports and a final report on the development and implementation of their systems. All fifty states, five territories, and the District of Columbia are eligible to apply. In November 2005, the first year of the grant program, IES awarded SLDS grants to fourteen states. SLDS grants were awarded to twelve additional states and the District of Columbia in June 2007 (FY 2007 Grantees), twenty-seven states—including fifteen new states—in March 2009 (FY 2009 Grantees), and twenty states in May 2010 (FY 2009 ARRA Grantees). NCES administers the grants and also provides technical assistance to grant recipients. Grant amount ranges from $1.5 million to $39.7 million and will be disbursed over a period of three to five years. The SLDS grant program is jointly sponsored by federal government and state governments. Lessons learned and nonproprietary products or solutions developed by recipients of these grants will be disseminated to aid other state and local education agencies in the design, development, implementation, and use of longitudinal data systems.

State Student Unit Record (SUR) Databases

Forty-five states have Student Unit Record Databases (SUR)[21] in place. Some states, such as California and Texas, have had such a system in place for a long time; others have developed these databases only recently. The SUR system is established by a state's legislature or Board of Regents for purposes that range from student tracking to resource allocation. Two-year and four-year public institutions are included in the SUR system. In some cases, as in Florida, the SUR system may also include K-12 institutions. The databases contain records of students enrolled in public institutions in a state. Data elements covered in SUR can be categorized into:

- Demographics—sex, race/ethnicity, date of birth, citizenship, geographic origin, and disability status.
- Academic background—admission test scores, high school attended, high school class size, high school rank, high school GPA, high school graduation date, prior college attended, transfer credit, remedial status, placement test scores.

---

[21]See http://www.nchems.org/c2sp/sur/ [January 2011].

- Enrollment status—degree seeking status, first term of academic, history, full-time/part-time, program/major, financial aid details, join enrollment status, distance education status.
- Academic activity—term data collected, term GPA, term credits attempted, term credits earned.
- Academic attainment—cumulative GPA, cumulative credits earned, degree awarded.

Most of these data elements are collected by forty-nine states. Other data elements, such as disability status, high school class size, high school rank, remedial status, placement test scores, and joint enrollment status, are collected by fewer than twenty state systems.

National Survey of Student Engagement (NSSE)

The purpose of conducting the National Survey of Student Engagement (NSSE)[22] is to understand the quality of education being offered by institutions. The survey focuses on college experiences—gains made in learning, program expectations, and future plans. The NSSE was conceived in early 1998 and supported by a grant from The Pew Charitable Trusts. The NSSE conducted a successful pilot in 1999 that involved more than 75 selected four-year colleges and universities. Approximately 275 colleges and universities participated in the inaugural survey in the spring of 2000. In 2010 the number of participating institutions rose to 603. In 2009, 363,859 students participated in the survey. The sample consists of institutions from the United States and Canada. An institution which registers for the survey is required to post a message to its students that it is participating in the NSSE. The institution has discretion to select methods to encourage student participation. Each student in the institution is sent an e-mail message with the survey questionnaire embedded or is mailed the paper questionnaire depending on the mode chosen by the institution. Survey components include college activities—class work and preparation, faculty interaction, peer interaction, mental activities emphasized by coursework, time use, activities planned before graduation; educational and personal growth—contribution of college education to knowledge, skills and personal development; opinions about the school—activities emphasized by school, relationships among faculty, staff and students; and background information-age, gender, ethnicity, nationality, educational status of parents, level, grade received till now, types of schools attended since high school, current term enrollment status, sorority or fraternity membership, residency status, living alone or with others (parents, relative, roommates), and field of major.

---

[22]See http://nsse.iub.edu/html/about.cfm [January 2011].

Beginning College Survey of Student Engagement (BCSSE)

In Beginning College Survey of Student Engagement (BCSSE),[23] the population of interest is students entering college. The survey is administered to first-year college or university students by Indiana University's Center for Survey Research and Center for Postsecondary Research. The BCSSE began in 2007 and had its fourth round in 2010. 72,954 entering first-year students across 129 institutions participated in the 2009 survey.

Administration of BCSSE is similar to NSSE. Survey components are high school experiences—year of graduation, high school grade, performance in math classes, years in a particular subject classes, completion of AP or honors or college credit courses, amount of reading and writing in the last year of high school, time use, class participation, faculty interaction, peer interaction, SAT/ACT scores, and participation in various activities; college experiences—expectation of time use, grades in coming year, highest degree attainment, expectations about involvement in class and course-related work, interacting with faculty and peers, expectation of difficulty level of course material, time management, paying college expenses, expectations from college or university, financial aid information; and additional information—gender, ethnicity, nationality, enrollment status, close friends attending the same college, parental education, and distance of college from home.

Faculty Survey of Student Engagement

Faculty Survey of Student Engagement (FSSE)[24] is a complement to the NSSE. Its purpose is to measure faculty expectations of student engagement and it can be linked to results from the NSSE. The survey started in 2003. Thus far, 140,000 faculty members from 590 institutions have participated. Institutions that are participating in NSSE or have done so the previous year are eligible to administer the faculty survey. With results from both surveys, it is possible to compare student and faculty answers to the same questions. The mode of the survey is Web-based only. Each institution selects its sample from faculty who teach at least one undergraduate course in the current academic year. Institutions provide the names and e-mail addresses of faculty to be surveyed. All other aspects of the survey administration are handled by FSSE (i.e., e-mails to faculty, follow-up, data collection, and analysis). Faculty responses to the survey remain anonymous to their institution. Survey components include items on faculty perceptions of how often students engage in different activities, the importance faculty place on various areas of learning and development, the nature and frequency of faculty-

---

[23]See http://bcsse.iub.edu/ [January 2011].
[24]See http://fsse.iub.edu/ [January 2011].

student interactions and how faculty members organize their time, both in and out of the classroom.

Community College Survey of Student Engagement

To address the specific needs of students enrolled in community colleges, Community College Survey of Student Engagement (CCSSE)[25] was initiated in 2001. The survey aims to fill the gap left by NSSE which draws its sample from four-year institutions only. CCSSE can be considered a partner survey of NSSE and is administered by the Community College Leadership Program at The University of Texas at Austin. The survey is administered to students in randomly selected classes (credit courses only) at each participating college. The required number of course sections to be surveyed is determined by the total sample size. Therefore, sample sizes range from approximately 600 to approximately 1,200 students, depending on institutional size. For colleges with less than 1,500 students, the targeted sample size will be about 20 percent of total credit enrollment. A unique feature available to participating institutions is that they can chose to oversample to provide sufficient data for analysis in an area of interest, such as how successful an institution is in educating students from an ethnic community. Community colleges have multiple campuses and classes are offered in various sites. Oversampling can help also them to understand the relative efficacy of different campuses.

Questionnaire items in CCSSE are similar to NSSE items except for a few questions tailored for community college students. Survey components are college activities, educational and personal growth and background information. Extra items included topics such as support from friends and immediate family, social life in college, Internet availability and use, reasons for attending community college, reasons which would force one to withdraw from college, financial sources, number and type of classes enrolled, credits earned, details about joint enrollment status, child care situation, and English as native or first language.

Starting in 2006, a few supplemental questions were added. Their focus has changed from year to year:

- 2006: item on academic advising—identity of advisor, whether advisor provided up-to-date information, quality of working relationship with advisor and whether advising helped the student in setting academic goals and achieving them.
- 2007: item on entering student experience—meeting with an academic advisor, completion of assessment test, teaching methods, satisfaction with quality of new student orientation.

---

[25]See http://www.ccsse.org/aboutsurvey/aboutsurvey.cfm [January 2011].

- 2008: item on student financial aid—submission of a Free Application for Federal Student Aid (FAFSA), reasons for not submitting details about other sources of financial aid.
- 2009: item on technology—usage of social networking sites or course management systems by students for communication with other students, instructors or college staff about coursework and usage of social networking sites by the college to communicate with student about various services.
- 2010: item on deep learning—usage of interdisciplinary ideas and diverse perspectives to finish assignments or participate in class discussions, evaluate own views, empathize with another's viewpoint.
- 2011: item on practices for student success—freshman orientation experience, participation in student development courses, clarity of instruction activity, usage of college-provided material and participation in brief or multi-day refresher workshop to prepare for placement test, completion of college placement test, kind of courses taken due to results of placement tests, help from academic advisor and participation in group learning or tutoring or supplemental instruction/learning.

Community College Faculty Survey of Student Engagement

Community College Faculty Survey of Student Engagement (CCFSSE)[26] is a complement to CCSSE. Its purpose is to measure faculty expectations of student engagement and can be linked to the results from CCSSE. The survey started in 2005. At that time, thirty-nine community colleges participated. For CCFSSE 2011, 180 colleges have registered. Institutions which are participating in CCSSE or have done so the previous year are eligible to administer the faculty survey. The mode of the survey is Web-based only. Administration of CCFSSE is equivalent to that of FSSE. Survey components are very similar to FSSE, with few extra items to take into account special features of community college students. Participating faculty members are asked questions on frequency of referral and usage and importance of services provided by community colleges. Services included in the questionnaire are academic advising/planning, career counseling, job placement assistance, peer or other tutoring, skill labs (writing, math, etc.), child care, financial aid advising, computer lab, student organizations, transfer credit assistance, and service to students with disabilities. Faculty were specifically asked about their work status (part-time or full-time), total number of credit hours scheduled to teach in the current academic term, components of teaching assignment, academic rank, tenure status, teaching experience, and educational qualification.

---

[26]See http://www.ccsse.org/CCFSSE/CCFSSE.cfm [January 2011].

Law School Survey of Student Engagement

Law School Survey of Student Engagement (LSSSE)[27] is a survey oriented toward law school students. The purpose of the survey is to gather information on law school experience, including how students spend their time, what they feel they've gained from their classes, their assessment of the quality of interactions with faculty and friends, and their view of important activities. LSSSE is housed in Indiana University Center for Postsecondary Research and is co-sponsored by the Association of American Law Schools and the Carnegie Foundation for the Advancement of Teaching. The survey is administered similarly to NSSE but is Web-based only. More than 160 law schools have participated since 2004. Around 25,000 law students participated in the 2010 survey. Survey components are very similar to NSSE except for few extra items tailored to law students. Extra items covered topics such as choice of law school, sexual orientation, enrollment in joint degree programs, time gap in years between undergraduate education and law school, expected amount of educational debt upon graduation, area of legal specialization, preferable and expected work environment.

National Study of Student Learning

The National Study of Student Learning (NSSL) was a longitudinal research project that ran from 1992 to 1995. It examined the influence of academic and nonacademic experiences on student learning, student attitudes about learning, student cognitive development, and student persistence. Eighteen four-year and five two-year postsecondary institutions participated in the study, with data collected from a total of 3,840 students. The eight areas of inquiry focused on the effects of: (1) attending a two-year college in comparison to a four-year college on cognitive development; (2) attending a historically black college compared to a predominantly white college on cognitive development; (3) teacher behavior on cognitive development; (4) first-generation college attendance on cognitive development and attitudes; (5) intercollegiate athletic participation on cognitive development; (6) institutional environment and students' academic and nonacademic experiences on students' openness to cultural and racial diversity; (7) affiliation with a fraternity or sorority on cognitive development during the first year of college; and (8) in-class and out-of-class experiences on first-year students' critical thinking ability. Analysis of the data found little difference in the cognitive gains made by students attending two-year versus four-year institutions, or historically black versus predominantly white institutions.

---

[27]See http://lssse.iub.edu/about.cfm [January 2011].

International Enrollment Survey and Study Abroad Survey

International Enrollment Survey and Study Abroad Survey[28] are two surveys conducted by Institute of International Education starting in 2000. They collect data on the number of international students attending various U.S. postsecondary institutions and the number of U.S. citizens studying abroad in foreign countries. The surveys was are carried out by the Institute of International Education (IIE) in cooperation with American Association of Community Colleges (AACC), American Association of State Colleges and Universities (AASCU), American Council on Education (ACE), Association of American Universities (AAU), Association of Public and Land-grant Universities (APLU), Council of Graduate Schools (CGS), and NAFSA: Association of International Educators. A total of 688 institutions participated in the 2009-2010 survey.

The international enrollment survey provide information on newly enrolled international students such as the countries of origin, kind of academic programs enrolled in, the most welcoming state, city and institution. At the institutional level, information is collected on total enrollment of such students in various programs. Similar variables are collected for students who are studying abroad— host country, academic program, and duration of program. The data are obtained each year through surveys sent to approximately 3,000 accredited U.S. higher education institutions, who report on the international students enrolled at their campuses. The IIE was founded in 1919 with a mission to collect information on enrollment of international students in the United States. The data has been published as part of IIE's Open Doors project since 1954. The Open Doors project is supported by the U.S. Information Agency.

IIE has been conducting the surveys on study abroad flows since 1985/86. The *Open Doors* Study Abroad survey counts only those students who received academic credit from an accredited U.S. institution of higher education after they returned from their study abroad experience. Students who travel and take courses abroad without receiving academic credit are not reported in *Open Doors*, nor are students who are enrolled overseas for degrees from non-U.S. institutions.

National Student Clearinghouse

The National Student Clearinghouse (NSC)[29] is a central repository of student enrollment and graduation information. Its purpose is to provide the required enrollment information to the servicers and guarantors of the Federal Student Loan Programs. The Clearinghouse was designed primarily to service the Federal Family Education Loan Program (FFELP) loans, which include Stafford, Supple-

---

[28]See http://www.iie.org/en/Research-and-Publications/Open-Doors [December 2010].
[29]See http://studentclearinghouse.com/about/aboutus.htm [January 2011].

mental Loans for Students (SLS), PLUS and Consolidation loans, both through traditional lenders and through the Federal Direct Lending Program.

More than 3,300 institutions and hundreds of school districts participate in the Clearinghouse, representing 92 percent of total U.S. college enrollment. It was originally created to provide lending organizations with enrollment verifications and deferments of financial aid students. Over time, it expanded to verify degrees of graduates to employers, background search firms, and recruiters. Other data users include federal government agencies, student health insurance providers, student credit issuers and student loan providers. The Clearinghouse also allows students who transfer from one participating school to another to continue their in-school deferment status without inherent delays. Participating institutions can send files of students of interest to the database and receive appended information containing number of schools and colleges attended, dates of enrollment and degree (if any) earned. The student tracker tool follows students across colleges/universities and across states. The Clearinghouse helps an institution to know about the educational background of currently enrolled students, educational pathways of drop-outs and prospective students who did not enroll, and also postbaccalaureate pathways of graduates. Even though it is a comprehensive database following most students over time, the number of variables collected is very limited. There is no information on college experiences, jobs or internships during college education, expectations, and plans for future, etc.

Unemployment Insurance Wage Record Data[30]

State Employment Security Agencies (SESA) collect employment and earning reports from employers on a quarterly basis. The data is collected by these state agencies to aid the process of administering the nationwide system of unemployment compensation. SESA uses the information to determine the tax liability of employers for unemployment compensation and verification purposes. Even though wage record data is collected by state agencies, there is commonality across states. The common factors are social security numbers of all employees in the state who are covered by unemployment insurance, their quarterly earnings, the standard industrial code, business name and address of employer. The employment and earnings data cover around 90 percent of the working population.

---

[30]U.S. Congress, Office of Technology Assessment, Wage Record Information Systems, OTA-BP-HER-127 (Washington, DC, May 1994).

Appendix D

Estimating Project-Related Departmental Research

Recommendation (7) calls for an "estimate of the departmental research (DR) directly associated with sponsored research projects (now typically considered part of the instructional cost in universities' accounts)," which should be excluded from faculty instructional labor. The algorithm will have to be developed through a special study, since it appears impractical to capture the data directly in university accounting systems.

Two options suggest themselves:

- **Alternative 1:** Acquire a sample of faculty reports that include time allocations and regress the average departmental research allocation, excluding academic year salary offsets, against the department's sponsored research funding. Minor public service activities might be included as well, if they are not separately budgeted. This could provide the basis for adjusting the institution's overall faculty cost for research, but some adjustment for field would be required. Nonfaculty costs would not be adjusted. (The research design needs to be elaborated.)
- **Alternative 2:** Array data for sponsored research per faculty FTE into deciles. Set the percentage of faculty time for the top decile to the results of a sample of reported time allocations for a sample of very research-intensive institutions. Scale the other deciles linearly to zero at the lowest decile.

These options need more research, particularly with regard to determining the time allocation percentages, probably through a survey on time use by faculty for a sample of institutions. The sample should be representative of the current institution segment mix. The Faculty Survey on Student Engagement has an item on number of hours spent in a seven-day week on various activities:

1. Teaching undergraduates
2. Grading paper and exams
3. Giving feedback to students
4. Preparing for class
5. Reflecting on improving teaching
6. Research and scholarly activities
7. Working with undergraduates on research
8. Advising undergraduate students
9. Supervising internship
10. Working with students on activities other than coursework
11. Interacting with students outside classroom
12. Conducting service activities

This structure may provide a good starting point for the analysis.

Appendix E

Biographical Sketches of Panel Members

TERESA A. SULLIVAN (*Chair*) was named the eighth president of the University of Virginia in January 2010. She was previously provost and executive vice president for academic affairs at the University of Michigan, where she was also professor of sociology in the College of Literature, Science, and the Arts. Earlier, she was executive vice chancellor for academic affairs for the University of Texas System, having served as vice president and graduate dean, vice provost, and chair of the sociology department at the University of Texas at Austin. She has also held faculty appointments at the University of Chicago. A member of the law school faculty at Texas in addition to the sociology department, her research focuses on labor force demography, with particular emphasis on economic marginality and consumer debt. She is author or co-author of 6 books and more than 50 scholarly articles, and her most recent work examined the question of who files for bankruptcy and why. Ms. Sullivan has served as chair of the U.S. Census Advisory Committee. She is past secretary of the American Sociological Association and a fellow of the American Association for the Advancement of Science. A graduate of James Madison College at Michigan State University, Ms. Sullivan received her doctoral degree in sociology from the University of Chicago.

THOMAS R. BAILEY is the George and Abby O'Neill professor of economics and education in the Department of International and Transcultural Studies at Teachers College, Columbia University. In 1996, he established the Community College Research Center at Teachers College, which conducts qualitative and quantitative research based on fieldwork at community colleges and analysis of national- and state-level datasets. Dr. Bailey has examined the role of community colleges in promoting educational attainment of black and Hispanic students in a recently completed study for the Ford Foundation. Since 1992, Dr. Bailey has also been the director of the Institute on Education and the Economy at Teachers College. He has served as a consultant to many public agencies and foundations including the U.S. Department of Labor, the U.S. Department of Education, the Office of Technology Assessment, the Alfred P. Sloan Foundation, the William T. Grant Foundation, and several state and local economic development and educational agencies. Dr. Bailey holds a Ph.D. in labor economics from Massachusetts Institute of Technology.

BARRY P. BOSWORTH is a senior fellow in the Economic Studies Program and is the Robert V. Roosa chair in international economics at the Brookings Institution. His research includes work on the determinants of economic growth in developing countries, saving, and capital formation. He was director of the President's Council on Wage and Price Stability in 1977-1979; visiting lecturer at the University of California, Berkeley, 1974-1975; and assistant professor, Harvard University, 1969-1971. Some recent publications include *The Economy of Puerto Rico: Restoring Growth*, with Susan Collins and Miguel A. Soto-Class (2006); *Services Productivity in the United States: New Sources of Economic Growth*, with Jack Triplett (2004); "The Empirics of Growth: An Update," Brookings Papers on Economic Activity (2003), with Susan Collins; "Increased Life Expectancy: A Global Perspective," with Benjamin Keys, in Henry Aaron and William Schwartz (editors), *Coping with Methuselah* (2003); *Aging Societies: The Global Dimension* (1998), edited with Gary Burtless; *Coming Together? Mexico-U.S. Relations* (1997), edited with Susan M. Collins and Nora Lustig; and "Valuing the Renminbi," Tokyo Club Papers (2004). He holds a Ph.D. from the University of Michigan.

DAVID W. BRENEMAN is university professor and Newton and Rita Meyers professor in economics of education at the University of Virginia. He previously served (2006-2009) as director of the public policy program at the Batten School of Leadership and Public Policy. From 1995 to 2007, he served as dean of the Curry School of Education. He also serves as a member of the Board of Trustees for Sweet Briar College. Dr. Breneman was visiting professor at the Harvard Graduate School of Education from 1990 to 1995, where he taught graduate courses on the economics and financing of higher education, on liberal arts colleges, and on the college presidency. As a visiting fellow at the Brookings Institution, he conducted research for a book, *Liberal Arts Colleges: Thriving, Surviving, or Endangered?*, published by Brookings in 1994. From 1983 to 1989, Dr. Breneman served as president of Kalamazoo College, a liberal arts college in Michigan. Prior to that, he was a senior fellow at Brookings from 1975 to 1983, specializing in the economics of higher education and public policy toward education. He holds a Ph.D. in economics from the University of California, Berkeley.

RONALD G. EHRENBERG is the Irving M. Ives professor of industrial and labor relations and economics at Cornell University and director of the Cornell Higher Education Research Institute. From 1995 to 1998, he served as Cornell's vice president for Academic Programs, Planning, and Budgeting. A member of the Cornell faculty for 28 years, Dr. Ehrenberg has authored or co-authored over 120 papers and books. He is a research associate at the National Bureau of Economic Research and a past president of the Society of Labor Economists. At the National Research Council, Dr. Ehrenberg has previously served on the Committee on Dimensions, Causes, and Implications of Trends in Early Career Events for Life Scientists and the Committee on Methods for Forecasting Demand and Supply of Doctoral Scientists and Engineers; he is also a member of the PGA Oversight Committee and previously served on the OSEP Advisory Committee. He holds a Ph.D. in economics from Northwestern University.

PETER T. EWELL is vice president at the National Center for Higher Education Management Systems (NCHEMS) in Boulder, Colorado, a research and development center founded to improve the management effectiveness of colleges and universities. A member of the staff since 1981, Dr. Ewell's work focuses on assessing institutional effectiveness and the outcomes of college, and involves both research and direct consulting with institutions and state systems on collecting and using assessment information in planning, evaluation, and budgeting. Dr. Ewell has authored six books and numerous articles on the topic of improving undergraduate instruction through the assessment of student outcomes. Prior to joining NCHEMS, Dr. Ewell was coordinator for long-range planning at Governors State University and was on the faculty of the University of Chicago. In addition to consulting in higher education, Dr. Ewell has been involved in program evaluation, organizational development, and strategic planning for a variety of nonprofit and arts organizations, including the National Endowment for the Arts and six state arts agencies. He holds a Ph.D. in political science from Yale University.

IRWIN FELLER is senior visiting scientist at the American Association for the Advancement of Science. He is also emeritus professor of economics and former director and professor of economics for the Institute for Policy Research and Evaluation at Pennsylvania State University. His research interests include science and technology policy, the economics of higher education, and program evaluation. He has published widely on topics such as the influence of the Government Performance and Results Act on research, technology diffusion from university research, research performance measurement, the university role in basic research, and state and federal technology policy. He has been a consultant to the President's Office of Science and Technology Policy; the National Aeronautics and Space Administration; the Carnegie Commission on Science, Technology, and Government; the Ford Foundation; the National Science Foundation; the National Institute of Standards and Technology; the COSMOS Corporation; SRI

International; the U.S. Government Accountability Office; and the U.S. Departments of Education and Energy. Dr. Feller is a member of the American Economic Association, the American Association for the Advancement of Science, and the Association for Public Policy Analysis and Management. He is currently a member of the National Research Council Committee to Review EPA's Title 42 Hiring Authority for Highly Qualified Scientists and Engineers. Dr. Feller holds a Ph.D. in economics from the University of Minnesota.

BARBARA FRAUMENI is associate dean of research, chair of the Ph.D. program, and professor of public policy at the Muskie School of Public Service of the University of Southern Maine. She previously served as chief economist of the Bureau of Economic Analysis and was a research fellow of the Program on Technology and Economic Policy at the John F. Kennedy School of Government at Harvard University. Her areas of expertise and research interests include measurement issues and national income accounting; human and nonhuman capital, productivity, and economic growth; market and nonmarket accounts; investment in education and research and development; and measurement of highway capital stock and the real output of government by function. Dr. Fraumeni served on the National Research Council's Panel to Study the Design of Nonmarket Accounts. She holds a B.A. from Wellesley College and a Ph.D. from Boston College.

JULIET V. GARCIA is president of the University of Texas at Brownsville and Texas Southmost College, and is the first Mexican-American woman in the nation selected to lead a college or a university. She is known for her pioneering effort to design and establish a unique partnership between the pre-existing community college and the newly created University of Texas at Brownsville. Under her leadership, the newly created "community university" has grown from 7,300 to almost 14,000 students, expanded its degree offerings to multiple new associate, bachelor's, and graduate programs, and transformed a 47-acre community college campus into a 380-acre university campus with new state-of-the-art facilities. Dr. Garcia serves on the board of directors for the Public Welfare Foundation, the Ford Foundation, Campus Compact, and the National Audubon Society. She is the former chair of the American Council on Education and the Advisory Committee to Congress on Student Financial Assistance and the former vice chair of the Carnegie Foundation for the Advancement of Teaching. She holds a Ph.D. in communication and linguistics from the University of Texas at Austin.

MICHAEL HOUT is professor of sociology and demography at the University of California, Berkeley. Dr. Hout currently chairs the Graduate Group in Sociology and Demography and the Berkeley Population Center. He has published widely in the areas of demography, inequality, religion, social change, and quantitative methods. His honors include the Clogg Award from the Population Association of America in 1997, and election to the American Academy of Arts and Sciences in

1997, the National Academy of Sciences in 2003, and the American Philosophical Society in 2006. At the National Research Council, Dr. Hout previously served on the Committee for the Redesign of the U.S. Naturalization Tests and is currently a member of the Committee on National Statistics, the Board on Testing and Assessment, and the Committee on Incentives and Test-based Accountability. He holds M.A. and Ph.D. degrees in sociology from Indiana University.

NATE JOHNSON is a senior consultant to HCM Strategists on higher education policy, funding, and student success issues. He has worked in education policy, planning, and institutional research at the national, state, and institutional levels. He previously served for five years as executive director of planning and analysis for the State University System of Florida in the office of the chancellor. He facilitated the first statewide strategic plan for the Board of Governors after it was created in the Florida Constitution in 2003. He also served as associate director of institutional research at the University of Florida and as a policy analyst in Florida's nationally recognized Office of Articulation, where he helped develop policies related to inter-sector transfer, high school graduation standards, and college admissions. He holds a bachelor's degree from Whitman College and a Ph.D. in English literature from Cornell University.

GEORGE D. KUH is chancellor's professor emeritus of higher education and founding director of the Center for Postsecondary Research in the School of Education at Indiana University. His research interests include assessing student and institutional performance to enhance student success and to improve the quality of the undergraduate experience. Dr. Kuh founded the National Survey of Student Engagement (NSSE) and related surveys for law students, beginning college students, and faculty along with the NSSE Institute for Effective Educational Practice. Since 1994, he has directed the College Student Experience Questionnaire Research Program. Dr. Kuh was a member of the National Research Council Panel on Student Processes and Outcomes. He holds a Ph.D. in education from the University of Iowa.

WILLIAM F. MASSY is professor emeritus of education and business administration at Stanford University. From 1995 to 2009, he was president of the Jackson Hole Higher Education Group, Inc., a specialist in the economic and leadership issues confronting today's colleges and universities. In the 1970s and 1980s, he held senior administrative positions at Stanford University, where he pioneered the use of financial management and planning tools that have become standards in higher education. After founding the Stanford Institute for Higher Education Research in 1988, Dr. Massy's research focused on institutional strategy, faculty roles and responsibilities, resource allocation processes, and universities as systems. He holds a Ph.D. in economics from Massachusetts Institute of Technology.

CAROL A. TWIGG is president and chief executive officer of the National Center for Academic Transformation in Saratoga Springs, New York, and an internationally recognized expert in using information technology to transform teaching and learning in higher education. Winner of the McGraw Prize in Education, she is former vice president of Educom (now EDUCAUSE), where she advanced the need for new models of student-centered, online teaching and learning, now commonly accepted in higher education. She also initiated the IMS Global Learning Consortium, which is establishing interoperable technical standards for online education and training. Before joining Educom, Dr. Twigg was associate vice chancellor for learning technologies for the State University of New York and held a number of senior academic administrative positions at Empire State College. She holds a Ph.D. in English literature from the State University of New York at Buffalo.

DAVID J. ZIMMERMAN is Orrin Sage professor of political economy and professor of economics at Williams College. He is also director of the Williams Project on the Economics of Higher Education and a research associate at the National Bureau of Economic Research. His research interests include labor economics, poverty and income distribution, and the economics of higher education. He holds M.A. and Ph.D. degrees, both in economics, from Princeton University.

COMMITTEE ON NATIONAL STATISTICS

The Committee on National Statistics (CNSTAT) was established in 1972 at the National Academies to improve the statistical methods and information on which public policy decisions are based. The committee carries out studies, workshops, and other activities to foster better measures and fuller understanding of the economy, the environment, public health, crime, education, immigration, poverty, welfare, and other public policy issues. It also evaluates ongoing statistical programs and tracks the statistical policy and coordinating activities of the federal government, serving a unique role at the intersection of statistics and public policy. The committee's work is supported by a consortium of federal agencies through a National Science Foundation grant.